Games Business Experts Play

Winning at the Games of Business

L. Michael Hall, Ph.D.

Crown House Publishing
www.crownhouse.co.uk

First published by

Crown House Publishing Ltd
Crown Buildings, Bancyfelin, Carmarthen, Wales, SA33 5ND, UK
www.crownhouse.co.uk

and

Crown House Publishing Ltd
P. O. Box 2223, Williston, VT 05495-2223, USA
www.CHPUS.com

www.crownhouse.co.uk

First published 2002.
Reprinted 2003.

British Library Cataloguing-in-Publication Data
A catalogue entry for this book is available
from the British Library.

ISBN 1899836721

LCCN 2003101968

Printed and bound in the UK by
The Cromwell Press
Trowbridge
Wiltshire

Distributed in Ireland By
Outside The Box Learning Resources
Jigginstown Commercial Centre
Naas, Co. Kildare, EIRE
Tel: 045 856344; Fax: 045 897819
outsidetheboxlearning@eircom.net
www.outsidetheboxlearning.com

Table of Contents

Preface

In this book you will read, as the title suggests, about *The Games Business Experts Play*. I'm personally interested in such "games" for one primary reason. Namely, I would prefer to do what I do as business efficiently, effectively, and productively so that I have even more time, money, resources, and influence to do all of the other things that make my life full and rich. How about you?

This book reveals the secret games of the experts:

- What allows them to play the Game of Business so effectively?
- What mindsets support their productivity?
- What frames of mind best support their everyday efficiency?

It doesn't take a rocket scientist to realize that we can't play *The Game of Business Excellence* or to operate as a business genius at work if we don't even know what games such geniuses play or how they play such games. For that matter, it will be hard to really transform our everyday business experiences if we do not know how and why we humans play games (frame games) in the first place, or how we can change, alter, refuse, refine, and/or set up new games. That's why we will first visit the *World of Games* and the *Frames that drive* them. We will do that to prepare ourselves for truly understanding *Games Business Experts Play*.

In the process of adventuring through the first part of the book, I will suggest a few of the basic *Frame Games* of the experts. Actually, these will be the games that make all the difference in the world if you really want to become a *Game Master*. They will set the foundation for all business and personal excellence.

There are games afoot in the world—in business, at home, among friends. They are everywhere. And there's no escaping from them even when we are by ourselves. We play games, *frame games*, even with ourselves. The real questions before us are these:

- *What* do we play?
- *How* do we play?

- What kind of a *player* are we?
- Are we playing the games that bring out our best or that bring out the best in others?
- Do we play the games or do they play us?
- What does it take to become a frame-game master?

I was not raised to know or care much about the business arena. My dad was a mathematics teacher and taught in the local high school and later in the math department at Indiana University. Having grown up during the Depression, he played *The Finance Game* that so many of his generation played: *"Play it Safe," "Don't Take Chances," "Anticipate All of the Losses that You Could Possibly Lose."* He liked having tenure. He wanted a large organization to provide him economic security, insurance, and retirement.

That was the world he lived in. And it made sense given the maps he had created over the years and absorbed from his culture. But they did not make for business excellence. One day after I had bought my first investment property, I asked Dad, "Why didn't you keep that house on Indiana Avenue and turn it into a rental?" He had bought the house for an outrageous amount—$11,000 in 1956. It was now 1964 and he had contracted to buy a new house for $18,000.

"Oh, I couldn't afford the payments if I had to have two houses."

"Dad, the renters would have paid the payments on the first house. They would have finished buying that house for you."

"Well, I was so busy with school in those years, I didn't have time to fix broken toilets."

"Why, was there a problem with the toilets in that house?"

"No, but you never know when one would break or when the house would need a new roof."

"Why, do you need new roofs more than once every ten years in Indiana?"

"The risk was just too much. What if there was a recession and …"

"Ah, yes, the 'Let's Always Play it Safe, Anticipate All Possible Contingencies of Things that could Go Wrong' Game!"

Before his death I had purchased five rental properties and he was always cautioning me about them, warning me about lurking dangers, and scratching his head about how in the world I could afford them. I teased and played with him, loving him dearly, and as I became increasingly aware of how his frames ran his games just as my frames run the games I play.

When I first began to play business games, I really didn't know much about how that world worked or how to play the games that would win. I didn't even know that I wanted to play such games. Having received my first formal training in the ministry, and then in psychotherapy, I bought into the games of my generation (the 1960s). "I'm more interested in helping people than succeeding in business." As a child of the human potential movement, I viewed business as a not so noble domain.

Of course, the amazing thing about that frame of mind is how well it worked. As a frame of mind, it drove, organized, and informed the games that I played so that I succeeded. I succeeded in *not* being very informed, efficient, or successful in "the ways of the world." I didn't really know much about finances, capitalism, marketing, and so forth.

Eventually financial reality knocked on my door. It wasn't until I played *The Divorce Game*, having spent everything in court fees in a child-custody battle, that I found myself back at square one. Starting all over again caused something to click inside. At that point I decided:

"I've had enough. I'm going to learn the business games, how to play them, how to succeed at them. I'm not going to suffer another financial loss like this."

I started over but in a new way. I began to play some very new and different games.

In the years since then, I feel as though I have been living an entirely different life. I did not study business, not at first. But I adapted some very different frames of mind. Recognizing that I could really help no one else as long as I lived from paycheck to paycheck, I decided that I would succeed in business. That meant that I would use my psychotherapy practice (which was my business at the time) to succeed, that I would make sure it made sense from a business and financial point of view. I also began extending myself to do other things. I began conducting communication trainings with businesses, which led to consulting, management training, and stress management training.

It was in that field that I first discovered the modeling excellence of Neuro-Linguistic Programming, or NLP So I took my training and immediately founded an NLP training center, and began partnering with numerous people on various short-term projects. Soon thereafter I found a "deal" that allowed me to purchase my first rental property. How did I know that would become a business in itself and that I would eventually buy multiple houses at a time? My passion for writing gave me eyes for turning situations into opportunities and so that launched a writing career. That led to partnering with my chief co-author, Dr. Bobby Bodenhamer, which then led to the founding of Neuro-Semantics, and Institutes of Neuro-Semantics around the world. And that led to a training career, which a few years later turned into an international training career. In the midst of these years, I finished a doctoral program, put an end to all debts, founded a publishing company, became financially independent, and, among other things, taught wealth-building workshops around the world.

After I stumbled onto the *Meta-States Model* (1994), I wrote several books about describing and applying that model. Later I began translating Meta-States to the business realm. That led to creating and conducting a business workshop, *Genius At Work*. Upon the development of the *Frame Games Model* (1999) I began conducting international trainings around several business themes: *Selling and Persuasion Excellence, Games Wealthy People Play* (Wealth Building using Meta-States), *Games Business Experts Play*.

What does it take to succeed in business in the twenty-first century? Obviously, it takes some basic business intelligence about how supply and demand work, what it means to create and use capital, what people want, how to work with people, how to keep learning, how to sell and persuade, how to keep balanced and healthy in mind, body, and relationships. It also takes a *great attitude*—a positive, optimistic, solution-oriented, can-do, playful attitude.

That's what this book is about. As the winds of change began to blow through businesses in the last half of the twentieth century and changed the very twentieth-landscape of business, it has made business much more *people-oriented* (and hence psychological). It has become so much more than just about the *product* created (or the *services* offered), it has become about *how we present and deliver* such products and services.

There is a new game in town. And that new game necessitates new frames of mind to play it.

Part I

Figuring Out the Games of Life

Overview

Games Business Experts Play

This book is about *games*. It's about all of the behavioural games, speech games, even the mental and emotional games that we play in the field of business. It's about the Business Games that the experts play that enable them to succeed as they do. It's about the games that we can learn to play to replicate the success of the experts. The book addresses how the experts think about the business games, and how to replicate their frames of mind. Why? To become much more productive and efficient in the games that we play. That makes this book about setting new frames of mind and refusing the old frames and the old games that undermine success.

In *Part I*, we will focus on *figuring out frame games*. This presents the idea of business as "games" and is the only theoretical part of the book. Here I will introduce and describe frame games and how to shift your thinking about your career in terms of frames and games. This sets the stage for everything else: how to detect and identify the games, how to appreciate the driving power of our mental frames and not get seduced by thinking that they are real.

Part II describes the most foundational games—the *games that make for personal effectiveness* in every realm. Games for personal empowerment establish the foundation for excellence and expertise in every field—personal, business, athletics, finances.

Part III then gets down to business—the actual business games that make for *expertise and excellence in business*.

A Template for the Games

While I have a more thorough model for thinking about games in Chapter 3 and have two worksheets there for more extensive frame analysis, I have used the following template as a simple way to think about the games in the following chapters. It follows from what we mean when we talk about a set of actions and interactions as a "game."

- The **name** and the description of the game: What is the game? How does it work? Does the game enhance or limit?
- The **rules** of the game: How is the game set up, structured? Who plays the game? When?
- The **cues** of the game: What are the questions that elicit the game, the terms that reveal the game? What triggers recruit us into playing the game?
- The **payoff** of the game: What are the benefits, values, and outcomes of the game?

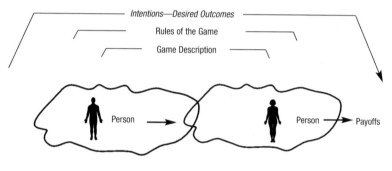

Intentions—Desired Outcomes
Rules of the Game
Game Description
Person → Person → Payoffs

Cues for the Games

Toxic or Empowering?

It doesn't matter what we call a game. I've invented lots of insight-ful as well as silly titles in the following pages and I invite you to do the same with the games you play. What matters is whether they work for you or against you. You need to know both. Business experts do. It's not enough to know the positive, won-derful games that you want to play and want to say *"Yes"* to. Frequently, we can't say a thunderous *"Yes"* to what we want until we've said an equally impactful *"Hell, No!"* to the games that undermine and sabotage our best efforts.

It's for this reason that I will constantly be contrasting *Bad Game/Good Game* in the following pages. Your clarity on toxic or enriching will give you the personal power to *cut* (de-*cision*) a clear path toward your desired outcomes. It will also empower you to stand strong and firm when the toxic games put on a seductive show and try to recruit you for them.

Becoming an Expert Game Player

Here's the overall game plan of this book. First, we learn to *detect* games. By naming the games we put the spotlight of awareness on them. This allows us to flush out the sick and morbid games that have terrible payoffs and empowers us to refuse them. Game detection means becoming mindful, aware, conscious. It's the wake-up call. It's like the wake-up call that Neo received in the movie, *The Matrix*. Until he took the red pill and woke up to the Matrix that he had been living in, he didn't even know what game he had been playing.

Second, we *access the personal power* it takes to play the games. It takes energy, power, and vitality to become conscious, to look the games in the face and to decide which ones get the thumbs-up and which ones get the thumbs-down.

Third, we access the higher frames of our mind to turn on even greater sources of power and insight. This introduces the human dynamic of frames into the picture and underscores the cognitive-behavioral nature of our lives. As we think and believe, so we play the games that we do. Games are governed and directed by frames. This provides us the central leverage point regarding how to transform things quickly. It doesn't take years of analysis: it takes the change of a frame. We use two raw and primordial powers to do that—our powers to confirm and to disconfirm, to say *"Yes"* and *"No"*. By these powers we exercise executive control regarding which games we'll play and which we will no longer tolerate.

Fourth, we will *temper this power* lest it go to our heads. We will qualify our frames with the kinds of frames that will texture our games so that we play the *Business Expert Games* with the kind of values, visions, and beliefs that truly keep us balanced, healthy, and sane.

5

Fifth, we will learn a *structural template* so that we can quickly or extensively analyze games. Frame analysis will enable us to become more strategic and thoughtful in our approach. It will enable us to not be blind-sided by facets of our games that we didn't see.

Sixth, after that we will explore the world of *the Business Games that the Experts play*. This is *Part III*, where recommended business games are introduced for your success. These are the games that allow you to take charge of your world, your responses, and your ability to make a difference. Here you'll get to decide which games to say *"No"* to and which ones to validate with, *"Yes!* Let's play!"

Seventh, in the area of business, as in most other complex domains of life, there will be games for different seasons. Games for positioning yourself (Chapter 10), games for making work meaningful and satisfying (Chapter 11), games for handling things with mastery when things get tough (Chapter 12), games for being your own best boss (Chapter 13), games for adding value to the lives of others (Chapter 14), games for resolving conflicts (Chapter 15), and games for inventing even better games (Chapter 16).

Ready to Play?

If you're ready to go to it, then I'd recommend you read the book in its entirety to get a sense of the overall game plan. Then return with a game-plan notebook and the ability to play the Implementation Game. Then you can pick and choose the games of business excellence that you want to make *yours*.

Chapter 1

What in the World is a "Frame Game"?

Welcome to the Wild and Wonderful World of Games

Every day when Jim gets up, gets himself ready and off to his job, he plays business games. Jim never thinks of them as "games." Yes, every once in a while he may briefly entertain such a thought, but usually he just thinks of the things he does as the everyday activities that make up his profession. It's just business.

I here speak about our actions, speech, and interactions as "games." Obviously, I am not speaking about *actual* "games." I am speaking metaphorically and accommodatively about the set of actions and transactions that we engage in with ourselves and others as a "game," that is, as

- a set of actions and transactions
- performance to obtain an outcome and payoff
- activities designed for efficiency and productivity

We do not do this consciously. Consciousness is *not* required. We can and do carry on without much awareness about what we're actually doing. Amazing, but true. We can get into habitual ways of acting, thinking, talking, and feeling and really *not* notice the "game" in play, how it affects others, or even how it affects us—at least not in the short run. If we step back, take a breath, and think about it using a larger vision of years, we can then "catch the game in play."

To get a clear view of the games we play at work, the games we play as employees, as managers, as supervisors, as CEOs, just step

7

back for a moment from your everyday experiences of work, career, and business and do something very special. For just a moment, view your everyday work experiences as though they were a game. Do this as a rejuvenating process to enrich your life, increase your effectiveness, enhance your productivity, and make you wealthier in mind, body, and pocketbook. If you are ready, then let's go. Get a notebook, or a tape recorder, and respond to the following questions:

- If you viewed the activities, actions, interactions with others, the roles, personae, etc. that you engage in, *what games* do you play?
- What games do your associates, bosses, supervisors, employees, and customers play? Name some of their games.
- If you're in management, what are the management games that you play? What games do you *intend* to play or would *like* to play? What games do you actually play?
- What games do you find really fun and enjoyable?
- What games bring out your best?
- What games do you experience as really sick or stupid?
- What games do you play unwillingly?

The Games of Alan

I first met Alan when he was 42. He owned a large and very successful construction company worth perhaps twenty million dollars. His own personal wealth was probably five or six million. He had forty men working for him actually running the equipment and ten people in the office handling sales, paperwork, and administration. Alan was one stressed-out person. His nerves were on edge, he was fearful, even paranoid, his wife was threatening divorce, he was working fourteen-hour days.

Alan was playing lots of business games that we might call:

- "Work is Serious Business."
- "You Can't Let Up: the Competition Will Overtake and Destroy You."
- "Don't Trust People: They'll Betray You."
- "It's a Dog-eat-Dog World."

- "It's Usually Just More Efficient to Do It Yourself."

No wonder he was stressed out. He could not delegate. He could not take a vacation—had not been on one in five years. He could not stop himself from micromanaging *everything*.

His doctor sent him to me for stress management. But every stress-management suggestion I made violated all of his frames of mind. The suggestions didn't even make sense. He thought I would give him even more efficient ways to micromanage, protect his legitimate fears of employees and competitors, and get his wife to back off her demands. He found that I was just adding to his stress with my psychological nonsense! Learning to trust, releasing worries and concerns, delegating, adopting a more relaxed and playful attitude, taking time off—all of these ideas were utterly ridiculous. So he didn't take any of them.

A year later he appeared in my office in an even more distressed state. The business had nearly doubled in the past fourteen months and Alan was at his limits: now his stress symptoms were even more intense. He couldn't sleep well, home life was a living hell, he avoided going home even more, his business was computerized and he was in total terror that the guy running the computer would "steal the business." Alan would constantly *not* give him necessary information for fear of betrayal. He now had an ulcer and his stomach constantly hurt. And his doctor was demanding change!

This time I was a little wiser and I knew how to talk the language of games. "So *The Dog-eat-Dog Game* is getting to you!"

"No, I'm just stressed, that's all!"

"Ah, *The Denying Reality Game*. That's what you want to play? How many experts and friends have to tell you that you need to lighten up, learn to delegate, and take care of your health and family before you'll believe it?"

"It's not that. In business, you have to watch the rear. You never know when someone will take advantage of you."

"Is this the secret of your success, Alan?"

"Yes, it is."

"So this way of thinking and acting, playing life this way—this really works well for you? Gives you health, peace of mind, riches, great family life, great sex, sense of fulfillment ...?"

"Okay, okay. I get it. Okay, no, it does not."

"Are you willing to learn to play some different games?"

"You mean do the things you suggested last time?"

"Yes, I'm afraid that it has come to that!"

Actually, it would take another three months of stress and stomach pain before Alan became willing to release the old games and learn some new ones. It was not easy. I had to keep leveraging by asking about the bottom line. "Are you really getting what you want?" But eventually he got it. Eventually, he began to play the game of *"Business is Just One Part of my Life."* Eventually, he also learned how to play The *"Efficiency through a More Relaxed Attitude Game."*

Work Games

If by "game" we refer to the sets of actions and interactions that occur in the workplace, then what games have you learned best?

* Do you play *The Expert Game,* presenting yourself as "the expert"?
* Do you play *The Caretaker Game,* ready to serve any and every need?
* What about the game of *"Pass the Buck"*?
* Have you ever played *The Blame Game* when you or someone you supervised messed up?
* Or perhaps you've played the (take deep sigh) *'God, I Wish It Were Friday!' Game."*
* *"Now I've Got You, You S.O.B.!"*

A game not only refers to talking and acting, but can also refer to a way of thinking, a style of feeling, a pattern for communicating, along with all of our roles and rituals. At the macro level of behavior, a game refers to any of the actions and behaviors that we could pick up on a video recorder. Using a video recorder, we could gather the sensory-based referents to describe how we actually play the game. We could *see* the game, we could *hear* the game, we could *feel the movements*, the impressions of pain and victory of the game.

First Cues

Watch someone play *The Blame Game*. Watch the index finger come out and shake furiously in the air at someone else. Hear the vocal chords become tight and the volume increase. Observe the facial expressions, the breathing patterns, the tense movements. "You should have finished that report! What's wrong with you? Do you know what you've done—the trouble that you've caused? Do you?"

You can actually *see* and *hear* the game.

Games give off cues and clues.

In chess, we see a particular kind of board set out on a table and two chairs facing the table. That gives us our first clues about the game. However, if we then see someone open a small box with black and red checkers (or draughts in the U.K.), we would shift our thinking, "They're not going to play chess: it's a checkers game that they're going to play." If we then notice them making the "right" kind of moves with the checkers on the board, we would feel confirmed in our guess. If they use the checkers as if they were chess pieces, or in some other way foreign and unfamiliar to us, we would wonder, "What in the world are they doing? They're *not* playing checkers. I don't know what they think they're doing, but I know that they aren't playing checkers!"

In a similar way, the games we play in business also have cues and clues, rules and procedures. There is a *structure* to the way we interact and the moves we make.

11

When a boss begins, "You didn't do this right ..." and has his or her index finger pointing at us, we can pretty well bet that someone is pretty close to stepping fully into playing a round of *The Blame Game*. At least those initial cues would suggest such.

If, however, the words and actions that next occur go, "... and what I really should have told you was X, then I would have communicated more clearly ..." we shift our thinking. "Maybe the boss is *not* going to play *The Blame Game,* but maybe he's setting up another kind of game to play with me. Perhaps, *The Solution Game.* Perhaps he wants to play, *'Let's Collaborate on How to Solve This Situation.'* Or perhaps, *The Mutual Responsibility Game:* 'I accept and assume partial responsibility for this.' "

Mind Games

We not only play *external* games that a video camera could pick up in sensory-based terms (terms that you can see, hear, and feel), but we also play *internal* games. We play what we commonly refer to as *"Mind Games."*

In this, "games" can also refer to our way of thinking and our pattern of perceiving. That's what the confirmed pessimist plays. He or she knows how to regularly and consistently play the game of looking at the world or any particular part of it *in terms of how things will go wrong, mess up, and make us feel bad* (the frame). And if they have that game really down pat, they will play it frequently, methodically, and persistently. When we point out their game, they will play, *"Ain't It Awful!"* with us.

This means that what we *do* inside our heads as we process information, construct maps that enable us to conceptualize and construct ideas, we can also view as "games." They describe the mental games that we play. They differ only in that we don't actually need another person to play those games, we can play them by ourselves.

That's the kind of games we play on our way to work. As we get up in the morning, get ourselves ready, and get to work, we run various patterns of thinking, imagining, feeling, and anticipating in our heads. What games do you play *about* work before you get to work?

- *"Oh, God, another day slaving for a buck!"* (Utter this with lots of sighs.)
- *"Oh, what a glorious morning; oh, what a glorious day!"* (Sing to the tune "Oh, What a Beautiful Morning" from the musical *Oklahoma!*)
- *"I wish I could get a better job!"*
- *"I have so much to do; there's just not enough time in a day!"*
- *"Great, I wonder what I'll learn today."*

As you'll discover in the following chapters, we not only play conversation games, action games, mind games: we also play games at various *levels*. We play games *about* our games.

- *The "Let's Pretend We Don't Play Games" Game*
- *The "I Hate the Games that I Play" Game*
- *The "I Love My Games, I Wouldn't Part With Them for the World" Game*

What explains this facet of games? Namely, that we do not merely think and feel at one level of awareness, but at multiple levels. After we engage in a *mental* game of some sort, we then experience thoughts and feelings *about* that game. Doing this shifts us up to a higher logical level. Technically, this takes us to the higher cognitive level that we call "meta-cognition." It's a little like the Boss of the first Thought. This means that we have layered a level of awareness *about* our awareness, by moving to a higher game, a game about a game.

In a way, it's like the levels within a business. At the primary level we have people who actually create products, perform services, and engage customers. The next level in the organization are the men and women who manage the front-line people. We can move up higher and find another level of people who manage the managers, their supervisors, and so on until we move all the way up to the C.E.O., who performs a very different kind of work than the front-line person.

A similar kind of hierarchy operates in our minds and bodies. We have levels governing and directing other levels. And, as you will discover, we actually will find the *power* residing in those higher "executive" levels. This explains why the highest personal empowerment, competence, efficacy, and authority involves learning to access and run that "executive" level of mind. In a nutshell, that's what this book is all about.

In the next couple of chapters I will introduce the *Levels of Mind Model* (known as the Meta-States Model). That model will provide the only theoretical understanding you'll need to navigate the Frame Games that you play with yourself and at work.

So, in these ways, the games that we play make up the very fabric of our lives. And, if they make up the fabric of our lives, then they control the quality of our lives, the quality of our mind and skills, the effectiveness of our actions, and so much more.

And Then There Are the Frames

By *"frame,"* we refer to the most basic process of human consciousness, namely *frame of reference.* Your "frame" first identifies *what* you are referring to. Without knowing that, we really can't communicate. This explains why we so frequently ask each other, "What are you talking *about?*" We especially ask that when we're not understanding another person. To talk or think, we have some *reference* in mind. These references govern the games that we play. The idea of *levels of mind* explains these layers of references, which we so easily develop from actual references and transform into our *mental structure*, which we then use to make sense of things.

You do something at work that goes wrong, something that creates a mess. Suppose that mistake costs the company money, time, and effort to put right. Suppose further that your boss comes down on you with some strong words, anger, and accusation. This experience now becomes a future referent—something you can refer to.

More than likely, as you see, hear, and feel the results of this "wrong," you will experience a state of fear, apprehension, concern, stress, and upsetness. If you then *use* that referent experience

Figure 1:1

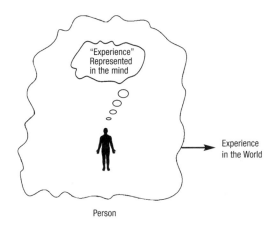

as your reference point and *way of thinking* about taking a risk, dealing with the boss, or working, you graduate to a higher level. Now the referent experience, which once occurred as an actual historical happening, becomes a *mental reference point in your brain;* now you use it as a template or a frame of mind.

That's what we do with the external references that we call "experiences." We use our life experiences to establish a reference structure for making sense and creating meaning, and to create *a map of the world.* We take our experiences and draw conclusions. We make generalizations from the events *about* the events, *about* the people involved, *about* ourselves, etc. It's as if we *mine* the events for the *meanings* that we think lie inside those events, as we would mine gold, silver, lead, or copper from the earth. Yet that it doesn't happen like this is precisely where we all go wrong.

Wrong? Why wrong?

> Because "meaning" does not exist *in* events and experiences. We **create** meaning—we invent it in our minds and then impose it on the brute facts of everyday life.

As you will shortly discover, it cannot exist there. "Meaning" is predominantly a thing of the mind—a function of our entire nervous system and brain. We *create* meaning. We *invent* it. It occurs only in the mind of some meaning-maker. In communicating with one another, we often seek to *find* and *discover* another person's "meaning." Yet that's fairly difficult to do. To do so means listening apart from all of our mental filters, intensive listening, reflecting back what we think we've heard, correcting our impressions.

Figure 1:2

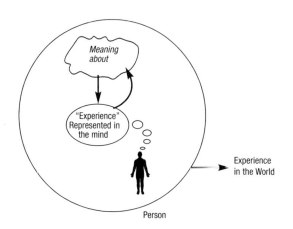

Because we internalize our experiences and use them as reference points, we build up a system of "meanings" and then see the world in terms of those frames or meanings. Eventually, we develop layers of nested frames within frames. Then we take our frame of mind, and with lots of repetition it habituates so that our way of thinking eventually becomes our cognitive *framework*. This entire framework of nested frames governs what and how we understand, think, perceive, reason, and believe. The framework forms and structures what we call "personality."

Eventually, we develop an entire reference system that we carry with us everywhere we go and use it to play work games. Depending on the meanings that we've made, our frame of mind prepares us for specific games.

- *"I must cover my butt and never take a chance"*—The *"Play it Safe"* or *"Making Mistakes is Terrible"* Game
- *"The bosses are always looking to 'get' me"*—The *"Us Against Them"* Game

- *"I can't make any difference"—The "I'm Just a Cog in the System" Game*
- *The "It's Just a Rat Race, Anyway" Game*
- *"It's all about working my rear end off"—The "Stress for Success" Game*
- *"It doesn't really make all that much difference: I'll just do what I have to do, collect the paycheck, and go home"—The "Don't Care" Game*
- *The "Let Me At 'Em! This Is Fun" Game*
- *"It's all about finding a passion and giving myself to it; that's the best way to live life!"—The "I Love To Contribute the Best I've Got" Game*

Frames describe the content and structure of our thoughts and so set us up with regard to the games that we are permitted to play, know how to play, and want to play. Within the term "frame" we include all of the higher-level cognitive structures. This includes what we commonly call beliefs, values, understandings, paradigms, mental models, expectations, assumptions, decisions, identifications.

Together we have "Frame Games"

Putting games and frames together gives us *Frame Games.* I use this to describe both the internal and external facets of our experiences, and the full range of mental and behavioral games that govern and to a great extent define the life that we live. In work, as in personal life, health, fitness, wealth building, and learning, we all play various Frame Games. Our frames establish the games, both the good ones and the destructive ones. Our games imply and flow from the governing frames. The governing frames create the games we willingly play.

With this introduction, we can now look at some of the not so desirable *frame games* that go on in the workplace. The fact that games occur is not particularly insightful or even helpful. However, that the games are functions of our frames *is* so. Awareness of the frames gives us insight into where the games come from, what endows them with *meaning*, motivation, and power. Knowing that frames give us choices with regard to what

Figure 1:3

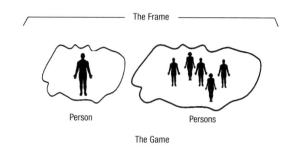

we want to do about the games. Conversely, when we lack awareness of the game, the frame, or the governing influence of the frame, we can easily get caught up in the game. When that happens, the *Frame Game* plays us, when we should be playing the *frame games* that we design and choose.

- What games are currently *playing* you at work, in your career and profession?
- Did you consciously choose to play those games?
- Do those games support you and move you in the direction you want for yourself personally and professionally?
- What game or games would you prefer to be playing?
- What cues and triggers hook you into the games?
- What frames drive these games?
- What do you believe about these games?
- What historical or conceptual references do you use to generate the frame to play the game?

Indicators of Unhealthy and Destructive Games

We have already enumerated some of the not-so fun games that sometimes we find ourselves playing at work. These reduce the quality of life and when unchecked can induce a sense of meaninglessness and futility. Did some of them particularly speak to you? Here's another quick check-list of games. Check those that you find yourself involved in that do not enhance your career. Identify those that undermine you and your success. Because this represents only a small sample of potential games, take a few moments to identify other not so useful games that are playing you.

Frame Games that don't enhance your life

The Helpless Game: "You can't really change anything. I'm just a cog in the system around here, powerless to change anything."

The Dog-Eat-Dog Game: "Only those who compromise their values can succeed in business. You have to be an asshole! The more successful I am, the more people will resent me and try to undermine my success."

The Peevishness Game: "I shouldn't have to do some of these things."

The Paranoid Game: "They're out to get me! They want to fire me, undermine my success. What if they steal my great ideas?"

The "If It Weren't for People" Game: "Why do people have to be so difficult?"

The Unfairness Game: "Why try? Life is so unfair and nothing ever really changes."

The Overresponsible Game: "I'm responsible for everything. I can't delegate. I can't trust others to do it as well as I can do it myself."

The Complaint Game: "They're all incompetents around here."

The Helpless Game: "One person can't make any difference."

The Stress Game: "I can't balance my energies between home and business. It's one or the other. There's too much to do. I can't juggle everything. Something's going to get dropped. I'm deluged with too many e-mails, too much information, too many demands."

The Competition Game: "In the business world you have to be cutthroat."

The Overwhelm Game: "I can't keep up—I'm not smart enough."

The Double-Bind Game: "It's a no-win situation. I'm damned if I do, damned if I don't."

The Scarcity Game: "We have to use these tactics to win."

The Unappreciated Genius Game: "If everyone would just listen to me, I could solve all of the company's problems! My amazing talents intimidate the mental weaklings around here!"

The Chaos Game: "I don't feel like I ever finish anything. There's no closure. I'm living on the verge of chaos."

Sorting for Games

If you have ever communicated with a boss or supervisor and felt that you lacked influence with him or her, then you experienced someone playing a game with you. Actually, it's a common one. Many managers actually *fear* giving employees much say, influence, or power. The *frame* in their head warns them, "If you give them an inch, they'll take a mile."

"If you let them have a little say, you'll open up a Pandora's box of complaints."

Given this way of thinking, their managerial behavior and style makes perfect sense. In fact, we can say that they *have* to act and talk that way. Given that frame, they have no choice about what game to play or what game they can play. And, even when a higher supervisor tells them to "cut that out" or sends them to classes for how to empower employees, they will play that game at one level, but at a higher level become more covert and subtle in how to deny employees true empowerment.

Why? Because a person's highest frames always win the day regarding the games we play. The higher frame is always *the boss* in our mind.

Figure 1:4

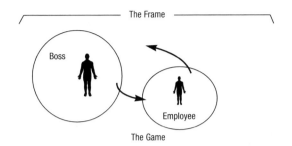

Statistics indicate that lots of people feel as if they live under the thumb of their boss or company and do not truly feel free to make a difference. In this frustration, they may come to work and play numerous games: *"Anger," "If It Weren't for You ...," "Injustice,"* and so on. In this way, one nonenhancing frame game invites and initiates another nonenhancing frame game. This can cycle around and around, creating a downward spiral of interactions and locking all participants into a prison of negative thoughts and feelings.

What nonenhancing games are you currently experiencing and playing? To check this out simply begin by noting your state of mind about work. What do you think? What comes to mind? Do you sense that there is little to no chance of moving up, being promoted, getting a raise? Do you feel or sense that there's a lack of respect and appreciation for you? What *games* are you playing in your mind, thought-world, feelings, and behaviors?

"States" and Frame Games

A great way to detect the games afoot at work is to examine your states or attitudes as well as those of others. I use the term "state" to refer to the sum total of your mental, emotional, and behavioral *experience* at any given moment.

- Are you in an excited state?
- A depressed state?
- Would you characterize your state as stressful, angry, pleasant, playful, or what?

In any given day, we typically experience a great many states regarding the games that we play. Some of these are appropriate and resourceful; others are inappropriate and unresourceful. When we "cop an attitude," we typically enter into an unresourceful state of mind and body. We're not at our best. *"State"* is a great word for this overall *"attitude"* because it holistically captures both the mental (cognitive) and emotional (bodily) facets of our experience.

As a leading researcher in the field of psychobiology, Ernest Rossi (1987), has noted, our states create a mindset or attitude set. This means that, once we get into a state, the state itself governs our learning, memory, perception, communication, and behavior. We call this *"state-dependency."*

For example, once in an angry state, we tend to perceive the world in terms of hostility. Anger becomes our "game." Our learning and memory do service to the anger. So do our actions and communications. So with every intense state (joy, playfulness, relaxation, tension, fear), once we are in the state, the state controls the rest of our psychological powers.

Imagine sprinting at full speed in a race on a track. How likely will you will be thinking and feeling "depressive" thoughts and feelings at that moment? Regardless of your thinking before or after the run, both your mindset and the bodily chemical processes required for depression (to play the Game of Depression) will in all likelihood *not* be available while you are running. Because the experience of running (as with every experience) involves a holistic mind–body process, it will typically eliminate certain states of mind and body. Even when you just *think* about running, if you do so intensely and vividly, you will often find that your thoughts will alter your state and your feelings.

What does this mean in terms of the games that we play at work? It means that our state, at any given moment, sets the physical and emotional background (and frames) for the games we play and determines the quality of our games. Our states are intimately related to the games that we do, and can, play.

- What state would you have to experience in order to blame?

- What state would you have to access in order to seek solutions in a positive way?
- What state would support you in problem solving?
- What state would support you to feel demotivated, fearful, or overcontrolling?

Motivated States and Frame Games

Thinking about work inevitably raises the subject of motivation. This becomes especially true with regard to becoming a "genius at work." In the field of work, the whole question of what motivates, how to motivate, external and/or internal motivators, and so forth describes an immense and critically important area. Here, the idea of *frame games* gives us a particularly helpful way to think about this.

- What games do you play regarding work when it comes to "motivation"?
- Do you wake up in the morning full of excitement and passion about getting to contribute significantly?
- Do you wake up and groan and moan and play *The "Why do I Have to Go to Work?" Game?*

Whether you play the game of loving or hating your job, you have some frame and frames-of-frames that govern and support those games. In this, they both create the state and reflect the state. Does it surprise you to realize that wanting to take action toward your goals and *not* wanting to take action both involve the same process—a process of setting a frame and then actualizing that frame. In both cases, we use our consistent focus on our goal to follow through. We move toward making something happen or we move toward making something *not* happen.

Consider the field of sales. How is it that a new salesperson, with little or no experience, could possibly outsell someone with many years of experience? Or, how is it that some people consistently go for their dreams while others, who may have as much or even greater talent, find themselves crippled by hesitation? It's all a matter of frames. Some people play the frame game of *Focusing on My Goals and Making them Happen.* Others play the frame game of

"I Sure Don't Want to Get Any Rejections Today. I've Had Enough of That." Frames are *that* important. They govern all of our experiences.

Summary

- We don't have to say, "Let the games begin!" because they have already begun. There are already plenty of games already going on in the workplace. We play games in how we work, why we work, what we seek to accomplish in working. We also play mental games with ourselves and others as we engage in our profession.

- Behind (or above) every game there is a frame. Frames drive games. To play a game, we have to learn the rules, the structure, the payoffs, etc.

- *Frame Games* give us a new way to think about the sets of interactions on the behavioral, communicational, and psychological levels for analyzing, understanding, and effectively working with the games that aren't enhancing. They also show us those games that are enhancing.

- As there are a lot of sick, toxic, and morbid games that can make people insane, so there are a lot of enhancing, empowering, and fun games that make for an increased sense of sanity and enable us to become highly productive.

- If we want to become a "genius at work" and develop the expertise and quality of business excellence we need only to know how to stop playing the stupid and destructive games, and learn how to play the ones that bring out our best. We also want to know how to make those work even better and more effectively.

Chapter 2

Frames: The Driving Force in the Game of Business Excellence

Where there's a Game, There's a Frame
(Frame Game Secret, Frame Games)

It's inescapable that you show up for work and participate in the everyday activities, and that you do so in some *frame of mind*. We're always in some state or frame of mind and body; we never leave home without our frames of mind. These mental and emotional states govern our everyday experiences as the driving force that animates our lives, and therefore animates all of our experience as we do business. Given that, let's then begin by asking some questions to raise our *frame* awareness:

- What *frame of mind* do you show up with when you go to work?
- What *frame of mind* do you have about *that* frame of mind?
- How well do these mental frames serve you?
- Do you find your emotional frame of mind empowering?

Now while "frame" and "frame of mind" are pretty common terms that we use frequently every day, there are other synonyms. We commonly talk about our frames in terms of our *"attitude"* or even *"mood."* And, as everybody in business knows, *attitude is everything*. It makes all the difference in the world.

It's All About Frames

When we're involved in a "game," especially one that we do not like, it seems like it's all *about* the game. Yet that's a trick. It is not about the *game,* even though that's typically what we are most conscious of.

When you experience someone pointing a finger at you and blaming, it seems like it's all about *The Blaming Game.* When someone is intimidating, manipulating, ordering you around, playing you off against someone else, running a scam, complaining, or bellyaching *inside* of the game, it certainly seems like the immediate talk, actions, feelings, and consequences are everything. But that's deceptive.

> *A game is only the game that it is because of its Frame.*

"Checkers" is only the experience and set of interactions that we call "checkers" when there are two players who are playing by the rules they have learned that make up the game that we call "checkers." The game is the game it is because of the rules that structure it. This highlights the *structure* within or behind or above games. That's what the frames provide—frames create the framework structures that we then live in.

The Game of Criticism

Consider *The Game of Criticism.* I used to criticize freely and so became pretty skilled at it. I would criticize any time I saw something amiss from what *I* thought ought or ought not to be. I would criticize to make things better. Yet I found that it seldom worked out that way.

I just could not find many people who *wanted to play that game* with me. I would start in at various times and places and offer my insightful critiques and lo and behold!—they didn't seem to want to play! The nerve!

Of course, come to think of it, I guess I didn't act much like an enthusiastic partner when people would want to play the game with or on me either. "You need to …" "You should …" "Have you ever thought of …?" They'd initiate *The "Let's Criticize What You're Doing Wrong" Game,* and somehow I didn't get the feeling or impression that this was actually a version of "I Want to Help You Make Your Life Wonderful!"

I have no doubt that one of my highest *frames*, and one of their highest *frames*, in criticism was to make things better. Yet there were some other frames involved.

For the one trying to play the game:
- I don't like what's going on and I'm going to let you know.
- I feel upset, angry, and frustrated and you're the cause.
- I think you're *wrong* and I'm going to set you *straight*.
- I wouldn't have done it that way, so you shouldn't!
- What's wrong with you? Are you stupid?

For the reluctant one who doesn't want to play that game:
- I hate being reproved, corrected, straightened out.
- Who gave *you* the right to criticize *me*?
- I'm in no mood to take this from you!
- Shut up! I don't want to know about my failings or fallibilities.

Of course, with those frames driving our thinking and feeling, no wonder the "criticism" seldom works as a way to make things better. No wonder both the person criticizing and the person receiving the communication do not use *The Game of Criticism* to improve things, gain deeper understandings, or feel honored that they are so engaged. No wonder *The Game of Criticism* more typically ends up being *The Push-Shove Game:*

- You ought to ...
- No, you're wrong, I ought not to do that!
- Well then, you are just stupid about these matters.
- Who are you calling stupid?
- I'm calling *you* stupid!

The Power of Frames

A frame of reference governs our thinking, emoting, speaking, and responding because it sets a context for how we view and interpret things. It establishes a *conceptual* or *mental* context that governs the meanings we use and create in our responses. Without a frame, a game has no meaning, no rules, no winners or losers, no time limits or any other kind of limits. The power that actually governs the quality of our actions, skills, and even our lives lies in our *frames*. So as we say with someone who has a powerfully positive attitude or who adopts an attitude in a negative and hurtful way, *attitude is everything*.

> *Frames create meaning. Or, more accurately, **we** create "meaning" by framing.*

In the first chapter, I mentioned that "meaning," as a crucial human phenomenon, does not and cannot exist in an external event or experience. We can further highlight this by saying *"Meaning is not real"*—it is not "real" externally. That's why you never walk out of your house in the morning or office at noon and stumble over a hunk of meaning.

"Hey, who left this hunk of meaning in the driveway?"

"Meaning" is not that kind of a thing. It's not a "thing" at all. It's a *way of thinking*. It is the process of *"holding"* an awareness or idea *"in mind"* (the literal meaning of "meaning" is to "hold in mind"). This is what makes it so slippery, so plastic, and so difficult to manage. Yet it is *meaning* that gives our lives significance and power. Meaning drives and motivates. Meaning governs what we can sell and what we cannot sell. It's meaning that brings out our best and enables us to reach into the depths and heights of our hearts and minds and become geniuses at work.

If meaning plays such a crucial role in our lives, in the expression of our actions and behaviors, in our communications and feelings, in the quality of our lives, then let's explore what we mean by "meaning."

- What does anything *"mean"*?
- What does your work or career *mean* to you?
- What *meanings* do you give to succeeding or achieving a particular goal that you've set for yourself?
- What *meanings* really turn you on?

- What *meanings* do you really believe in and will invest yourself in?
- What's so *meaningful* about those meanings?
- What doesn't *mean* that much to you?

In asking these "meaning" questions, we are asking about our frame of references at many levels; we are asking about our frame of mind at many levels; and we are asking about such frames as our

- Belief Frames
- Value Frames
- Destiny Frames
- Identity Frames
- Expectation Frames
- Outcome Frames
- Emotional Frames
- Theological Frames
- Philosophical Frames

It's Frames All the Way Up

"Mind" has levels. We never just think: we are a class of life that has the most amazing ability to *think about our thinking*. We call this "self-reflexive consciousness."

Upon thinking about what went on in the board meeting on Monday (first level thinking), we can then think about *the quality or nature of our thinking*. We can step back, so to speak, and reflect on ourselves—our thoughts, our feelings, our experiences, our history, future, ideas. We call this recursive nature of thinking, "meta-cognition." The term *"meta"* here refers to a higher level, something that is above something else:

- A thought *about* another thought: (What's the quality of my thinking?)
- A feeling *about* another feeling: (I'm *afraid* that my *confidence* in that task isn't strong enough.)
- A thought *about* a feeling: (I wonder if that's real fear or just a worry.)

- A feeling *about* a thought: (I feel so stressed out when I think about his communication style.)
- A feeling about a thought about a feeling: (I worry that our decision to go forward on that project will only confirm my fears that it won't work.)

Our ability to denote a word, idea, feeling, experience, or event with a word or a symbol enables us to move conceptually up the levels of awareness. This creates our ability to think conceptually, to abstract to more complex understandings of things, to create sciences, philosophies, and higher psychological states of mind. It's a great power. It's also a terrible power when misused or abused. When we do not handle it well or when we abuse it, we can create living hells of closed-ended spirals that only take us into more confusion and limitation (*Dragon Slaying*, 2000).

As with the hierarchy of a corporate business, the higher frames govern personality or consciousness as a boss or CEO governs a corporation. In any living system of interactive parts, the higher levels organize, modulate, and control the processes of the entire system. The boss, CEO, board of directors, or someone at the top creates the policies, sets the rules, establishes the operational directives.

Correspondingly, our higher frames govern our thinking, feeling, speaking, acting, relating, development, and use of skills. Our higher frames establish, among other things, the existence of certain games, the rules that we play by, the limits we recognize or refuse to recognize, and who can play. The games we play with regard to our jobs, careers, and professions, the motivation, commitment, quality of investment, and ways of interacting are all derived from our *frames of mind* about it.

Quality-Controlling our Frames and Frame Games

Given this, it seems appropriate that just as soon as we recognize and detect our games and frames, we should quality-control our frame games, doesn't it? Quality control simply refers to checking out our frame games to make sure that they support and contribute to our business excellence. We Quality-Control our *frame games* when we ask such things as:

* How healthy are the games that I play at work?
* Do the games enrich my skills, relationships, or development?
* Do I have any frames of mind that get in your way and undermine my ability to achieve?
* What frame games limit or hinder me?
* Which ones support, empower, enrich, and bring out my best?
* What frame games enable me to be a genius at work?
* Do any of them get me to play *The Work Idiot Game*?
* Do I need that game?

The Total-Quality Movement has raised awareness in the workplace about the role and value of excellence. It also gives us a human "technology" for bringing quality to our brains and to the games that we play. In business, we have learned that quality sells, it makes money, and it creates long-term, enduring business relationships.

Quality thinking and feeling at the personal level has a whole list of similar benefits in terms of business excellence. When we ensure that the games we play with ourselves and others are *quality* games, it supports our long-term success. It makes work fun and enjoyable. This reduces the stress and tension of forgetting to be human in our professions. It's not just about money and success: it's about *how* we spend our lives.

When we learn how to play *Quality Games*—we find that others want to play along with us. This creates quality relationships that not only support our financial and professional success, but enable us to enjoy ourselves and become more of who we can become along the way. This keeps us balanced and healthy. We then don't sacrifice family, friends, or health to "the job."

Then There Are the Frame Wars

Jean worked as the office manager of a busy construction company and, owing to her efforts, efficiency, and intelligence, she really kept the place going. Few recognized that. Her immediate supervisor and the owner of the company especially did not seem to see that. Yet they did know that she was efficient, quick, intelligent, and dependable. And Jean thought (this was the game she played) that merely being productive would bring the approval, rewards, and recognition she desired. It did not.

I met Jean during the years when I worked as a psychotherapist. She called for an appointment due to "work stress." Later, the owner of the company continued to send her because "she just didn't seem to have what it takes to fit in, and yet we really need her here."

Ah, the conflict of games! *The Frame Wars.*

Jean wanted to play the game called *"If I'm Skilled, Talented, and Productive the Company Ought to Beat a Path to my Door with Appropriate Rewards and Approval."* Her supervisor and the company's owner were playing other games: *"If You Want to be Noticed, then Stand Out from the Crowd and Make Yourself Noticed, but By All Means, Never Complain, for Complaining is for Wimps!"*

What got Jean so stressed out? The teasing of some of the guys at the construction company. They would come into the office on payday and act like construction workers. And when they discovered that they could "tease" Jean, that they could "get her going," and "rattle her cage," well, she couldn't get them to stop.

"What do you expect of 'construction workers'?" I asked just to flush out what kind of mental frames she used about it all.

She immediately shot back with,

"This is business! This is no place for that kind of behavior. Jokes are inappropriate!"

"And I suppose you try to get them to stop it?"

"Of course! I am the office manager and they have no right to tease me when I tell them to stop."

"So, does it work?"

"What?"

"Telling them to stop it?"

"No, but it *should*. They *should* listen to me. Even Mr Thompson told them to cut it out, but they don't."

"So you keep telling them to stop it?"

"Yes, of course."

"Does that empower you as a person or enhance your work situation?"

"Well … ah … no, not really."

"So would you say you're ready to try some different games than *The Game of Shoulding* on them, or being so sensitive to teasing? Would you like to operate from a sense of your own personal power and resourcefulness?"

"But they *shouldn't* …"

"Yes, *The Shoulding Game*—and yet does 'shoulding' on them work? If I said, 'Jean, you shouldn't "should" on them,' does that make you want to immediately stop 'shoulding'?"

Jean had not run a quality control on the games that she was playing and got so caught up playing and trying to win that she had lost perspective. That's what *The Quality Control Game* provides us—the ability to step back and make sure that we're playing games that we want to play.

Frames for Changing Games

If frames operate as the driving force within the games that we play, then when we change a frame we alter a game. Transforming our frame of mind (or attitude) can involve many different transformations. We could change the rules of the game, the name of the game, the conditions and situations for the game, the players, the way we score, how we value the game, what we believe about the game. Sometimes the tiniest change in the frame can irrevocably alter the game. At other times, a frame change will refine, hone, and heighten a game—make it more sane, humane, compassionate, and fun.

We call a change or alteration in a frame, a *reframe*. In the place of one reference point, we substitute another. This could involve a change of perspective, another set of criteria, or a transformation in the structure of the frame. Reframing, as a mental shift, invites us to try on a new perspective. Accordingly, reframing operates as one driving force that can renew, rejuvenate, and refresh the game that we play.

The Frames and Reframes of Business

In the 1960s and 1970s, the Swiss completely dominated the watch market. In terms of history and mechanics, they controlled that market. In 1968 watches still had mechanisms composed of gears and springs (some still do, of course, but fewer in this digital age). If you wanted to make quality watches, you would use gears and springs for the composition of the watches. Joel Arthur Barker in *Future Edge* tells about the Swish watchmakers first learning about electronic quartz watches, which were actually developed in Switzerland's Nauchatel Research Institute. Yet they dismissed the idea.

Why? The new watch did not have what all top-quality watches have to have—gears or springs. It was a new paradigm. A new way of thinking.

Consequently, by 1981, the Swiss had lost 50,000 of the 62,000 jobs in that industry. Why? Because the Japanese, unencumbered in terms of their frames, simply took to making electronic quartz watches. They didn't have limiting definitions, rules, and knowledge about "quality watches," or what a "real watch" was like. So they simply captured the market.

In this case, the Swiss watchmakers simply suffered from what we call "frame blindness." As they overtrusted in their frame of reference and failed to keep updating it or even questioning it from time to time; they treated their mental way of thinking as the only reality. And, confusing their mental mapping with "reality," they were unable to see the changing market. Knowing full well what a watch was and how to make it (their frame) they validated their thinking ("We have history on our side as proof,") and just knew that the new electronic watch was not the wave of the future.

Framing our Framing

> *Everything you say and do, every emotion you experience, and every meaning you discover or create—occurs in some frame.*

In human experience, frames are all-pervasive, and all-determining. Everything you do or say *in the context of business*, in selling, negotiating, producing, marketing, relating, and writing, also occurs in some frame-of-reference. That frame determines your success or failure. How you frame a change in procedures governs how others will think and feel about that change, more than "the change" itself.

How do you typically go about *framing* change? What does *change* mean to you? What do you think it means to others?

To ignore these meta-level concerns ignores the neurosemantic context of our subjective experiences. Further, you have many choices about how to frame the change that you're proposing and wanting.

- "This offers *a whole new way* of working."
- "This will *revolutionize* this entire company."
- "You're looking at *the future* of this business."
- "This will really upset the old diehards around here!"
- "This procedure simply offers a way to make your job *easier*."
- "It's not a big change, just a way to achieve our tasks in a *more straightforward way*."

What frame does each statement presuppose? Which frames would have the most impact in terms of making the change seem less upsetting?

As expressions of frames, each of those statements give us "mind-lines" that allow us to set up games. As frames are made up of thoughts, ideas, concepts, we encode them in statements or "lines." And often, if we don't have a succinct and compelling line, it's near impossible to set and solidify an enhancing frame. Yet when we use one of these lines for thinking and conceptualizing, each line creates a new and somewhat different effect. How do these affect you? How does another line change the way you think about the same thing?

Daniel C. Dennett, a philosopher of the mind, describes words and language as *"mind tools"* (1996). I like that. He speaks of the human technology par excellence, the one that enables us to externalize and unload our cognitive "overhead."

> "Words make us more intelligent by making cognition easier ... When *Homo sapiens* became the beneficiary of this invention, the species stepped into a slingshot that has launched it far beyond all other earthly species in the power to look ahead and reflect." (Pages 146–47.)

This explains the power of *mind-lines as frames* for creating our conceptual contexts or games. And by them we can just as easily reframe a mental context as we re-evaluate something and attribute new and different meanings to it.

Frames for Business Excellence

Our focus here is on developing *business excellence*. This involves excellence and mastery of our work and embedding what we do in frames of quality. Doing so is what makes us "geniuses at work."

Excellence in any field involves finding and replicating the strategies of those who show the highest expertise in their area. At the surface level, this directs our focus to the *content* of what the expert does, which defines him or her as an expert. What are the necessary skills, activities, understandings, and so on?

Yet excellence involves more. Much more. We all know people who have excellent skills, but who spoil their expertise with their attitude. Their attitude undermines what they can do and contribute and makes others not even want to be around them. In addition to skill and competence, excellence involves attitude, the right kind of attitude—spirit.

- What are the beliefs, ideas, and attitudes that support the expert in attaining, sustaining, and demonstrating such high-level performances?
- What is the expert's attitude about the boring details that are involved in the process?
- What attitude does the expert take about any given facet of the work?
- How does the expert think or feel when experiencing failure, rejection, frustration, etc.?

Such questions enable us to look at not only the external factors that contribute to excellence, but the internal and psychological factors of success. In terms of the model here,

- What are the mental games that experts play that set them head and shoulders above the rest of the crowd?
- What are the verbal and linguistic games that they play that enable them to control their frame and stay fresh and creative?
- What are the behavioral games that they play?
- How do they frame things about X or Y that enhances and supports their performance?

Summary

- There is a *structure to excellence* and within that structure, the driving force for genius in any field involves *the higher frames of mind*. These govern our internal world and set up a self-organizing influence that patterns our external world.

- A game is the game it is only because of the frame that drives it. This makes *frame-game detection* critical if we want to develop business excellence.

- It's frames all the way up because we are a special class of life—a class that lives and thrives on symbols, and especially language. We not only play games: we play games within games, games about our games.

Part II

Games for Personal Empowerment

Chapter 3

How to Play and Master the Games of Business

Frame-Game Analysis

I think you will find playing *The Business Expert Games* easy when you fully appreciate the significance of frame games in our lives. In one sense, you've been playing games all of your life anyway. Yet in another sense it is more the case that the games have been playing you. Now it's time to change that. Now it's time to learn to *play* the games that make life fun and productive and that put you in charge of your own life.

A *"game"* simply refers to a set of actions and interactions that allow you to structure your energies so that you can achieve some desired objective. In fact, that's why we play "games." We want to accomplish something; we want to "win" at something, express our skills, show off or discover our knowledge and abilities, relate to someone in a certain way, and/or simply enjoy the process of living and expending our energies. Games have payoffs.

Further, as we play games, we play according to the rules of the game. These rules set up the structure, form, and nature of the games. The rules give us an understanding of when we play, whom we play with, how we play, why we play, how we score, when to start, when to quit, exceptions to the rules. Without the rules of the game, we could not play. Without the rules, there would be chaos.

All of this holds true for *frame games.* The games that we play arise from, and are giving form by, our frames of mind. This highlights the very first thing we need to do as we learn any new game. We need to clearly identify the *frames* that initiate, institute, and structure the game for us and others, and they may be different. When we first learned chess, Monopoly, baseball, tennis, or any game, we began by asking, "Okay, how do we play? How do we get started?"

Typically, we do not learn games by formally studying rule books. We learn just enough rules to begin and then we play around with the game until we get the hang of it. *We learn games best by trying them on and giving ourselves a chance to learn the ropes. We also give ourselves a chance with the new game by not expecting* that we have to begin as experts or masters the first time out. We know it will take some time and lots of practice, and that we will improve our game through experience. We also know that, if we begin by just having fun with it, learning, making mistakes, using the feedback of what works and what does not, we will learn the new game more efficiently.

With that in mind, as you read about some new games here, do the following:

1. *First, get an initial impression about the game.* Start with the name of the game. What is it called? Often, just knowing the name of the game is enough to get you started in that new domain. This is also the value of naming games colloquially in memorable ways. *"The No-Blame, No-Shame Game,"* for instance, provides a nice initial impression that specifies the governing frame.

2. *Begin playing the game and experimenting with it.* We learn best and most thoroughly as we experiment, test, and play around with the game. Take the *governing idea* and play with it. Toss it back and forth with someone. Get a feel for it. Express it in numerous ways. Apply it to work, home, exercise, friendship, whatever. Don't aim to do anything with it except just testing and playing with it.

3. *Visit the description of the game to begin filling in some of the details.* One reason for *not* starting a new game by reading the rule book is to avoid overwhelming ourselves with details. Another reason is that the rules become more meaningful and understandable if we learn them bit by bit, trying out what we know, testing it in experience, getting a feel for the initial structures, experiencing the contexts in which they make

sense, and then returning for the next piece. It's similar to learning to work with a computer or computer program. We start by reading a step or two, acting on those, seeing if we get those right, making sure that we are orienting ourselves to the computer or the program properly, and then adding one or two pieces at a time.

This incremental approach to learning and mastery makes the *game* the primary thing, rather than the rules. The rules and frames are there to support the game, not to become a substitute for the game. Weird things can happen to a person when the rules become uppermost and the game secondary.

4. *Continually renew your focus and awareness on the objective of the game.* What is the purpose of the game? Why do you want to play this particular game? What's the payoff that you want from it? What enlivens and energizes any game is its sense of direction, outcome, and purpose.

   In the *frame games* of our lives, many of our games actually operate as sub-games within some larger game. The purpose of one game may therefore be to enable us to play a larger game. Knowing this gives our playing more meaning and purpose.

5. *Have fun as you play.* No matter where you are in the process, whether you are a novice at a new game or a master, don't forget to have fun and to enjoy the process. This will support your learning, development, and expertise. Remember also that most of the fun is in the play itself rather than in the prize for winning the game.

6. *Keep aiming for mastery by developing more skills and taking on more challenges.* In any game there is a relationship between your skills in playing the game and the challenge the game offers you.

When we experience a low skill level with high challenge, we typically feel overwhelmed and anxious. When that happens, our fun and delight in the game itself is reduced. We then begin to get serious, stressed, and often will feel inadequate. And that will lessen our interest. This is why we need to start off slow and easy.

When we feel a low skill level and there is a low challenge, the game does not seem worth even learning. It feels boring. As it doesn't matter much to us, our interest wanes. We feel no passion about the game. Games are then easily dismissed with a "So what?"

We can also get bored when we develop high-level skills, and yet face a low challenge from the game. "Why bother?" we ask. The game seems like a child's game, offering no real challenge to our skills. It's too easy. And, as it becomes too easy, our interest and passion wanes.

The best situation occurs when we face bold challenges with our high-level skills. This calls to our highest passions. Then we not only feel drawn into the game, compelled to play at our best, but we also get lost in the game. We enter into a "flow" state. As we do, the world goes away, time goes away, a sense of self goes away, all of the higher levels of the mind vanish (we lose awareness of this mind) as we become totally present in this moment and fully experience the *frame game*.

In the following chapters we have lots of "games"—*frame games* that you can learn to play for greater management over yourself, your time, energy, schedule, or relating. Treat them as games. Treat the frames as all of the rules, structures, and formatting that allow you to play the games. As you identify the old games that you have been playing (and their corresponding frames), and the new games that you can play if you so choose, you move to a new position. You can now choose how and why you play the game of life as you do.

Mastering the Games of the Business Experts

Via Frame-Game Analysis

There is rhyme and reason to the games we play. They do not arise as mere happenstance events. Unique and personal reasons and understandings govern them. The following sets of questions will enable you to engage in a process that's nearly magical. We call this process, *Frame Analysis.* By thinking through the structure and form of our games, we bring insight and clarity to our minds. This empowers us to take charge of the games that we play and the frames that we allow to control our minds.

One way to make this a true research and transformation of your work and business habits is to grab a notebook and use it to record the *frame games* that you catch. Then you can analyze them. The following questions will lead you not only to describe, but to name the game. And *the name of the game is to name the game.*

By naming the game, you take control over it. It's the first step. As long as the game plays you and you don't know it, you don't know *how* it plays you, nor the structure of the game as it plays you—you are its patsy. You then become an unconscious participant in the games others play with you. As you stubbornly refuse to tolerate that kind of mental and emotional slavery, you'll be able to develop true mastery over the games that you choose to play.

Game description: What's the Game?
- What's the game you're playing at work ...?
- With your career plans?
- With being a team member?
- With working hard?
- With adding value?
- With disciplining your responses?
- With running your own brain?
- With managing your own states?

Who are the Players in the Game?
- Whom do you play the games with (just yourself or others)?
- How many people do you invite into the games?
- Are all of the players living?

How healthy, productive, useful, or enhancing is the game?
- Do you like the games you're playing?
- Do they serve you well?
- Do they enhance your life?

- Do they empower you as a person?
- Are they useful, practical, or productive?
- Would you recommend them to your children?

What would you like to call this Frame Game?
- Now that you have described many of the facets of the game, what would you like to name this game so as to take control of the frame games that you play?
- What funny, silly, memorable, and colloquial name would really summarize this *frame game?*

What Frames of Reference support and drive this game?
- Are you using historical referents?
- Are you using imagined referents?
- Are you using conceptual referents?
- Are you using vicarious referents (something that happened to someone else)?
- Are you using healthy or unhealthy referents?
- Are you using enhancing or limiting referents?

What's the emotional intensity of the game?
- How much intensity from 0 to 10 does the game generate?
- Are there any somatic responses that the game produces?
- Are there any other symptoms that the game produces?

What are the leverage points in the game?
- What ideas, thoughts, emotions, beliefs, or expectations operate as leverage points in how the game is set up?
- If you wanted to change the game, where is its weakest point?
- What would be the easiest thing to do to mess up the game?

Game cues

What are the Hooks that Pull you into the games?
- What starts the game? How does it begin?
- How do the games hook you?

- What's within the games that's seductive, tempting?
- What's the payoff that pulls you into the game?
- What are some of the triggers that get you?
- What bait does the game depend upon to get you?

What are some of the Cues that indicate the presence of a game?
- How do you know when you're involved in playing a game?
- What lets you know?
- What are some of the linguistic cues (the way that you talk)?
- What are some of the physical cues (things that you are doing)?
- What are some of the environmental cues?
- What begins and ends the game?
- When is it over?

Rules of the game

What are they?
- How is the game set up?
- How do you play?
- How do you "score" points in the game?
- What comprises a "win"?
- What lets you know that you are "losing"?
- Who makes up the rules?
- Do you like the rules?

Payoffs of the game

What's the Agenda?
- What's the intention or motivation that drives the game?
- What payoffs do you get from the game?
- What hidden agendas outside your awareness may be motivating the game?
- What do you get from the game?

Game transformation

What New Frame Game would you prefer to Play?
*   If you had a magic wand and could play a better, more empowering, more enhancing, and more productive game, what game would it be?

How would the New Frame Game go (New Description)?
*   How would you play it?
*   With whom?
*   At what times?
*   How would you set up the new game?

What would be the objective of the New Frame Game?
*   What would be its outcome or goal?
*   Why would you play it?
*   What would be the outcome for the others?

How would we Establish the New Game and Install it?
*   If we can shift from the old to the new, how would that occur?
*   If we have to reject the old entirely before initiating the new, how strong a definitive *"No!"* do we need to say?
*   What processes would help us to establish and solidify the new game?

Analyzing Frame Games

These questions now enable us to analyze the *Frame Games* that we play, others play, and, most importantly, that business experts plays. By using *Frame Games Analysis* we can blow the whistle on the games that will only waste our time and energy on our path to become business experts. The process of analyzing our games also increases our mindfulness about what's occurring. That, in turn, then increases our clarity about our choices. Then we can power-fully say *"No!"* to the toxic old games and *"Yes!"* to the empowering life games.

As a short version of all of this, in the coming chapters I will provide descriptions of the new games, the rules of the games, their payoffs (benefits) and the cues that indicate when to play, when to start, when to stop.

On the following pages I have provided a more extensive analysis of *Frame Games.* I use this in our trainings to analyze more thoroughly the structure of a game.

Summary

- Life comprises *games*—games driven by frames.

- When you know how to view your actions and interactions in terms of games, it gives you the choice with regard to what games you'd like to play.

- We cannot *not* play games. It's only a question of *what* games we'll choose, and why.

- By the questions within the model of *Frame-Game Analysis*, we can now take charge of the games and opt for those that are truly healthy and productive *Win/Win Games.*

Frame Games: Worksheet 1

Diagnosing a Toxic Game

1. *What's the game?* Describe the "game" being played out in terms of states—Meta-States, gestalt states. *What's the script of the game?* What sub-games or sub-frames are part of it all?

    _____

    _____

    _____

2. *Cues and clues*: What are some of the cues (linguistic, physical, environmental, etc.) that indicate the presence of a game? How do you know? What cues you to it?

    _____

    _____

    _____

3. *Players*: Who plays the game? With whom? Who else has games going on? What's the larger social system of the game? (Use another Worksheet 1 for each additional person.)

    _____

    _____

    _____

4. *Hooks (triggers, baits)*: What hooks you into the game? How does the game hook others to play?

    _____

    _____

    _____

5. *Emotional intensity of the game*: How intense (0 to 10)? Are there any somatic responses or symptoms?

_____

_____

_____

6. *Rules of the game*: How is the game set up? How do you play (commands, taboos)?

_____

_____

_____

7. *Quality control*: Do you like this game? Just how toxic is this game? Ready to transform it?

_____

_____

_____

8. *Agenda of the game*: What's the intention, motivation, or payoff of the game?

_____

_____

_____

9. *Name the Frame Game*:

_____

_____

_____

10. *Style*: What is your frame of mind? Style of thinking? Meta-Program or attitude?

☐ Matching/Mismatching   ☐ Reactive/Thoughtful

☐ Fast/Slow   ☐ Rigid/Flexible

☐ Aggressive/Passive/Assertive   ☐ Self/Other

☐ Options/Procedures   ☐ Global/Specific

11. *Leverage points*: Where is the leverage in this game to stop it, change it, transform it?

_____

_____

_____

12. *Preferred Frame Game*: What game would you rather play?

_____

_____

_____

Frame Games: Worksheet 2

Design-Engineering a New Frame Game

1. *Desired game*:

   _____

   _____

   _____

2. *Target*: Name the person(s) you want to influence (this will undoubtedly include yourself, and may even exclusively be yourself).

   _____

   _____

   _____

3. *Emotional Agenda/Motivation*: What concerns, him or her most? Values? What's really important to this person? What would hook him/her into this game? Vested interests?

   _____

   _____

   _____

4. *Larger Systems*: What's the larger social system of the game? Who else is involved?

   _____

   _____

   _____

5. *Objective and outcome*: What do I want in this? What do I want for the other(s) in this?

_____

_____

_____

6. *Description*: How will the New Game be played? What frames will work best?

_____

_____

_____

7. *Leverage points*: Where is the leverage to change or stop the game? What frames will best leverage this person?

_____

_____

_____

8. *Process*: How can I set up these frames? How can I implement my persuasion process?

_____

_____

_____

9. *Checklist stages*: Will you need to interrupt, shift, loosen, and/or transform the frames? Which patterns or techniques would provide the most leverage?

_____

_____

_____

10. *Patterns for installation*: Which *Frame Game* (patterns) could you use to install the new *Frame Games* in yourself?

_____

_____

_____

11. *Frames*: What frames of mind do you need in order to play the new game?

_____

_____

_____

Chapter 4

The Power to Play Frame Games for Business Excellence

The First Games

Have you ever attempted to play some game, whether it be something vigorous such as gymnastics, swimming, or skiing, or more cerebral such as chess, Monopoly, or cards and just didn't feel like you had the energy for it?

"I'm just too tired."

It takes energy to play. Maybe that's why kids do a lot more playing of games than do adults. Fatigue in mind, emotions, and body can undermine our ability to play games. And yet, when we get that tired, that depleted, that stressed, we become most vulnerable to becoming the victim of those who might like to play some games on us or with us. Then, we become a target for someone who wants to push our buttons and rattle our cage. We become more susceptible to reacting.

Concerning the *frame games* that govern how we play *The Game of Business Excellence*, it obviously takes mental and emotional energy, verbal and linguistic energy, behavioral and relating energy. We don't find business excellence in the lives of the lazy, the slothful, the indulgent, or the ones searching for "the path of least resistance." We find business excellence emerging in the lives of the passionate, the searchers for adventure, the dreamers who act, and those who love to rise up to meet a challenge.

Frames for Energy

If *frame games* so thoroughly govern our lives, and if we actually have to enter into the fray to play the games to achieve excellence, then where do we find the source of power to play, the power to be alive and vigorous, and to keep rejuvenating our playfulness? What mechanisms govern the source of personal power to rise up to meet this challenge?

The power that enables us to frame, to create mind–body states, and to play the games that we do are four in number: the two *private* powers of thinking and feeling, and the two *public* powers of speaking and behaving. It is from these basic psychological and personal powers that all of our other powers emerge. These basic powers support our mental, emotional, verbal, and behavioral powers needed to think, choose, create mental models, represent and process information, invest ourselves, value, generate meaning, and take effective action.

In these mind–body powers (or neuro-linguistic powers) we have the source of all of the mental and emotional framing needed to establish the games that we want to play. After all, we set frames by the way we think, by what we think about, by the emotions we evoke regarding the frames, and by how we then speak and act.

To "power up" and to tap into and develop more energy for playing expert business games with conscious mindfulness, we begin here. We begin by recognizing and owning our core "powers" or functions, the functioning of our neurology and "languaging." By doing this, we establish the basis for personal empowerment, responsibility, and proactivity, as well as many other higher level states that make the difference in creating business excellence.

Figure 4:1

Power Zone

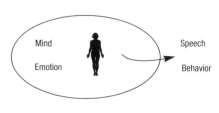

The Powering-Up Frame Game

I like to ask people what *core* powers supply and support all of their other powers. "What are the most fundamental powers?

"If you really wanted to power up, what core powers would you focus your attention on?"

Most people don't know. They haven't been let in on the secret. And, when they hear the secret, they often have a tendency to dismiss it because of its simplicity.

"What core powers can we access and then use at the higher levels of our mind for frame-setting?"

The answer is simple and awesomely profound. It is this: we have four fundamental powers. Two occur deep inside and comprise our private powers and two occur more openly and comprise our public powers. Each of us has these four central and inescapable powers, which enable us with the ability to fully respond to things. Two of these human powers operate very privately (thinking and emoting) and two operate as our public contributions to the world around us (speaking and behaving). In these four powers lies our ability to cope with and master the challenges we face. This describes the essence of our *response-ability*, that is, our ability or *power* to respond. I refer to these four powers as our "power zone."

1) Thinking-feeling
In the private recesses of our mind we *think-feel*. Thinking-feeling makes up the central "engine" that drives all of the rest of our responses and gives shape to the very structure and tone of our personality. And, just as nobody can "make" you think a certain way without your consent (but can only invite you to try one way of thinking) so nobody can "make" you *feel* a certain way. At best, others can invite and provoke you to feel, evoke certain responses.

Traditionally, we have separated thinking and feeling so much that most of us actually think of these as separate powers. They are not. They operate as part of the same mental mapping process within the same mind–body system. In fact, when we separate them and

59

treat them as different "faculties," we misunderstand the way thinking and emoting interface and influence each other.

2) Speaking and acting
While thinking/feeling occurs inside and can be almost entirely hidden, not so our speech and behavior. We express our thoughts and feelings by talking and acting. These two public powers describe *how* we express what we've been thinking and feeling. They express our power to affect the outside world and to make real (realize) our thoughts and emotions in our engagement with the world.

As we take specific *actions* we give our thoughts and emotions expression and thereby influence things in the outside world. We can also talk, use language, formulate ideas in linguistic forms be it story, poetry, prose, news releases, books, problem solving, or whatever. Herein lies our power to affect events, people, systems as we use higher levels of symbols to affect the minds and emotions of people.

Power Zone Ownership

If our most fundamental and core powers boil down to the processes of thinking-feeling, speaking, and behaving, then there are only a few questions left to ask.

*   Do you recognize these basic powers that give you the ability to order and organize your own responses to the world?
*   Do you fully accept and own these powers as your own?
*   Have you cultivated and developed these powers?
*   Do you give way to others by disowning your powers of thoughts and emotions, speech, and behavior?

The Empowerment Game

"Empowerment" and "proactivity" have been a key concepts in business for a couple of decades. Yet all too often these words have come *not* to stand for actual and personal powers of taking effective action and doing so as an initiative rather than waiting for a crisis. More often than not, the words have been used as the latest business jargon to try to get employees more involved without actually empowering them.

True empowerment would lead to a very different set of games. It would lead to managers and supervisors turning over the power and authority for making decisions to the people who they hold accountable. It would lead to employees, managers, and others feeling the right, privilege, and responsibility to act, to significantly contribute, to move into a solution-oriented frame of mind.

To play *The Empowerment Frame Game*, we first of all have to recognize, accept, and own all of our *powers*—our powers of thinking and emoting, and of speaking and acting. This means adopting the following attitude:

> "I, and only I, ultimately determine what I think and feel. Nobody can *make* me think or feel anything. I always play a determinative role about what I let into my mind and what I give attention to. I have the power of mind and heart over this ultimate human freedom of what to think and how to think."

Do you *own* that way of playing *The Game of Life*? Would you like to? Would you like to say the same thing about your linguistic and behavioral powers?

> "I, and only I, ultimately determine what I say and how I say it, what I do, the actions I take, and the quality of the behaviors I use as I relate to the world of events and people. My actions and behaviors are mine just as are my words, metaphors, stories, and language patterns, etc. By these powers I can make an impact on myself, on my world, and on others. I fully accept my power to influence others and do so responsibly."

Games Business Experts Play

To be an expert at work, and to rise to the level of expertise in your given field, you have to play these games. *The Proactivity Game, The "I'm the One Responsible for My Success" Game, The "I'm Personally*

Empowered and Centered" Game, etc.—these are the games that the business experts play. They are the games that the experts first played that turned them into experts. When we play these games, the games that undermine expertise (those of Blame, Victimhood, Whining, etc.) have no power to recruit us.

Powering Up Frame Game

To fully and mindfully *own* your *power zone*, you need to do three things. First, recognize these powers of your personality as your central powers to affect the world. You can check that one off by taking a little time to really notice these formative facets. Next *accept* them. Acceptance refers to acknowledging what is, whether we like it or not. It refers to welcoming and adjusting to such factors. How well do you accept your mind and mental powers, your heart and emotional powers, your tongue and linguistic powers, your body and behavioral powers? Finally, *own* them. If you're ready to play, then here's a pattern for making this real inside your mind–body system.

1. Access and amplify the resource state of ownership
Think about a time or place when you strongly felt that something was yours. That it "belonged" to you. That you "owned" it free and clear. Think about something so that, when that thing comes to mind, every fiber in your being, in your body, can fully and congruently say, *"Mine!"*

I would recommend that you keep your referent experience small and simple in order to get a discrete sense about it. Pick something such as, "My hand," "My eye," "My cat," "My pen," "My book." Stop now and try that on for size. If you have any difficulty with that, try "My toothbrush," "My underwear." If someone came up and said, "Could I use that toothbrush? Would you mind?" Do you immediately think, "Sure, go ahead." Or, does your mind go, "Well, I don't know: it's my toothbrush." Or does your mind say, "Absolutely not! That toothbrush is *mine*!"

There are some people who have theoretic concepts that actually get in the way of accessing a simple sense of ownership. They believe, "Nothing is mine, I'm just a pilgrim through this earthly pilgrimage." An example of a higher frame setting the rules of the game we play. Invite such a person to recognize and accept that,

"Yes, you are just a pilgrim or steward of these possessions, and they are *yours* to be treated with care. You are responsible for them, are you not?"

2. Apply that feeling of "ownership" ("Mine!") to your awareness of your four core powers
As you feel the sense of ownership, turn up those feelings so that they become stronger and stronger. Having picked some small and simple referent such as "My toothbrush" enables us to obtain a pure and discrete sense of what *ownership* feels like. Make your pictures and sounds of that referent bigger, bolder, closer, until you can feel that mind–body state. When you do so, *apply that state* of thinking and feeling of "mine" to your core powers.

Notice your power of thinking and say, "My thoughts, my brain, my mental processing!" Notice your power of feeling and emoting and say,

"My emotions, my sensations in my body, my feelings, my investment of my heart, my bonding, attachment, caring, rejoicing …"

Repeat this same process with speaking and behaving:

"My words, my languaging, my use of symbols, my storytelling, my metaphors, etc." and "My actions, my behaviors, my movements, gestures, and patterns of relating."

In so *owning* your core powers, gesture naturally and freely as if exploring how to fully express the idea of ownership in the way you move your arms, breathe, stand, and walk. Without the sense of ownership, we tend to treat things as interesting items to observe, talk about, and visit, but not fully use, take charge of, or embrace. Developmentally, we see *the ownership stage* in young children as they yell and assert themselves. They shout, "Mine!"

and grab a toy, cookie, or crayon from another. But, sometimes, unwitting parents set out to beat this sense of ownership out of the child, confusing it with ideas of selfishness or something. They are not the same. So, for some, reclaiming this power, granting oneself the right to *own* these powers, and asserting permission to do so will radically change the very structures of their personality.

As you *feel the sense of ownership*, just revel and enjoy that as you apply this to your core powers. Stay with that experience for a moment and then begin to notice the transformation of how you experience your thinking, emoting, speaking, and behaving when you fully *own* them as yours. This allows you to embed your core powers within a frame of ownership.

3. Access states of acceptance and appreciation and apply to the state of ownership

To enrich this even more, do the following. Think about a small simple item that you "accept" and then another that you appreciate. In *acceptance*, we welcome something into our world, but we may not particularly like it. We acknowledge it, we even embrace it, but do so matter-of-factly and without much emotion. Think about accepting a rainy day, the traffic at rush hour, interruptions during the day, the baby who'll mess his diaper—things like that. In *appreciation*, we not only welcome and embrace, but we do so with warmth and excitement, with a sense of seeing its value. Think about the appreciation you have for a beautiful sunset, a warm bath, a card from a special one—things like that.

Again, access these experiences, hold the feelings that they initiate in your mind and body, and then just step into them even more fully, letting them grow stronger and more powerful. When they feel pretty intense (8 or 9 on a scale from 0 to 10), then *apply* that feeling to your sense of ownership. In this way you will set two higher frames *about* the ownership of your own power zone as you accept and then appreciate your core powers.

4. Amplify all of these states until your neurology begins to radiate

"I accept and appreciate these powers as mine... I welcome, receive, and warmly embrace these neurolinguistic powers that give me the ability to take charge of my world. I appreciate and will continue to grow in appreciation for my thinking-and-feeling powers as an expression of how I can become much more effective in the world."

While you're at it, let your words emerge as you "language" (yes, we're using that word as a verb) this *Powering-Up Frame Game* in as effective a way as you can. Play with your words until you find those that really excite and give you a vision of the empowered you.

"This is my *zone* of power. I am totally responsible for my *responses* of mind, emotion, speech and behavior."

5. Now project yourself into the days and weeks to come
Now imagine all of these thoughts and feelings and ways of operating as you see yourself moving out into tomorrow and the days and weeks to come.

Vividly imagine taking the ownership of your essential powers with you to work tomorrow, next week, next month, in the way you relate to others, in how you communicate, and with the energy and investment you put into your plan and goals for your life in business.

Empowered to Reject The Blame Game

Intellectually, it's fairly easy to recognize, realize, and accept that *nobody can "make" us angry*. Our anger is our own. It arises from our angry thoughts and our angry state.

It is much more difficult and challenging to practice this higher level of consciousness in the presence of someone who seems to know how to "push all of our buttons" and get under our skin. How can we say *"No"* to *The Blame Game* when it feels so pleasurable to blame, when we have a motive to blame or when we have been falsely accused, and want to give our blamer a taste of his or her own medicine?

Here clarity strengthens us for the challenge. Being crystal clear about owning our power zone and having mentally, verbally, and behaviorally practiced a set of effective responses enables us to say *"No"* to defaulting to the Blame Frame.

Certainly, others can *invite* us to feel angry and upset. To do that, they have to communicate or act in such a way as to provoke us, so that we *think* upsetting thoughts. If we then buy into their frame, we will inevitably *feel* upset. Others can provide incredibly powerful stimuli that invite, urge, provoke, incite, and elicit upsetting thinking-and-emoting responses from us. Yet our *response* is always that—our response. It begins with a mental response and it shows up as a behavioral or language response.

We can play *The Blame Game* only by failing to distinguish between the *stimulus* that others offer and our *response*. There is a difference: one is a trigger; the other is a response. When I *think* that I have no choice, that I *have to* get angry, I give my power away. I become the other person's slave and do his or her bidding. Yet doing so disempowers me to become a victim of the other's provocation.

Listen to the frames that people set that send them into *The Blame Frame Game:*

*   "My boss makes me so angry that I can't stand it."
*   "I know that he uses that tone of voice with me in the board meeting just to make me feel put down and degraded. I just hate the way he controls me."
*   "I had to retaliate in the way I did, she made me feel worthless."

This kind of talk assumes that the speaker has no power, no choice, and no response ability. No wonder such people become *reactive*. They have no other choice. Their frame induces them to live in a deterministic world and they have to play that game. As long as they frame their thinking to *believe* that others control their responses, that frame will govern how they feel their emotional states and how they respond.

To play *The Empowerment Game* we shift to a new way of thinking-and-feeling. We proactively recognize and own our powers:

"My responses of thought and emotion result from the way I think and emote," we say. "No one 'makes' me think in a certain way. My thoughts arise from how I choose to think. No one 'makes' me feel in certain ways. My emotions also arise from my thinking and valuing. I will not play the victim and give all my power away to them."

The Validating Game

Did you like that?

Would you like to even more fully recognize and own your own basic human powers so that you can take charge of your life?

By asking questions that evoke a *"Yes"* response, I am not only seeking clarity, but also inviting you to *validate* the thinking, attitude, frames of mind, and their subsequent games. Asking rhetorical or straightforward *"Yes"* questions do that. In saying *"Yes,"* we essentially move up in our minds to validate an experience (a meta-cognitive move).

Saying *"Yes"* to your mental and emotional powers will further build up a higher quality, an emerging quality that we call "ego strength." This means the ability to use your ego sense (your sense of self) to face reality for what it is and to look at it without blinking. This also gives you the ability to affirm your values and visions and to *"disconfirm"* things that do not fit or that violate what you consider important. When you utter a *"Yes"* and/or a *"No"* to an experience, thought, choice, emotion, and response available to you, you have in your hands the dynamic duo of *affirmation* and *disconfirmation*. (We will explore that much more fully in the next chapter.) Recognizing that as you now say *"Yes"* to some things and *"No"* to other things allows you to control the inputs to your mind.

What's the very first item on the list of things to say *"Yes"* and *"No"* to? The *content* of your consciousness. What do you want to say *"Yes"* to in terms of the frames you set? What do you want to say *"No"* to?

- What games at work do you want to affirm? Which one would you like to disconfirm?
- What beliefs will you *"Yes,"* what will you *"No"*?
- What values and visions?
- What decisions and commitments?
- What self-definitions and identifications?
- What ideas and frames?

When you say *"Yes"* to your power zone, you also say *"No"* to blaming, excuse making, and irresponsibility. As a result, this automatically and effortlessly shifts you from playing *The Blame Game* to playing *The Aim Frame*. You will then focus on what you want to achieve—your aims and desired outcomes. When you don't get the responses you want, simply treat it as feedback (the Feedback Frame). You can then go into a learning mode (the Learning Frame) to discover what you can learn about how to do things differently. Then you shift your responses (the Flexibility Game) and keep varying your speaking and acting responses until you get the response that you want (the Persistence Game).

Summary

- It takes *energy* to play games; it takes power to play frame games—mental energy, emotional energy, verbal energy, physical energy, and personal energy. When we're depleted, tired, or fatigued, others can more easily play games with us without our awareness or ability to stand up to the games and refuse them.

- The core of personal power resides in our neuro-linguistic powers of thinking, feeling, speaking, and behaving. These are essential and fundamental. They arise from our innate neuro-logical and linguistic processes.

- You begin to play *the first game* that will build and support your business excellence when you recognize, accept, own, and validate your *Power Zone*. This enables you then to play such games as *Proactivity, Responsibility, Initiative, and Self-Efficacy.*

The Empowerment Game

- *Description:* This is the sense of power to make a difference in life and work and arises from owning our core powers or responses. Acknowledge the powers of mind, heart, language, and behavior; accept and appreciate them.

- *Rules of the game:* No one can *make* or *force* you to think, feel, say, or do anything. You always have choice. Refuse to buy into anything that seduces you from fully experiencing your power zone. Use the language and posture of empowerment. Proactively choose your games and responses.

- *Payoffs:* These are the sense of mastery, high-level sustainable motivation, and sense of optimistic hope in the face of challenges.

- *Cues to play:* these are any word, phrase, idea, feeling that would attempt to recruit you to play the victim, to lie down and give up, to throw up your hands in pessimism, to act defeated, to blame and accuse others for your experiences, etc.

Chapter 5

Advanced Power for Playing

The Yes/No Game For Powering Up

"Do you feel up to playing a game of chess with me?"
"Yeah, that's fine."
"Are you sure?"
"Yeah, I can get through it."

That ought to be an exciting game!

Not.

It takes not only energy to play actual games and *The Games Business Experts Play,* but it takes vigorous energy, vibrant energy, playful energy. It takes the kind of energy that allows us not just to "get through it," but to have a ball in the process. That's the kind of power we need. So, with that frame of mind, let's initiate that game.

We gain such power by accessing, owning, and validating our basic core powers, those neuro-linguistic powers that enable us to take charge of our lives, run our own brains, and determine our own pathway toward excellence. As you have now discovered and practiced *accessing your power zone*—that zone of energy in which you can *center* yourself in knowing and experiencing your ultimate freedom, the freedom to determine *what* you think and *how* you think—this, in turn, puts into your hands increased mastery over your emotions, languaging, and acting.

While that's a great beginning, it doesn't end there. Actually, by refreshing our awareness, appreciation, and use of these thinking-and-emoting powers, these linguistic and behavioral powers, we have just begun to put them to use, not only at the primary level of everyday experience, but at all of the higher levels of mind.

71

Playing the Frame Game of Validation

I invited you to play *The Validation Frame Game* in the previous chapter. I did that by simply asking you questions that presupposed a *"Yes"* answer. Now what were those questions? Oh, *yes* ...

Did you like that?

Would you like to even more fully recognize and own your own basic human powers so that you can take charge of your life?

What happens when we ask any question that invites a natural and strong *"Yes"* response? Notice for yourself:

*   Would you like to increase your personal skills and competence?
*   Would you like to become more intelligent in the way you think, make decisions, and respond?
*   Would you really like to increase your wealth and influence with people?
*   Really?
*   Would you find that valuable?

"Yes"-eliciting questions obviously put us into a particular frame of mind. They put us into a particular mental-and-emotional state. What frame of mind does it induce in you? Where do you go? What do you feel?

"Yes" questions, especially strong ones that activate our highest values, goals, beliefs, and purposes, typically elicit in us an *affirming*, *validating*, and *confirming* state. In such a state we welcome something into ourselves, such as an idea, feeling, choice. It enables us to create new possibilities for ourselves. In saying and feeling *"Yes!"* we access a state of mind in which we feel affirmative. It puts our mind and body into a place where we are much more ready to do something about what we are saying *"Yes"* to.

Sales people have known this for a long time. They call it *"the Yes set."* They know that if you get a person to say *"Yes"* seven times in a row it will be very difficult for them to shift to a *"No."* It's the state of confirming that *"Yes"* elicits that creates this motor response, this neuro-linguistic orientation.

Notice also the positive sense of direction that simple word *"Yes"* can provoke. In saying *"Yes"* to something, we develop more of a positive orientation, a solution orientation, a proactive sense of taking action to fulfill our dreams and outcomes. It makes sense, doesn't it? To say *"Yes"* is to validate, and in validating we come close to making a pledge, a promise, a commitment.

"Yes, I will give myself to becoming much more resourceful and productive."

Doesn't that feel good? Isn't there a basic healthfulness to saying *"Yes"* to a valued objective or a valued belief? It seems that when we rise up in our minds to affirm with a hearty *"Yes!"* we rise up to access some of our highest levels of mind. We become more; it brings out the best in us.

Wouldn't you like to experience that kind of state on a daily basis?

Wouldn't that create an ongoing and rejuvenating sense of purpose and meaning? And wouldn't that revitalize your energy?

Ah, and that's what this *frame game* is all about. By learning how to affirm, we learn how to amplify our basic powers. The fabulous thing, of course, is that we have to use our thinking, representing, valuing, emoting, speaking, and acting powers to access this power.

The Magic of Saying "Yes!"

Saying *"Yes"*—especially a strong and vigorous *"Yes!"*—enables us to establish higher frames of mind about things and to solidify those frames. You may have noticed this with the exercise in the previous chapter. Once you have recognized, accepted, and appreciated your power zone, and then accessed a strong—or maybe the strongest representation you have—of a powerful and overwhelming *"Yes!"* and then connected that sense of confirmation to

73

your power zone, you have embraced it and embedded it inside a frame of confirmation.

"Yes, by God," you say, "it's my zone, in which I do have the power to respond, to think, to imagine, to create, to feel, to connect, to invest myself, to love, to celebrate, to talk, to put ideas into language, to act on my beliefs; and I refuse to let anyone or anything take this power away from me."

That sense of validating your core powers then generates a sense of what we call *self-efficacy.* This relates to your confidence in your own competence to be efficient, effective, and able to take productive action. Would you like that as your everyday frame of mind— a frame of mind to wake up in and operate from? Really? You'd enjoy that? That would enrich your life?

Getting Your Vigorous "Yes!"

The idea of saying yes to something gives voice to confirming, validating, and affirming. *"Yes"* is the neuro-linguistics of confirmation. It's one of our most basic states, one of our prime states, a developmental stage that we all negotiated when we were very young, and one in which some people have suffered damage. That is, their ability to affirm has been lost or weakened. Numerous experiences can make it difficult for a person to even think, let alone feel, about things affirmatively. Such events can tempt us to create mental maps that prevent us from experiencing affirmation: disappointments, frustrations, confusions, failure to be loved and valued, traumas, and son on. How is your power to confirm and validate? How alive and vital is it?

Let's refresh our ability to affirm. Here's an exercise to renew and rejuvenate this *"Yes-ing"* power.

1. Access a discrete and intense referent that you can clearly say "Yes!" to
What can you say *"Yes!"* to with every fiber of your being? What brings out the biggest, strongest, wildest, and most powerful *"Yes!"* in you? Would winning a million dollars or pounds? Would

recovering your youthful energy? Would touching a loved one's life with some real healing power?

Think of something you can absolutely say *"Yes!"* to in the most powerful way possible. After you get your first *"Yes,"* access four more references for an empowering *"Yes!"*

Find your referent and then let yourself feel that *"Yes!"* fully and completely. Stay with it and experience it in all of the sensory systems: *see* the sights and images; *hear* the sounds, tones, volumes, music, words; *feel* the physical sensations in your body: warmth, excitement, relaxation. As you stay with the feelings and let them grow, allow yourself to gesture with your arms and hands, even with your full body. How do you gesture a strong and vigorous *"Yes!"*? What does *"Yes!"* look like, sound like, feel like in your movements? You may even want to experiment with finding seven different tonalities for uttering your *"Yes!"* Utter a series of three yeses, each with a rising crescendo of intensity and emphasis: **"Yes, Yes!, YES!"** Continue to juice up your *"Yes!"* until you begin to drool!

2. Apply your sense of "Yes" to your core powers
When you have the biggest and most ferocious *"Yes!"* that you can experience today (knowing, of course, that it will double and triple in intensity in the days to come), bring it to bear upon (that is, apply it to) your *awareness* of your sense of personal power and mastery. Say *"Yes!"* to the idea of taking charge of your life and becoming proactive in the way you live it. Validate that as a concept, as a belief, and as a value. Confirm it repeatedly in as many ways as you desire to confirm it.

When you have confirmed it thoroughly, read and answer with a *"Yes!"* the following questions, or, better, have a friend read them to you.

- Do you really want that idea in your head?
- Would you want it in your body?
- Would you like it in every muscle of your body?
- Would you like it as your way of being in the world?
- Would it enhance your life?

75

- Would it make you a better person?
- Would it contribute to your everyday experiences?
- Would it enrich your work and career?
- Would it begin to develop your "genius at work" state?

3. Confirm the confirmation
So you really would want this? You're not kidding me about this? You are fully okay with becoming more empowered? You really want to say *"Yes"* to that?

"Yes-ing" our ideas, concepts, understandings, and beliefs enables us to set an even higher frame of validation for our validation. We confirm our confirmation. In doing that, we solidify our frames. This embeds our thoughts within a frame of confirmation and elicits within us reasons for the validation. So just keep right on *"Yes-ing"* these ideas and representations until you begin to hear a matter-of-fact voice commenting on your inner movie and saying, "Why, Yes, of course!"

"Yes-ing" Yourself Into New Beliefs

We call this the Meta-*Yes*-ing Pattern and use it as a belief-change process.

A "belief"-change pattern? Yes.

Can you *think* of something without *believing* it?

Can you read something in the local newspaper, hear something on television, talk with a friend about his or her different point of view, understand with clarity and precision that different opinion and still *not* believe it?

Can you listen with appreciation to a discussion of business ideas and alternatives and come away still not *believing* that's the way the company ought to go?

Yes, I know, rhetorical questions. Of course, you can *think* without believing. You'd be in a poor place (mentally) if you believed everything you saw, heard, or read! Of course, some people seem to live their lives that way. They won't read, view, or think in any depth about anything that they don't already agree with or believe in. It's as if they fear reading, learning, and understanding. They are playing *The "I Already Made Up My Mind" Game*—a game that prevents new learning and discoveries.

If we can fully and completely represent, encode, and understand data without believing it, then what's the difference? What's the difference between a "thought" and a "belief"?

In Neuro-Semantics, we have discovered that a "thought" remains just a thought as long as we do not confirm it. Once we *confirm* it, however, we turn it into a "belief." A belief exists as something more than a mere thought: it exists as a higher-level experience, as a very special kind of thought, as a *confirmed and validated thought*. This means that a mental-emotional transformation occurs when we confirm and validate an idea. What once was just a representation now becomes something more than the sum of the parts, an energized, dynamic "belief," a command to the nervous system to actualize and make real the content of the belief.

This *structure* of a belief explains why beliefs operate as self-fulfilling prophecies. It explains the power and danger of beliefs. It explains why mere "thoughts" seem so innocent and harmless, yet when we turn a "thought" into a "belief" it turns us inside out. Beliefs, as higher frames of mind, operate as the governing influence in a living system that will self-organize after the image and likeness of the belief. (See *The Structure of Excellence: Unmasking the Meta-Levels of Submodalities* (1999), Hall and Bodenhamer, for an extensive description.)

Blowing Out Old Beliefs By Meta-No-ing

The converse of saying *"Yes"* to something is saying *"No."* As *"Yes"* confirms and validates, *"No"* disconfirms and invalidates. As *"Yes"* turns thoughts into beliefs, *"No"* undoes the gestalt and reduces a belief to a harmless and mere thought. *"No"* invites us to play an entirely new *frame game*. By finding, accessing, and applying a definitive *"No!"* we can refuse *frame games* and so use our core powers to set boundaries and limits on the games that others can play with us.

There's a funny thing about beliefs. You can learn better, you can gain new knowledge and awareness that updates your old maps from some old outdated or toxic belief, and yet you can still act and feel *as if* you believed something. It's a strange phenomenon. You "know" intellectually that criticism will not hurt you, but, when you experience it, you act and feel as if it were the worst thing in the world, as if you'd been slugged in the stomach. What's going on? Probably an old belief. Probably an old belief operating outside of conscious awareness as your actual frame of reference.

So how can we use a nicely placed *"No"* to blast out old and toxic beliefs that still run the show? How can we disconfirm that old frame and completely reject it, fire it, decommission it?

Once we have detected such a belief frame, especially a pathetic belief that only sickens the mind or spirit and creates a crappy attitude, how can we say a definite and resounding *"No!"* to it so that it blows to smithereens? In a word we access a state of *"No!"*—a state or frame of mind where we can powerfully and absolutely reject and disconfirm it. It's a strong mind–body state. For it you will need to find a very strong and definitive *"No!"*

1. Access and amplify a strong disconfirmation state
Think of something to which every fiber of your being can say *"Hell, No!"* and do so fully and completely. Identify five different items or situations to which you feel a strong, powerful, and definitive *"No!"* Would you eat a bowl of filthy crawling worms? Would you push a child in front of a speeding bus just to watch it get smashed? Would you cut your own throat? Would you strip down naked at work? Would you walk blindfolded across a busy road?

As you do, access each experience separately and as discretely as possible. Again, as you did with the *"Yes!"* gesture, use your hands, arms, and full body in such a way as to shove away from you, and your "space," that old toxic belief. Upon accessing this *"No!"* each time, *amplify* it so that it feels stronger and stronger in your neurology, and continue to do this until every fiber of your being wants to shout out with all of the energy that you can muster, *"Hell, No!"*

2. Enjoy and relish this power to stubbornly refuse things
When you get all of that definitive energy pumped up so that it energizes you thoroughly in mind and body, take a moment to *enjoy* this power of refusal, disconfirmation, rejection, and stubbornness. *Relish* this power of self-determination as you commission it to have the final word about what you will and what you will not admit into your mental and emotional theater.

Your parents or teachers or others in early life may have tried to beat this power out of you—so be it. That was then. Today is now. And today you can give yourself permission to have the right, the privilege, and the responsibility to say *"No."* It's never too late to access and develop the personal resources needed for effectively navigating life. Refuse to whine as you learn to really say *"No!"* in a powerful way!

3. Apply this disconfirmation to the toxic belief
Holding all of these feelings of *"No!"* constant, begin to direct them to every belief, idea, and activity to which you want to utter a final and definitive *"No!"* Bring this neurological *"No!"* to bear upon various toxic ideas, beliefs, behaviors, and habits and, it becomes a "meta-no" to the experience that you will no longer tolerate, repeat the *"No!"* until you feel it pushing away the unenhancing state. Do so until this neurological *"No!"* becomes a matter-of-fact no: "No, of course, not. Are you crazy? Why would I want *that*?"

There are some really sick games. There are some really sick ideas, thoughts, beliefs, and frames. Is there any idea, experience or game that you'd like to refuse right now? Feel that *"No!"* about that.

What are some of the sabotaging beliefs about your work? What sick and unhealthy ideas still seem to run the show even though you know better? List them and then blast them to smithereens with a strong, *"Hell, No!"*

The Power to Say "No"

Now with this power, add another power to your arsenal. The power to decide what will and will not gain entrance into your mind. You can now use your mental-emotional energies to refuse things, to set boundaries, to establish limits, to differentiate your-self from others, to individualize, to discover and create your own identity.

Developmentally, we all experience two periods of life where we have to engage in saying *"No"* in order to individualize and dif-ferentiate as we learn to become our best selves. We do this during "the terrible twos" and during the turbulent storms of adoles-cence. These developmental stages enable us to differentiate in order to create the kind and quality of *independence* that ensures we can become healthily *inter*dependent later.

But, of course, lots of parents didn't graduate from *Parenting #101* and so failed to understand the importance and value of such dif-ferentiation. They took the *"No-ing"* of their children personally and set out to squelch it in them, or they tried to beat it out of them. They forbade their kids the right to say *"No."* And lots of kids grew up with a taboo rule about saying *"No."* This led them to begin to play *The Non-Assertiveness Frame Game:* they learned to fear their own strength of character. The taboo frame forbade them from knowing their own mind, emotions, values, and strengths. Permission to do this was taken away from them. Years later, of course, they find themselves feeling like wimps, beaten pups, like Jell-O personalities with no fiber of will, no willpower, no deter-mination or persistence to go after their own visions and values. It's not a very fun game to play.

This explains the importance of rediscovering and refreshing our power to say no—and to say it powerfully.

Summary

- If we really want to develop mastery in playing the games of life and the games necessary for business excellence, we have to have the twin abilities to say *"No!"* to sick and toxic things, and to less valued choices, and to say a full and affirmative *"Yes!"* to the things that fulfill our vision of the good life.
- Affirming and disaffirming, validating and invalidating put into our hands the very powers that can transform inspiring thoughts into full-fledged *beliefs* and that can unglue the danger and damage of old beliefs that no longer serve us.

- Recognizing that *beliefs* represent a higher level of mind than mere *thought* alerts us to the fact that thoughts differ. There are *levels of thought*. The higher thoughts become beliefs and frames of mind—the mechanisms that really govern the games that we play. And therein lies an even higher power, which is the subject of the next chapter.

The Validation Game
- *Description:* The power to say *"Yes,"* the power to affirm and validate, to welcome new ideas into the theater of our minds. By *"Yes-ing"* we experience a neurolinguistic state that can create new possibilities.

- *Rules:* Think about a strong neurological *"Yes!"*—one that gets your entire body into the experience—and relate this *"Yes!"* feeling to any and every idea that supports expertise and mastery in business.

- *Payoffs:* To fill up your mental and emotional world with the ideas, frames, and feelings that support your effectiveness, enrich your sense of control in life.

- *Clues for knowing when to play:* Whenever you see, hear, read, or discover a great idea or experience expertise in others.

The "Hell, No!" Game

- *Description:* The power to say *"No,"* the power to refuse, invalidate, and prevent sick and toxic ideas from gaining entrance into our minds. It's the power to set self boundaries, to individuate, and to be true and to be yourself.

- *Rules:* Refuse to tolerate things that violate your values and visions. Draw a line in the sand and use your stubbornness to "make up your mind" about crucial things to your wellbeing. Say *"No!"* with power.

- *Payoffs:* To stop sabotaging ideas from poisoning your mind; to slay mental and emotional dragons.

- *Clues to when to plan:* Whenever you see, hear, or read anything morbid, stupid or boredom.

Chapter 6

The Frames at the Top of the Mind

How We Build and Play Mind Games in the First Place

When it comes to playing games.

Whoever sets the game's rules controls the game.

We all know that and we have known it for a long time. Even as kids, we knew that. That's why we so frequently said or heard,

"Hey, why do *you* get to make the rules? Who appointed you the boss?"

It is for this reason, if we want to get to the most powerful and controlling factor in human thinking and feeling—the mechanism that provides us the most leverage in terms of change, transformation, and renewal—we have to go *up*. We have to move up to the *highest frame* of all. We have to go to the top frame.

The Person Who Sets the Frame Controls the Game

In the field of business, we easily understand *levels*. That's because the business world pervasively uses levels. We talk about "working up to the top," "starting at the bottom," "top dog," etc.

If you got to work one day and had an office memo from your secretary, a letter from a colleague in a competing company, and an email from the CEO of the company, which of these do you respond to first? Which person would rank highest in priority?

Bosses and CEOs carry a lot more influence, weight, power, and authority because they operate from *a higher level*. That principle holds true for all living systems that are also organized hierarchically. The higher level (or frame of reference) governs. In self-organization theory, systems theory, chaos theory, logical levels, and multiple other theoretical disciplines, the higher frame governs because it modulates, organizes, and controls the lower frames.

As a psychologist I can tell you that this is eminently true of human minds as well. That we can and do think about our thinking reveals a special quality about human consciousness. It reveals one of the key secrets for truly becoming a master of yourself and of your area of expertise. The secret is that we operate from *levels of thought* or *levels of mind*. And if frames describe the *driving influence* in the games that we play, then when we specify the higher frames of mind and/or the highest frames, we put our finger on the leverage point for transforming and setting new frames for new games.

To describe the *levels of mind*, and the way we mentally and emotionally set up levels of thought in various forms to govern the games that we play, let me tell the story of how our mental-emotional levels develop in us. In doing this, I will provide an overview of the basic *Frame Games Model*, the only theoretical information you will need in this book to understand and work with the processes for accessing and developing your own "genius at work" state

(For more on this, see *Frame Games: Persuasion Elegance* (2000), *Dragon Slaying: From Dragons to Princes* (2000), *Secrets of Personal Mastery* (2000), *Meta-States: Mastering the Higher States of Your Mind* (2000))

In the Beginning, There Is a Reference

It all began when we first discovered and related to *a referent event* beyond our skin. With that discovery we found that there was a world "out there." Then, over the weeks and months and years of our lives, our nervous system and brain (the stuff that makes up our neurology and linguistic skills) enable us to become aware of various referents. We become aware of such references as people, experiences, events, ideas, statements, stories, concepts, movies, and all kinds of things.

"Mind" works in this way: it feeds on references. "Minds" respond to referent structures that stimulate us to respond. At first we merely react in a mindless and pre-programmed way, but eventually we begin to respond more thoughtfully and with conscious awareness. Mentally we begin to record, represent, and encode. In this way, our mind (actually, mind/body) starts to fill up its memory banks with referents—pieces of history, statements about things, learnings, experiences, conclusions, expectations. It is in this way that we create the uniquely personal "files" that we use to "make sense" of and understand the world, others, and ourselves.

When we want to elicit this level of awareness, we need only simply ask ourselves or someone else about the referent. The answer will identify the given person's *reference points* and *frame of reference*.

What do you think about when you consider working at X company?

What experiences have you had with promoting the career that you want in this business?

What *authority figures* have you encountered in your life that stand out in your mind, either positively or negatively?

What do you feel about *criticism* in terms of your work performance (or *mistakes, friends, succeeding, sense of self, etc.*)?

Figure 6:1

What are you referring to (the Referents)?

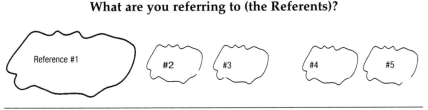

Time-Line ... Of Events

Then the Referent Develops as an Internal Code

Now with the human *mind* (again, the mind–body) you can count on one thing. The referent experiences that we recognize and note *on the outside* do not stay there. They do not stay out there because we *bring them inside ourselves*. In a way, it's like magic. We are a class of life who have to map the world so that we can deal with the world. Without the "instincts" of animals, we have to create our own programs—our own "software." Once we do that, then we relate to the world *in terms of our maps*. We call these internal maps "thoughts."

In this way, the *Referents* out there become uniquely personal and inside us as we *represent them*. This begins the *representational life* of our thoughts. Neurologically, our cortex somehow maps over from what we see, hear, smell, taste, and sense of the world out there and creates on the inside "a sense of" those sights, sounds, and other sensations.

Now we know in neurobiology that there are *no actual or literal* pictures, sounds, and smells in the brain. We have no actual movie playing in there. There's no theater in the mind. Yet it seems is if that were the case. If I ask you to think about where you live, your house or apartment, and to see your bedroom, and to be there, to walk about in it, to sit down on your bed, to hear the sounds that you typically hear in that place—just a "thought" as simple as your bedroom can initiate what "seems like" an internal movie of that external referent. As I *refer* to your "bedroom," you are able to call forth a *reference* and to experience it. So with the Great Pyramid of Egypt, Bugs Bunny, Adolf Hitler, the smell of fresh bread baking, success in business, Albert Einstein's formula …

If I ask you about a time in your life when you really felt down and despondent, or conversely when everything surprisingly fell into place and you experienced so much more than you were expecting—I bet your brain will do what most brains do. It will call forth some movie-like series of images, memories, sounds, words, and sensations of a reference. Or it will invent one! And if we evoke a reference that has a lot of emotion in it for you (in other words you give it a lot of meaning and value) then it can seem and feel as if somehow you'd *entered into the movie again.* You enter into that Matrix—that biocomputer-generated world of your own making.

How does that happen? What makes that kind of mental and neurological "magic" occur in this way? How is it we take our mental theater with us everywhere we go?

Well, it's actually as simple as "thinking," and as complex as our ability to work with symbols and to represent experiences and ideas, and to hold them constant in our minds. Our representational powers are really fabulous, incredible, and mysterious. Somehow we can map the world out there and make it our internal referential world, which we can live in, carry with us, and use for thinking, perceiving, feeling, and being. This profound mystery still amazes and delights me as it teasingly fascinates me with its possibilities.

Once we create an *encoded representation* of the world and of our thoughts and feelings about that world, we keep it with us. In *Frame Games,* we designate this as our *Represented Frames.* So from an event, we take the experience inside our mind, where we represent it. We encode it. We create a mental picture of it. We begin doing this as infants and we continue to encode more and more throughout life.

At first we can't hold constant the images and sounds. Yet, with brain development and maturity, we quickly learn *constancy of representation.* Then, even when we no longer see, hear, smell, or feel something in our immediate environment, we can still recall the referent and respond to it as if it were present. More "magic."

As in the movie, *The Matrix,* we similarly use our brain to create the "computer-generated" world. It's a world filled with people, events, words, ideas, and meanings. How do we do this? We do so with our *representational power.* And, as we move up the levels, we add more and more richness and complexity to our own personal matrix. That's why we never know what referents another person carries around in his or her mind and uses to filter and color what that person says and does. Sometimes, however, when we just don't understand another person, we say, "What are you referring to?" "How did you come up with *that*?" They, like us, live in a mental and emotional world of their own making (their matrix of frames). That's what creates and sets the frames that then direct the games they play.

If you want to elicit this level of mind in yourself or another, simply ask about the mental coding of some "thought" or awareness.

- What are the audiovisual qualities of your internal movie as you remember that reference?
- If I were to peek into your mind and see, hear, and feel what you do, what would I see, hear, and feel?
- What words and language do you use to talk about this thing?

Figure 6:2

How do you represent that reference?

| Close | Far | Color | Loud | 3-D | etc. |

Represented Frames (Frame after Frame) of a Mental Movie

Then there is a "Frame of Reference"

"Mind" doesn't stop there. After we have a represented image, we create a "frame of reference." We use the experience that we recall to frame other events. We have an experience with "an authority figure" such as Mom or Dad, or some teacher or early employer; we then use that experience not only as an internal movie that we can play over and over and feel bad about (if that was the experience), but we can now use it as our *reference point* for other experiences. It becomes our *frame of reference*. That's why we often respond to people, events, and situations—not for what *is* there, but in terms of our historical references. We project. As current situations remind us of previous experiences, we use the early referent as a bookmark. This saves us mental work.

We draw conclusions as we think *in terms of* that experience. This explains why "first experiences" often have such a lasting impact. The frame of reference creates our orientation and perspective. We come to use it as our reference point—as our perceptual filter, and eventually as our conceptual filter.

We also do something else that seems "magical" in terms of our internal life. We take the experience and our memories of it and turn it into "principles" and "understandings" about life, about work, about our profession, about what it takes to get ahead. We create maps of higher-level understandings. In doing this, our reference becomes less concrete and more conceptual. The reference of the teacher who slapped our face and embarrassed us in front of the class now becomes *ideas*: "School is stupid," "Learning is for nerds," "Learning only leads to pain" …

When we do this, the frame of reference becomes so much a part of our mental world that it "gets into our eyes." As we make it more and more *embodied*, we incorporate it into our muscles. We find it increasingly difficult to discern *the frame* from our *perceiving*. We now perceive the world of events and people through the frame. They become one. Our perceiving becomes our frame. It seems so much a part of what we perceive that we often confuse our frame with external territory and tend to project it onto the world.

In this way we create *conceptual frames*. This term refers to how we not only use *actual experiences* as reference points, but we use *created conceptualized understandings* as reference points. Well, what would you expect from "a symbolic class of life"? We take a "concept" (a belief, idea, understanding, proverb, story) and use it for how we perceive things. In this way we create mental filters from the ideas and concepts that we grow up with in our culture, family, school, or nation and store them in the back of our mind as our "library of references." At this level, our frames operate as our rules, and as our mental thinking patterns, and reference systems. And the Matrix of our mind continues to grow.

The Frame of Reference Becomes Our Frame of Mind and then Our Matrix

All we have to do now is just repeat the frame. Repetition causes the frame to habituate. This then gives us a well-rehearsed frame, so well patterned that it becomes our frame of mind. Typically, we never notice. We live inside our Matrix. As the frame becomes our way of seeing the world, it also operates as a self-organizing and self-fulfilling set of beliefs. The frame operates as an attractor in our mind–body system.

Figure 6:3

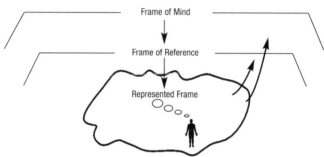

As you have used a given frame of reference as you've moved through life, what attitude or frame of mind has it generated within you? Each level or layer becomes yet another semantic environment. Our frames structure or format what we call "personality." Now the Matrix of our mind, the matrix of our frames, gives us a mental world in which we live and move and have our being. Yet, surprisingly, we commonly *don't notice it*. Perhaps that's the greatest "magic" of all, to live in and operate from our matrix of frames and *not notice*! That is also why we use the succinct phrase of Fritz Perls, the pioneer of Gestalt therapy, as a pattern for empowerment: "Lose your mind and come to your senses."

The solidification process that habituation creates continues transforming our frames of mind into frameworks—systems of beliefs, matrices of ideas, that encode our highest models of the world.

Given this frame of mind, what do you believe about self, life, others, the future?

Working simultaneously, this neuro-linguistic and neuro-semantic system or network creates the overall "gestalt" of our felt sense of life, our everyday "states." Every emotional state *is* a game and arises from a frame. Every state involves a set of actions and trans-actions with others as we act out our emotions, ideas, concepts, mental maps. Every state is also a *motivated state*. It operates for some purpose, some payoff. It seeks to achieve or accomplish something.

Figure 6:4

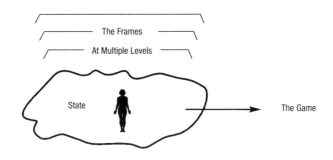

Levels of Mind/Levels of State

We naturally and inevitably set higher frames about previous frames. We think *in terms of* various ideas. We *bring* various ideas, feelings, and even physiologies to bear upon other ideas, thoughts, and feelings. In this way, whenever we think *about* our thinking, feel *about* our feeling, we set a higher-level set of thoughts and feelings upon other thoughts and feelings. *Reflective* thinking creates states-upon-states or meta-states. We react to our reactions. We fear our anger. We rejoice in our learning. We feel embarrassed about our sadness. We desperately want to succeed while we fear that we may not, and would hate to have to face what that would mean.

This level of thought or mind enables us to distinguish between three very different kinds and qualities of states (states of mind and emotion, mental and emotional states, physiological states) that we experience as we play personal and business games:

1. **Primary States**. These are those states we experience when we have direct and immediate reference to something "out there" beyond ourselves. In these states we base our thinking and emoting upon primary consciousness and emotions as we reference external events. Examples of primary states are tension/relaxation, fear, anger, sadness, joy, attraction, aversion, love, apathy.

2. **Meta-States**. When we reflect upon our awareness to consider previous thoughts and feelings we layer thought and emotion upon thought and emotion. This moves us to a higher level of awareness, meta-awareness. Meta-States include self-esteem, self-appreciation, self-contempt, proactivity, joyful learning, and self-motivation.

3. **Gestalt States**. These states *emerge*. They emerge from the overall process of layering or laminating the levels of mind with other thoughts and feelings so that our entire neurosemantic system or network generates a larger whole, an emergent state that's "more than the sum of its parts." Examples of gestalt states necessary for business excellence are courage, self-efficacy, resilience, and seeing and seizing opportunities.

Whenever we *think* or *feel* about a previous state or experience— we shift to a higher level. This sets a higher frame. When we do this intentionally and mindfully, we meta-state ourselves with a resource or limitation that then sets or establishes a new frame of reference which then invites new frame games and that qualifies and textures our frame games. Ultimately, because we live our lives at these higher or meta-levels, the quality of our lives depends upon the quality of our frames and the matrices of our frames. The quality of our work frames determines the quality of our work and performance.

Welcome to the Matrix of Your Mind

We all live in a *matrix* of our mind—the layers of states upon states and the gestalts that arise from these meta-state structures. When we frame, and frame our frames, we create and enter into a Matrix of our own making. The Matrix is our assumed world and we become its occupant—typically blind to it and unaware of it, unquestioningly compliant to it.

The *matrix universe* (the structure of multiple frameworks about numerous subjects and concepts) of each game gives to each participant the perceptions, anchored responses, and self-contained environment that make the world inhabitable. And people can get lost in those worlds. We often do.

So too with the *personal Matrix,* which each of us inherits and creates and then imposes upon the world. The world that we see is a *virtual reality* in this sense. And, because we all live in a frame world of our own making, our ability to *wake up* to the Matrix and to question it is, at the same time, our ability to master our Matrix. Then we can run a quality-control check on them:

- How's my frame world?
- Is it a nice place to live?
- Does it bring out my best?

Figure 6:5

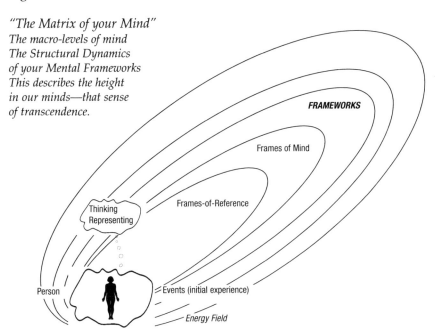

"The Matrix of your Mind"
The macro-levels of mind
The Structural Dynamics
of your Mental Frameworks
This describes the height
in our minds—that sense
of transcendence.

FRAMEWORKS

Frames of Mind

Frames-of-Reference

Thinking
Representing

Person

Events (initial experience)

Energy Field

The frames of our matrix describe and formulate the *structure of meaning*. To create such "meaning" for our lives and work, we construct or formulate what leads to, contributes to, or causes something else, what something means, for instance, or the value and importance of something. *Meaning only and always occurs in frames.*

From our frames we play games with ourselves in terms of how we experience ourselves, the mind games that go on in our interior selves. From our frames also we set up and play games with others. Typically, our games with others can be no better than our self games. If we don't play a *Game of Unconditional Esteeming* and are always trying to become a someone, our "ego" tends to intrude into every achievement, performance, and relationship. We take things personally.

The matrix of our frames operates in a self-perpetuating and self-organizing way. Once we have constructed and commissioned them, they take on "a life of their own." It begins with the frames that we use to punctuate events and activities. Then, in the process of framing, we set up classifications, categories, concepts, and thus the *frames that create our neuro-semantic* states (or meta-states). Then the frames become energized so that they operate systemically. As this transforms them into self-organizing systems, they become attractors—attracting experiences, ideas, and emotions that support them.

From a reference to a frame-of-reference, frame-of-mind, and higher-level frameworks, as a semantic class of life we frame and so we enter into *frame games*. This provides us a way to describe the overall structural dynamics of our individual matrix.

Summary

- This model of the mind comes from numerous sources: Alfred Korzybski's General Semantics and his "levels of abstraction"; Bateson's meta-levels and "levels of learning" model and his formulations about cybernetics and information theory; cognitive psychology's feedback loops governing feedback loops; Maturana's biology of language; systems and chaos theory about recursiveness; and more.

- Recursively tracking the flow of "thought" *up the levels*, from referent to frame-of-reference to frame of mind and so on, enables us to sort out and understand the higher levels of "mind" and how they operate so powerfully and pervasively in the games that we play.
- This model can now enable us to detect frames at various levels and to distinguish receptionist frames from CEO frames. Each carries a different level of authority.
- And, with that model in mind, *let the games begin!*

Chapter 7

Playing Business Games with Elegance

Playing the Games of Business with Grace and Charm

Let's review our progress in understanding and establishing the foundational games as we learn to play the *Games Business Experts Play*.

We began with a wake-up call. There are games afoot in the world and especially in the world of business. From the moment we wake up in the morning and get ready for work to the moment we walk into our workplace, and then to the last moment of the day when we retire, we are all *playing games*. We cannot *not* play games.

Yet we play a very special set of games that we are here calling *frame games*. The frames of reference and frames of mind that we have in our heads govern, control, and determine the games that we play. In this sense, we always and only play *mind* games, because there are no other kinds. The matrix of our frames has us— and controls us.

It takes energy to play these games. If you want to be successful and achieve your desired outcomes, you're going to have to have the necessary mental, emotional, personal, verbal, and physical *energy* to enter the fray. Weak, frail, fragile, depleted, and de-energized people are prey to be recruited for toxic *frame games*. It takes power to play.

The ultimate source of personal power, the basic equipment that you came with—your powers of thinking and emoting, speaking (languaging), and acting (behaving, relating)—are neuro-linguistic (mind–body) powers that enable you to have the energy to play.

That's why we introduced some of the basic *frame games* to play right from the start:

The Empowered Frame Game*:* Play by recognizing, accepting, and fully *owning* your own powers. Designate them as your *Power Zone,* and power up inside them so that you know your area in which you can take effective action by the responses (mental, verbal, emotional, and behavioral) that you can have in making a difference in your work environment.

The Validation Game and the *"Hell, No!"* Game for Invalidating*:* By knowing and owning our powers of affirmation and disconfirmation (*Yes-ing* and *No-ing*), we can totally take charge of and reconstruct the frames that we have inherited, absorbed by osmosis from our culture, and built over the years. In this way, we can turn great inspiring ideas into self-organizing beliefs and we can deframe old toxic, morbid, or out-of-date beliefs into mere harmless thoughts. Now we can fully play the game, "It's my Brain and I Can Run It My Way!" What a game!

Powered Up but Not Intimidating

A danger arises at this point for those of us who want to play *The Games of Business Excellence.* Playing the first three games can leave us feeling so empowered, so focused, and so passionate about our goals and outcomes that, as we power up, we can shift into overdrive and steamroller anyone who gets in our way. This is always a mistake and will cost us dearly. Accessing a state that allows us to discover and experience our "genius at work" inevitably involves good healthy and balanced relationships. Caring about others, taking their wishes, states, understandings, skills, and capacities into account, plays a crucial role in business excellence.

So, if we want to "work *with* and *through* others" (the art of interpersonal "power"), we need to temper our empowerment states so that we don't run over others, so that we don't intimidate others, and so that we don't mistreat others. Certainly, if you know about *frame games,* how to play them, how to manage them, how to set the highest frames, you can manipulate others to their disadvantage. You will have the *power* and *persuasion skills* to do that.

But (and that's a really big *but*) if you do you will eventually pay for it. The manipulations will eventually catch up to you and then you'll be friendless and without interpersonal resources. There's always someone who is more skilled at manipulating. Play the games in a Win/Lose manner and eventually no one will trust you or play with you. They'll just pack up their marbles and go home.

And (and this is a really big *and*) you don't need to do that! Not at all. True empowerment involves knowing that you can get your way *while at the same time enriching and empowering others to get their way*. This is called playing *The Game of Abundance*. It comes from a special frame of mind that says, *"There's enough for all—and more!"* It's called *"Playing the Win/Win or No Game."*

Manipulate we will. We cannot *not* manipulate any more than we cannot *not* communicate, influence, persuade, relate, and interact. All of our *public powers* of speaking, languaging, telling stories, describing situations, brainstorming, gesturing, moving, acting, relating, even breathing—all of these actions *influence*. All communicate. All have an impact on persuasion. All relate. All "handle" ourselves and others with words and tones and volumes. In other words, "manipulation" (from the Latin *manipulus*, handful, to handle something) is inevitable. Only the kind and quality of the manipulation is at question. We can manipulate respectfully in a way that honors the dignity and value of others, or we can do so in a way that views others as just someone to use. One form has a future; the other does not.

The Elegance of Being Gloriously Fallible

When we power up and fail to temper our sense of empowerment, adventure, and passion, it seems that we humans can easily get seduced into playing *The Infallibility Game: "I Know Everything and am Omnipotent in my Abilities."* Certainly, we know better than that, and yet with expertise, with business excellence, or excellence in any arena, with increased effectiveness and success—we lose our elegance and grace when we forget about our fallibility or fail to consider it.

This may not be what you were expecting. Most of us don't want to face our fallibility, or like facing it. That seems to disempower, to undermine our passions. And yet *all* of our powers, no matter how well developed, are still *fallible*, that is, liable to error. This seems to be one of the prerequisites of genius: the ability to be quite open and vulnerable about one's fallibilities and, in fact, to put errors, mistakes, and blunders to good use. The genius who has nothing to prove, but thoroughly enjoys his or her level of excellence, typically is quite open about how so many insights came as results of mistakes. And they are quite okay with being wrong.

Typically, it is the insecure, the fearful, and the person inadequately trained for a task who more often adopt the know-it-all attitude, and then, without any grace or charm, seeks to impress and oppress others with all their credentials, wisdom, knowledge, and rightness. Such are the signs of a small and insecure mind.

- What kind of a relationship do you have with failures, mistakes, errors, blunders, your human inadequacies?

- How secure are you with your fallible thinking, emoting, speaking, and acting?

- Do you maintain your personal sense of value and dignity when you experience and face up to some error, failure, mistake, or blunder?

- What game do you play with yourself when someone points out some inadequacy?

Since there is no escape from our human fallibility, what frames can we set that will promote excellence within the context of being fully fallible? Suppose we establish some new frames regarding any and all expressions of human fallibilities. Suppose we reflexively bring back some positive ideas regarding the everyday states that we so often take and use for self-contempt, self-depreciating, and self-judging. Suppose that, instead of bringing some negative thoughts and feelings *against* ourselves, we set more neutral or, even better, positive frames of reference.

Consider what this would mean with the experience of *frustration*:

- *Acceptance* of frustration creates "welcomed frustration."
- *Curiosity* about frustration leads to the game of "Learning about Frustration."
- *Anticipating* what *good* will come out of this frustration generates a sense of "anticipatory frustration."
- *Calmness* and *relaxation* about frustration generates the game of "Calm Frustration."
- *Loving self and others* in the midst of frustrating situations calls forth "Thoughtful-and-Considerate-of-Others Frustration."

How about those frames around the experience and feeling of frustration? Wouldn't these establish some very different *frame games*? Do you think of them as strange altered states of consciousness? Would you like to go there? Would accessing such frames give you a more resourceful handle on things when you feel blocked? What games would they create for you?

If we play *The "I'm Okay" Game*, or *The "My Self-Esteem is a Given" Game*, then we don't move through life feeling that either we or others are broken, defective, or substandard. We're just perfectly fallible human beings—nothing more, nothing less. This enables us to leave *The "Perfect and Flawless Matrix"* and to live in a world of fallibility and to do so with the grace and charm of using mistakes for learning, growth, and humor.

The Self-Esteem Game

Let's set an empowering frame for *The "Self-Appreciation, Self-Esteem, and Gloriously Fallible" Game*.

1. Check for a sense (and frame) of internal permission to play this game
Do you have permission to esteem yourself highly, unconditionally, with potential, as a lovable person *and* to be a fully fallible human being at the same time?

2. Access awareness of your Power Zones
Just notice your basic, inescapable, and undeniable "powers":
your thinking-emoting power and your speaking and behaving
powers. As you did before, *center* yourself in these powers as you
recognize that they function as the powers of your personality that
allow you to take charge of your responses. If you think of any
event or any reference, you can then notice your mental and emotional powers as well as your linguistic and behavioral powers in
regard to that event.

Earlier, you set frames of acceptance, appreciation, and ownership
over these core powers, and so you can refresh that again and
enjoy it.

*3. Outframe with self-esteeming thoughts that fully accept your
fallibility within these powers*
Take a moment and just notice the fact that your mind, emotions,
speech, and behavior are always "liable to error" or fallible.
Welcome this sense of fallibility into your awareness with appreciation. It means you don't have to be perfect.

What would it be like if you fully accepted your fallibility while
holding on to your sense of appreciation for yourself? Notice how
that frame invites some new emotions to temper and texture your
sense of empowerment. And do so while esteeming and valuing
your self as a person with dignity that no error or fallibility can
take away from you. Let this acceptance of your fallibility become
richer as you accept *your right* to be fully fallible, dependent on
others, ignorant about thousands of things. Notice how your
thinking and feeling of your innate worth, value, and significance
transform your sense of the frustration or whatever other fallible
piece of behavior that you'd like to apply this to.

4. Step into this experience and feel it fully as a state
Let all of this now engulf you as a canopy of awareness as you
vividly imagine yourself moving out into the world so that you
use this as your way of "being in the world." Imagine going into
your future *with this*.

Tempering and Texturing our Games

We can actually temper and texture the *frame games* that we play at home and at work. This occurs by accessing even higher frames *about* the game, about the experience, about ourselves, about others, about purpose, about quality. In fact, this is one of the incredible secrets about moving up the logical levels of mind.

> *Each jump upward to the next highest level involves a qualitative jump.*

This means that each higher frame provides a new *quality* to the overall experience. This naturally flows from the fact that each higher level organizes and modulates the lower levels. In this way, the higher frames determine the actual *quality* of our experience or states. Knowing this informs us that if we want to know the quality and character of someone's way of playing a game, we have only to ask about it.

- What's the quality of your frame of mind when you compete?
- What's the quality of your frustration when a negotiation gets bogged down?
- What's the quality of your anger?
- What is it like when you get down, stressed, or overwhelmed?

Your answers to these questions provide insight into the higher frames that govern the games that we and others play regarding these states or experiences.

"You wouldn't like me angry."

"I wouldn't? What are you like when you get angry about something at work?"

"Well, I just lose it. One minute I'm fine; the next minute I've hit a threshold and can't stand it any more. I get so angry, so wired up. I feel like I'm going to burst ..."

"So what do you say or do at that point?"

"I just lose it. I scream, I accuse, I hit. You just wouldn't like me angry."

103

"Yeah, it sounds like it. Guess *you* don't like yourself when you're angry either, huh?"

"Of course not. I hate it."

"You do? So you don't welcome your anger and warmly accept it as a positive and powerful sign that lets you know that something important to you seems or feels like it's being violated? You don't enjoy your anger as an inborn power to enable you to protect yourself against true violations?"

"Well ... no. I never thought of it that way. That sounds really weird."

It may be. But personally, I enjoy and celebrate my anger and as I welcome it into my awareness, especially when it's first being stimulated, I just check it out to see if it's all that appropriate, and, if I find something that rightly angers me, I just calmly talk about it with the person in a respectful way. Works for me. Works for you?

Frame-Game Texturing

That's *frame texturing*. We take a frame of reference—upset, frustrated, or angry about something that's not working right, someone doing something that we dislike, and then we frame our anger with, say, acceptance, appreciation, welcoming, calmness, or respect. Each layer textures the base experience with another *quality* or *character* and so gives it a new richness. As we do this, it changes the character and quality of the game.

In this, the sky is the limit in terms of all of the rich qualities that we can invent, create, and mix up for our everyday states. And I'm sure you're already jumping ahead and wondering about what qualities would temper and texture your "genius at work" state so that it will give it a richer and fuller quality, one that will support and enhance your own business excellence. If not, you can begin to do that now, can you not?

Actually, this describes one of the things we will do in the following chapters. We will not only identify some great frames and great games that make for business excellence, but we'll also hint at some of the marvelous possibilities about how to add some higher dimensions for creating more elegance, charm, and warmth to our passion and power.

Summary

- The games that we play are governed by not one level of frames, but multiple levels of frames. For that reason, we can now move up the levels and set even higher frames, knowing that each jump upward is a *qualitative jump* and gives us the power to make *The Business Expert Games* richer and fuller.

- *The Power Frame Game* can intimidate and scare people if we do not temper and texture it with our own humanity, with a modest sense of the constraints of our own fallibility. So we set the frame that allows us to play the *frame game* of being gloriously fallible.

- Playing that *frame game* with ourselves and others enables us to be warm and charming. It grants a grace and elegance to our style of interacting. People feel safe in our presence since we really don't have any agenda in *using* them for our own ego pleasures.

- Knowing how to esteem ourselves, to maintain our basic sense of dignity even when making mistakes, blundering, and recognizing our fallibility, enables us to put mistakes to good use.

The Gloriously Fallible Game
- *Description:* We never perfectly think, feel, or act. All of our actions are tainted with flaws and liable to error. Acknowledging and celebrating this within a frame of self-respect and dignity enables us to play *The Glorious Fallibility Game*. Then we're not shocked by mistakes or failures, but maintain our sense of value and dignity as we focus on learning to do better.

- *Rules of the game:* Acknowledge your right to be fallible; embed your fallibility in the larger frame of self-worth; view your self-worth as a given, as part and parcel of being human. Be open to mistakes by welcoming them as opportunities for learning.

- *Payoffs:* Operating with a sense of self and self-value will get your ego out of the way so that you can stay calm and relaxed even in times of stress and distress, then you'll keep your head while all about your are losing theirs.

- *Cues for when to play:* When mistakes, errors, upsets, setbacks, insults, and criticisms occur.

Part III

Let the Games Begin!

Frames for Business Excellence

What are the games, the *frame games*, that we have to play in the context of business that allow us to develop business excellence and replicate *The Games Business Experts Play*? What are the frames and the higher-level frames that make these games possible? Are there any sick or morbid games that I need to develop skill in detecting and refusing? What are some of the skills and patterns that allow me to become much more effective in playing the most excellent *frame games* at work?

In this and the following chapters you will discover numerous healthy and honorable games that will allow you to wonderfully and wildly succeed in business. Conversely, you'll discover some truly sick and morbid games that will undermine effectiveness. May you set about your discovery to find and incorporate those *frame games* that you find favorable for your long-term wellbeing, that enable you to experience a fuller and more satisfying life, that challenge your potential and that bring out your best—and that allow you to have lots of fun in the process.

Chapter 8

Flexibly Adjusting to the New Games

There's a New Game in Town

Games in this chapter
The Flexibility Game
The "Know Thyself" Game
The Self-Responsibility Game
The Aim Game
The Personal Boundaries Game
The "Managing Your Own Behavior" Game
The "Learning and Unlearning" Game
The "Accepting Uncertainty and Taking Risks" Game
The Context Game
The Personal Resourcefulness Game
The Implementation Game
The Discounting Game

- What *frame games* do I need to play in order to succeed?
- What are the central features of business today that I need to know about and deal with effectively?
- To be a genius at work, what models, skills, and states do I need in order to get to the top?
- How often do you think about *fully* accessing your personal work genius?
- What specific understandings support and empower us in developing excellence for work tasks?

When it comes to business in the twenty-first century, there's a whole new set of new games in town. "The times, they are a changin'" has become especially true for the work environment.

In *Smart Work* (1995), Lisa Marshall and Lucy Freedman describe the new workplace that has been emerging, and that will continue to evolve, in the new century. They primarily focus on the new workplace as becoming increasingly knowledge-intensive and service-based. These are the new games. Work demands, and will continue to demand, more from us as we face greater diversity and an ever-increasing global economy and world market.

In this new century, we can expect the continual growth of technology, an increase in information, and an ever increasing pace of change that will challenge all of us in new and different ways. Marshall and Freedman have suggested nine guiding principles for anyone who wants to survive in the new workplace (see Figure 8:1). I quote these guidelines here to highlight that the new games fall into two categories: *intrapersonal* and *interpersonal*.

The interpersonal category comes as no surprise. Yet it does highlight how work has become more and more people- and knowledge-intensive, and how it will continue in this direction. This means the building and maintaining of rapport games will become increasingly important. Getting along with others will become less and less optional. As business becomes more sales- and service-oriented, listening, questioning, and connecting skills will play a crucial role. Business will become more *psychological* in the sense that we will be called upon to understand and relate to others.

This domain of interpersonal relations will also highlight the significance of communication, conflict management, "getting to resolution," or defusing hotheads.

The big surprise for many people, if not for most of us, involves the intrapersonal category. *Psychological awareness*, intelligence, and skills are going to become increasingly important. Are you ready for that? The features in this category indicate that business success will become much more dependent, not on what you do or can do, but on your attitude, your state, your self-awareness and self-knowledge, and your ability to manage your own mind and life. Yet business experts already play these games, and with skill. They embrace the "psychological" nature of business knowing that they cannot eliminate the human factor, nor do they want to.

Figure 8:1

Guidelines for the New Workplace

1. Develop self-knowledge
2. Take self-responsibility
3. Hold clear vision and values
4. Manage personal boundaries
5. Manage your behavior
6. Build bridges
7. Manage conflicts
8. "Unlearn" and learn
9. Accept uncertainty and take risks (pages 4–7)

It is precisely in this that the magic of *frame games* becomes exceedingly useful and powerful. These intrapersonal skills support and comprise the structure of excellence or genius at work. This generates a new perspective about the games of business. It allows us to view the first five items listed in Figure 8:1, along with item number 8 and, as some of the new games that we will need to learn. All of these have to do with our mind–body states of consciousness or our frames of mind. These make up our basic attitude as derived from our model of the world and govern the games that we can and cannot play.

The Flexibility Game

Cues: It's the tremendous turbulence of change in the field of business that calls for the need for flexibility. Even the pace of this change is increasing. Though change has always been with us, the acceleration of change, along with the explosion of knowledge and technology, suggests that we most fundamentally need to learn *The Flexibility Game* if we want to effectively adjust to the changing times.

Descriptions: *The Flexibility Game* contrasts with *The Rigid Inflexibility Game*. Traditionally we have used the black-and-white thinking of Aristotelian logic to create a rigid business plan and then stay with it for a lifetime. That doesn't work any longer. While both flexibility and inflexibility as frames and games have their place and usefulness, today's business climate has shifted in such a way that only the flexibility frame works.

Certainly there are some things toward which we should adopt more of a black-and-white orientation, yet in most things we need a more flexible attitude. This is especially true in the business context, where change is the great constant, where markets fluctuate, where new products come and go.

In addition, with the growing complexity in today's world, we need more ability to flexibly shift gears and to keep adjusting to the ever changing environment. Some writers describe this as "sensitive to context." This means that, as such things as contexts, technology, environment, infrastructures, and information change, so do we. Flexibility enables us to become change *masters*, rather than its victims. We need the flexibility of the tennis player who never knows where the market will serve the next change, but is ready to move there quickly to stay in the game.

Cues: Successful business people learn how to ride the tides of change—and even pioneer the coming changes, rather than resist, resent, or become rigid about change. As they play *The Ever Ready to Change Game* it allows them to stay abreast of new developments and to waste no time pining over "the good ol' days." Excellence in this area emerges from leading the way in creating the changes and in mastering coping with changes. This calls for flexibility. This also calls for a new way of thinking. It calls for a whole new set of questions, questions that allow us to recognize the cues as to when to play the game.

- What changes are currently taking place?
- What changes can we anticipate in our field in the next one, three, five, or ten years, or even in the next six months?
- What forces, factors, and influences are contributing to these changes?
- What will people need and/or want in order to handle and master this area in the future?

- What resources, tools, technologies, and processes will best give people a handle on the future?
- What information will give us the best mapping for forecasting future changes?

Contrast: *The Rigidity Game* emerges from a different kind of thinking. Black-or-white and Either/Or thinking punctuates the world in terms of only two choices: this or that. In attempting to bring order and structure to the world, it *oversimplifies*. Yet in doing so it creates delusions and blind spots. Very few things are of the bivalent Either/Or form. This old form of Aristotelian "logical" thinking (the excluded middle) fails to deal with and therefore accurately map a world of multiple choices, the grays, and the things in between.

This is a problem of levels. It is the meta-level structure of *believing* in our beliefs. Believing is one thing. Believing in something means we are *confirming* a thought that maps some territory. But, when we believe in our beliefs, we then become so convinced in our belief that it shuts out new information and feedback. Information that may call the belief into question is eliminated. This makes for fanaticism. It creates what the sociologist Eric Hoffer called "the True Believer"—the closed-minded, narrow-minded, convinced-even-against-the-facts type of thinker. Now that's a very different game.

The need for flexibility arises from the very nature of our mental maps. We need flexibility to update and change our thoughts because all of our representing and validating of beliefs is fallible, and because at best they are just a replica of the territory, and not the territory. Given this fallibility, we need to constantly check our maps against the external situations and make appropriate adjustments as necessary.

When you appreciate the value of flexibility and develop some skill in adapting, changing, and transforming, then the following games of the new workplace become easier.

Payoffs: The payoffs of this game are many: relevance, fittingness, ability to stay sharp and current, ability to anticipate trends and to respond appropriately, proactivity, wise and profitable choices.

The "Know Thyself" Game

Rules: Plato established the mandate of this game millennia ago when he wrote, "Know thyself." This is the ultimate rule in this game. This once informed only psychology, yet now it informs the business experts.

Description: In practical terms we need to truly know our own desires and passions, our abilities and temperaments, our perceptual filters, our skills, and our state management abilities.

Cues: In today's market, most of us will change careers and professions at least two or three times, and possibly many more. This consequently calls upon us to operate from a fuller and richer understanding of our skills, passions, and aptitudes.

Description: Stability no longer operates by finding a company and staying with it until you retire. In the twenty-first century, "stability" operates more dynamically. We maintain stability from a higher level of mind as we discover, nurture, and develop what we truly care about, what we're good at, how we define ourselves. From that foundation, we constantly translate it in terms of the current market. As the pace of change in the world, the markets, the information explosion continues, we will we need to deepen and expand our self-assessment skills and our flexibility to more quickly fit into newly invented realities. Today this type of adaptability is very important, and it will become even more important in the years to come.

Payoffs: When we know ourselves, it becomes easier to develop our full potential and to know where to invest our skills and energy.

The Self-Responsibility Game

Description: I began describing this game when I introduced the core powers and *The Empowerment Game* in an earlier chapter. In terms of self-responsibility, this is going to be a crucial game and one that will change how most workers will view working and the work context in the future.

"Responsible? Who Me?"

In the coming years, it will become less and less appropriate for employees to look to their employers or their companies to "take care" of them. That game has ended. The final whistle has blown. "Game over!" The age of personal responsibility, initiative, ownership, and proactivity has arrived.

Rules: Individual workers at all levels will have to assume and own personal responsibility for their own career development, professional growth, retirement, interests, and initiative. The pace of change, the demand for greater flexibility, the unpredictability of the markets, and many other factors call upon all of us to take charge of our own success, professional development, and financial security. Depending on others to tell us what to do, when to do it, and how to do it is no longer appropriate at all. Business experts take charge of their work, learn to initiate, and take responsibility in new and different ways. This demands a higher level of maturity and mindfulness.

Description: Business experts assume responsibility for themselves, willingly invest themselves in their work and consider themselves "self-employed" regardless of the source of their income. Employing themselves, they assume both responsibility and ownership of their success. They fully assume ownership of their professional career. They look at their everyday activities in terms of considering where and how they can add value where they are.

This represents a revolutionary attitude both to ourselves and our organizations. This represents a game that every business expert plays (and has always played). The business experts, wherever they are in the process (just starting, or at the top), always look about them, even if it is in the mail room, and ask,

"How can I add value to what I'm doing here?"

"How can I make myself more valuable to my employer?"

Payoffs and Cues: Yet this attitude itself represents the heart of the expert games. The non-experts do not operate from that attitude and so do not play that game. They are more likely to be selfish, ego-driven, impatient, and dependent, and operating from a frame of entitlement. Yet, when we operate from that frame of mind, then ways of creating new products and services, of seeing opportunities, of becoming more of a team player begin to transform the way we see and feel life. Then a new game begins. And we play it when problems arise, and when new challenges present themselves.

The Aim Game

A central facet of self-responsibility involves a sense of purpose and direction. In Chapter 10 I will fully describe *The Aim Game.* When we *own* our response-able powers, we willingly engage in becoming mentally clear about our desired outcomes. We clarify to ourselves what we really consider important. We enter into *The "Living Life on Purpose" Game* and become intentional, focused, purposeful.

As we own the response-ability for developing our own sense of purpose and direction, this evokes a proactive clarity of our values and visions, our beliefs and higher frames of mind. This leads to greater expressions of self-motivation and initiative.

The Personal Boundaries Game

Payoffs: The sense of personal boundaries and the ability to set and respect our own personal boundaries describe a subgame within the larger *Self-Responsibility Game.* This quality emerges from self-knowledge and responsibility and leads to the payoff of a healthy balance between work and play, career and relationships, health and vacation, and more.

Description: People who don't play *The Personal Boundaries Game* confuse the boundaries and then suffer from one of the two extremes. When they take on far more than what belongs to them, they burn out. When they fail to accept their legitimate responsibilities, they bum off the work of others.

Rules: We play *The Personal Boundaries Game* effectively in the following ways: balance different polarities. Develop greater skills and elegance in communicating, asserting, resolving conflicts, making requests. "Draw the line" between different kinds of responsibilities—things you are responsible *for* (accountability) and things you are responsible *to* (relationship).

Description: Assuming responsibility *for* ourselves and our personal powers differs very much from assuming responsibility *to* others. That describes relationship to others and does not generally (except with babies and those who are not capable of personal responsibility) include responsibility *for* their responses. We assume responsibility *for* our responses *to* the other.

The "Managing Your Own Behavior" Game

Description: When we enter into *The Responsibility Game* (*see* Chapter 9) and play it well, we are enabled to play this game as well. This game expresses the excellence that comes when we truly learn how to "run our own brain" and manage our own states. When we take charge of our behaviors, we can choose when and where to produce a particular response. We will *have* our behavior and emotions, rather than suffer them as a victim.

Payoffs: Those who won't or can't play this game will end up playing various other games. Typically, they will play *The Blame Game*, *The Victim Game*, and/or *The Entitlement Game* as they accuse others of causing their behavior or being responsible for their circumstances. The payoffs for this game include a sense of control, increased ability to take our dreams come true, and self-confidence.

The "Learning and Unlearning" Game

Description: Business experts know how to play another game. They know how to both learn and unlearn. The abilities involved in learning and unlearning, of course, support, create, and enhance the flexibility that's necessary to keep up with the speed of change. This game enables us to ensure that our mental models won't get in our way, but will serve us. Then our ideas, beliefs, and understandings actually function as *maps* that enable us to navigate the territory.

Rules: Of course, learning and unlearning means a higher degree of mindfulness as we move through life, and an awareness that our maps are just that: maps, symbolic representations of the territory. Using our maps in this way leads to an increase in creativity. As work has continued, and will continue, to become more and more knowledge-intensive and companies *learning organizations* (Senge, *The Fifth Discipline*), learning itself becomes increasingly more important in order to be an effective player. Those who don't keep learning are being left behind.

Cues: Play this game daily as you read and work to stay current in your field, play it when you receive criticism, and when you are brainstorming about new ideas.

The "Accepting Uncertainty and Taking Risks" Game

Description: This state or frame of mind describes a structuring of mind that allows us to accept and tolerate ambiguity, confusion, and unknown factors with calmness, presence of mind, and playfulness. Given the accelerated speed of change, we will have increasing opportunities to experience ambiguity and confusion. Use this frame of mind to acknowledge such, validate it as useful and welcome ambiguity into consciousness. Refuse to get into a battle over ambiguity. Let this frame of mind support you in accessing and maintaining your personal work genius.

Cues and Payoffs: Many today don't want to play this game at all. They hanker for "the good ol' days" when change didn't occur so quickly, and when there was more of a sense of stability. Gracefully tolerating ambiguity, as a business game, may seem contradictory at first. Yet, with the pace of change accelerating year after year, those who succeed and those who excel will learn to live graciously with ambiguity. They will not only wed graciously, but will see and seize opportunities that exist in the midst of the ambiguity. As they do, they'll experience less stress and more satisfaction, and accomplish a lot more.

Excelling in the New Work Environment

To access our *work genius* so that we can precisely identify the structure, strategy, and skills of *excellence*, the very skills that will get us to the top and enable us to fully enjoy the process, to be at our best, and to stay there, we have to maintain a two-fold perspective and hence, two further games.

The Context Game

First, we have to have a clear and unmistakable understanding of the *work environment*, and how it is changing, and will continue to change. Awareness of this continual updating regarding the environment and context of our profession will allow us to stay current and relevant. If we lose touch with the work environment, our responses will become increasingly ineffective. Our skills and responses will become more and more out-dated and irrelevant.

The Personal Resourcefulness Game

Second, we also have to have a way of accessing our personal skills and resources so that we can rise up to meet the challenges that lie ahead. This means ongoing learning, development, and discovering. It means developing greater effectiveness at integrating and utilizing new skills.

Flexibly Shifting to the Best Frame of Mind

If the aforementioned skills, attitudes, and competencies make up the things that enable us to *get to the top by developing expertise*, then these describe the secrets of the successful game. We need only to change our thinking, emoting, speaking, and behaving in ways that fit these games.

This highlights the expert game of taking ownership over the basic powers. This also provides an excellent test for our personal *flexibility*. Ask yourself these questions:

- How easy do you find it to change your mind?
- How easy do you find it to alter your emotions?
- How easy do you find it to transform the way you talk and act?
- How flexible are you with these responses?

If we first identify the highest and best frames of mind, understandings, responses, and behaviors of the experts and then replicate them, these will make our personal flexibility a critical skill.

How do we play *The Flexibility Game*? First, we ask, "What skills, understandings, beliefs, values, attitudes, styles of handling things do we need in order to truly excel in our career?" Getting to the top in every field involves learning specific knowledge and developing specific competencies. What field of expertise will you give yourself to?

Rules: What really matters in your choice? Make sure that it's something that you *love*. Begin your search for those things that you feel *passionate* about. Then learn everything you can about that one passion. Play *The Passionate Game* in such a way that it inevitably cultivates your natural expertise. This happens to be the central strategy of those who become wealthy or financially independent. (I have noted this in *Wealth Training: Games Wealthy People Play*, 2001.)

Identify the specific understandings, skills, and experience you need in a given field, then, above and beyond that, identify the specific states for excelling. You need permission to develop, pursue, and understand your passion. Do you have that? If not, then you'll want to begin with *The Permission Game*, which I'll describe in a later chapter.

Yet aptitude alone will not guarantee success. Nor will intelligence alone. Nor yet past achievements. Each of these factors will certainly *contribute* as a component for high performance, but, in itself, each is insufficient.

Above and beyond them, you need to depend upon certain mental and emotional states of excellence to carry you through. These states, comprising such qualities as the achiever's *attitude*, beliefs, values, and visions, identify the true secret for playing *The Games Business Experts Play.* Since you do have complete control over these higher frames of reference, you can build them if you want to and take the effort to do so.

Success comes from flexibly shifting your mind to your best states. You need only to identify these states that support your passion. Do this to develop your personal work genius. Plant these question and keep revisiting it month after month, year after year.

- What states do I need to access and step into in order to truly be at my best?
- What are the most resourceful frames of mind that will allow me to play the games experts play in my line of business?

Begin with the Marshall–Freedman list if you like and use it as a checklist of career skills and states. Then go on to specify others that uniquely describe your situation. Doing this allows you to begin to truly *design-engineer* a particular kind of excellence for yourself. Stop now to do this.

The Implementation Game

Ultimately, every business expert (every expert in any field) *takes action and does something.* This is the *implementation state* and it is the one state that every person who pursues excellence needs. This game enables us to actually do what we know how to do. It's the moment when the truth becomes implemented into everyday actions.

- Do you play this game?
- Are you good at playing *The Implementation Game?*
- Is it an automatic game in your repertoire of games, or do you play *The Hesitation Game?*
- Have you become skillful at *The Procrastination Game?*
- Do you prefer *The Sit On Your Fat Butt Game?*

At the end of the previous section I mentioned an exercise, something to do. Did you do it? That exercise is only one of many in this book. It actually gives you an opportunity to exercise your *imple-*

mentation muscles. Did you frame it that way? When you think about so framing it as exercising your "will do" and "can do" muscles, what happens? Do you have a good relationship with the idea of taking action? Let's see what you do.

Get a sheet of paper and write out a list of *customized states of excellence* that you need in order to pull off your highest performance. Let these states correspond to the understandings and skills that you need to become an expert in your field.

My Business Expert Games

Have I done this myself? You bet. Want to peek at them? Sure, I'll give you an inside peek. The expert role that I want to play involves being a researcher, writer, trainer, and entrepreneur. Those are the business games that I want to play with ever increasing skill, elegance, and power.

So, in plotting out the states of excellence that I absolutely need in order to *be and perform at my best*, and to play the expert well in these areas, I need the following. Anything less will lessen the quality and productiveness of my work. These make up the basic prerequisites for the attitude (or frame of mind) that I need as I move through my day learning to play these games.

* *Playfulness:* A light-hearted attitude of fun, delight, joy.
* *Discipline:* The ability to manage my states.
* *Purposefulness:* Having a focused vision, an awareness of both my long-term and short-term goals.

Figure 8.2

The Expert Game: _____

Prerequisite Knowledge Needed:	Required Skills & Expertise	Corresponding Frames of Mind:	Best States Needed for Taking Action:

- *Concentration in the moment:* The ability to release the past and future time zones and to become lost in the now, to access a state of flow.
- *Creativity:* Free-floating ideas in a relaxed environment that's rich with sensory stimuli.
- *Curiosity:* A state of wondering, openness, explorative attitude.
- *Flexibility:* Easily shifting with interruptions and adapting to current demands to follow a flow of ideas.
- *Vitality:* The physical and mental energy that arises from a healthy life, physical fitness, etc.
- *Commitment:* The ability to invest the time and trouble to keep learning, reading, and thinking to stretch the mind into new areas.
- *Cooperation:* A collaborative state of partnership with others of like mind, the ability to work as a team member, to lead and to follow.

Going higher

Is that all? Can we take these states and develop them further? Can we expand them and enrich them? Yes, of course. How? By identifying the *driving beliefs and values* frames which will support, elicit, and enhance these states.

So, here's another exercise to get your implementation muscles involved. For each state that you identify, write out several beliefs that you would like to commission as personal convictions governing your mind, emotions, and actions. Write these in a form that you find compelling—this will add *juice* to your states of excellence.

- What *ideas* put you in the states of excellence?
- What *physiologies* best represent these states?
- What does each particular state of excellence *look* like, *sound* like?

As an example, regarding the frame of mind that I identified as "playfulness" (the first on my list), I wrote the following beliefs:

- Business, like life, is just a game; it's a game that I will enjoy and learn to play well. So play I will.
- Having fun along the way is a powerful way to become more effective and efficient. So I shall have fun every day.
- Humor makes everything more enjoyable and human. It helps me to keep things in perspective. So I will laugh more often.

Humor is a healing force that reduces stress and enables me to keep things in balance. This will be one of my way of transforming stress into excitement.

Setting Frames to Stabilize the Expert's States

Not only can we specify the number and combination of *states of excellence* that go together to create the overall gestalt of the business genius or expert, we can do something even more important. We can establish higher level frames that will prevent our gestalt frames of genius from deteriorating.

How can we find and build such supportive higher frames? What can we do that will solidify and stabilize the higher frames of our mind?

You may have noticed one thing I did in the list of empowering beliefs that I just wrote. I cheated a bit. I not only wrote some empowering beliefs, but I stuck in some empowering decisions. Those are the statements that begin, "I will …" and "I shall …" If you really want to solidify your higher frames, do what the American philosopher and psychologist William James suggested more than a hundred years ago: never leave the site of an emotion or insight without exercising your will to take some action. It's powerful. Also, notice the causes and/or contributing influences that diminish your best intentions, beliefs, and plans.

- What sabotages you?
- What causes or influences you to *lose* a given state of excellence?
- What knocks the playfulness out of you, or the centeredness, your peace of mind, your creativity?

- What diminishes your ability to accept ownership of your powers?

When you explore these questions, you begin to identify the various external environmental triggers as well as the internal thoughts and feelings that undermine your resourcefulness. Get as clear, precise, and specific a description as possible. The more precise you describe these triggers, the more you empower yourself to know specifically what to do to reverse them.

Solidifying Your Attitudes of Excellence

When you know *what* to think and feel as well as *how* to speak and act, you're on your way to becoming an expert in your field. The only thing left is to make sure your *attitude* supports your knowledge and skills. As we all know, *attitude* as much as anything determines success or failure.

Now we know why. Because an *attitude* operates as a high-level frame of mind over multiple meta-states and so creates the Matrix of our frames, or our canopy of consciousness. Once we have entered into an empowering attitude, the attitude of an expert, we then come to see the world through that lens. We feel the world through it. It controls and governs our "intuitions." It also operates as a self-organizing attractor, magnetizing to us what this higher-level attitude or Frame Matrix allows and creates. It also solidifies the whole mind–body dynamic of the attitude so that we can take it with us wherever we go and wake up with it every morning.

The Discounting Game

"Yeah, yeah, but it won't last!"

Here's a game that many play, but a game that experts do *not* play. It's *The Discounting Game.* While we might be tempted to think that competence in the necessary skills, knowledge, and intelligence and development of the right states might suffice in putting us at the top in our field, they do not. Once there, you have to play another game, a game that allows you to sustain these qualities.

Many intelligent, knowledgeable, gifted, and even positive people can induce themselves into a state of excellence but they cannot *maintain* it. They have the flexibility and skill to get there, but for some reason they keep losing it. Consequently, they have to repeatedly remotivate themselves—again, again … and then again.

Their excellence comes and goes, as do their bright, positive, and motivated states. Like those who come and go with exercise routines, healthy eating habits, and renewed commitments to relationships, they come and go about their career goals and activities. Of course, this tremendously undermines long-term effectiveness.

So, what's wrong with this picture?

In spite of their having so much of *the right formula* in place and even activated, there are yet some other frames of references (operating at a higher level) that prevent them from maintaining their resourcefulness. These other frames make up the very sabotaging influence that prevents the stabilizing of the states of excellence. That explains why they don't move to the place where their expertise becomes "second nature" and their competence becomes automatic and unconscious.

To address this, we have to deframe or bust those sabotaging frames. Typically, the ones that I have found in consultations with people who have an On Now/Off Now motivation involve the following frames, which induce corresponding states:

- "Why can't I have immediate success?"
- "I want it to be easy. I don't want to have to 'pay my dues.'"
- "I get tired of this focus …"
- "It's just not 'me' to do it that way."

Frame Busting

One of the very best tools around for blowing out sabotaging frames involves a simple set of questions. If we use questions to *index the specifics* about *how* a person does whatever he or she does or knows whatever the person knows, *the simple exploration questions* will operate to deconstruct the old frames.

Doesn't this make perfect sense?

After all, thoughts as representations about some reference, idea, or event make up the very stuff of our frames in the first place. This means that we ourselves glue our frames together with images, sounds, sensations, and words. This is especially true for conceptual and semantic states. So as a dragon-slaying tool, the *indexing questions of specificity* enable us to unglue a neurolinguistic construct—to deconstruct it. I wrote *Secrets of Magic* (1997) as an entire work on this technology.

When we play *The Specificity Game,* we endow our thinking and communicating with more precision and clarity. It allows us to keep things in perspective and not to be easily deceived or deluded.

Let's now apply this to the toxic and diseased thinking of this nonsense frame, "Success just ought to come more quickly and easily." We only need to exploratively index what this means:

* How do you know this?
* When did you build this map?
* From what experience did you learn to think this way?
* Have you found this to be accurate and true to your experiences of developing high-quality skills, abilities, learnings?
* Success just ought to come more quickly and easily than what?
* Why should you not have to pay your dues?

Ownership of Your Response-abilities

Want to solidify your *frame games* even further? Then use your basic core powers to fully *accept* and *own* your responses. Doing that initiates the grand state of "responsibility." Since this will be the focus of the next chapter, I'll wait to describe it fully there.

Summary

- There's a new game in town. The face of business has been changing and will continue to change. This challenges us to learn to be flexible, ever learning, and always able to adjust.

- We also need easy access to the kind of knowledge, states, beliefs, and skills that support expertise and that will get us to the top. This calls for such *frame games* as ownership, proactive implementation, decision, and refusal to discount. These are the beginning *Business Excellence Games*.

- It takes special frames to enable us to play the game of business skillfully and to take advantage of the career opportunities. Once we have the frames, the games come easily.

- There are frames that will enable us to succeed. We only need to identify them and translate them into the *states of excellence*.

Chapter 9

Playing As If Response-able

Games and Sub-Games in this Chapter
The Responsibility Game
The Ownership Game
The Responsiveness Game
The Competency Game
The Control Game
The Know-How Game
The Ability Game

The Power of Responsibility

Tremendous power comes when we operate from feeling *responsible* or "at-cause" state. You have undoubtedly felt the surge of power, energy, and motivation in your own personal experiences. For business experts this higher-level awareness is a turn-on. Yet for others it is either a turn-off or a state of fear. It all depends upon whether positive or negative emotions were originally attached to our awareness of response-ability.

Do *you* personally recognize and *feel* the power of *responsibility* as something robust and vigorous? Surprisingly, a great many people do not.

• Why do we not immediately *feel the emotional charge* to this high-level state?
• What can we do in order to put the *ummph!* back into this state so essential for business success?

Setting a new frame for "responsibility"

Let's begin by examining our frames. What comes to mind when you think about or hear the word *"responsibility"*? Does it initiate positive thoughts and emotions? Positive memories, associations, and meanings? Or does it evoke negative ones?

It really does not take a lot of thought about *"responsibility"* to recognize that *ability* (or *power*) lies in the word itself. It literally refers to our power, or ability, to respond. Given that, you would think that it ought to be a real turn-on word.

It is not.

Everyday use of "responsibility" does not consistently present it as a *power* term. At least, we do not think of the term in the same way as we think about other power words: authority, rights, privilege, empowerment, proactivity, promotion.

Yet business experts consistently and consequently play *The Game of Responsibility*. For them, accepting and owning responsibility for what they do, think, feel, and experience simply describes the common sense understanding that they will not succeed if they just sit around waiting for someone else to take responsibility for their success. In the business context this *frame game* shows up as, for instance, initiative, proactivity, empowerment, creativity, leadership, risk taking, ownership.

- What respectable business expert do you know and want to model lives a life of *ir*responsibility?
- How many of these people would you describe as responsible and response-able persons?

If playing *The Responsibility Game* endows us with the resourceful state that brings out our best and facilitates our success in business, how do we play this game? What frames of mind do we need to adopt? What frames will we need to lose?

Reframing "Responsibility"
The term *"responsibility"* has taken a real hit when it comes to effectively communicating that it is a very powerful and desirable state. Let's rephrase the term right up front as "response power." In this way, the term will remind us that it refers to *ownership of our ability to choose our responses.* In earlier chapters, I described our personal *power zone* and our four ultimate and undeniable *powers* that enable us to power up.

- *Powers* of *mind*—to think, believe, conceptualize, value, understand, imagine.
- *Powers of emoting*—to feel, somatize our values (incorporate them into our neurology and physiology), empathize.
- *Powers of speaking*—to "language," create symbols, to conceptualize higher understandings, to communicate.
- *Powers of behaving*—to do, gesture, relating, develop skills.

These four powers define our zone of influence and bathe us with a special awareness, a sense of being in control of our lives. In response to everyday events, we intuitively know that we can *do* something. We can think, create mental maps, emote, respond with our heart, talk, and act.

Imagine this *power zone* as a *circle of influence* surrounding you like a sphere or globe in which you live and move and have your being. Feel the tremendous power that you have and can exercise in it. In this zone, nobody can *make* you think anything without your permission. Others can attempt to entice you to think in a certain way. Yet ultimately, whether you do or not, lies within your power of choice. Others can attempt to *make* you feel a certain way. Yet, inasmuch as your emoting results most directly from your thinking, this also lies within your arena of power. And so it goes with how you talk and act.

What triggers seduce you into giving up this power and resorting to blaming, accusing, excuse making, victimizing yourself, "awfulizing," pouting, catastrophizing, "tantrumming," and other reactions that undermine your ability to own your own responses? *These* response states contradict and undermine the response-ability state.

What external and internal experiences could get you to give up your power, toss it away, and acquiesce to the triggers of others? Are you fully committed to playing *The Personal Empowerment Game?*

If you misbelieve about your *powers*, and erroneously think that others can *make* you think or feel in ways against your will, that idea as a frame will certainly disempower you. That frame will induce you into *The Victim Game* and off you'll go to act out the pouting script, forgetting to access your sense of ownership. Or you will have contaminated your sense of response-ability with other misbeliefs that are trying to get you to equate owning your responsibility with feeling wrong or blamed. Or, if you do not have lots of *pleasure* attached to the idea of ownership, that might have the same effect. All kinds of things could get you to fail to fully and completely access this state of excellence that business experts play by owning fully and completely their power zone.

Frames for The Responsibility Game
- What does responsibility feel like?
- How are you thinking when you're feeling responsible?
- What components come together to make up this resourceful state?

To explore the structure of this *frame game*, think about a time when you felt responsible in a positive and enhancing way. When you identify that memory, step into that experience fully so that you can become aware of the various elements that comprise this experience. What variables and facets create this gestalt for you?

Next, think back to a time and place where you did *not* feel or take responsibility, but later you wished you had. Recall it fully so that you relive what you saw, heard, felt as well as what you said to yourself. Use this to attach lots of pain to failing to operate from a vital state of responsibility.

While some states are simple and direct, such as fear and anger, attraction and aversion, tension and relaxation (primary states), other states are much more complex and layered. These higher or meta-states involve concepts, self-reflexive consciousness, and "gestalts." These states *emerge* in the mind–body system as they are greater than the sum of the parts. You can add all of the parts together and still cannot explain the new emergent properties. This describes the nature of systemic processes. This holds true for systemic states such as "responsibility," courage, resilience, optimism. The overall configuration of thought and feeling that emerges arises as a more highly developed state. Here I will talk about this as the subgames that combine to make up the larger *Game of Responsibility.*

1. The Responsibility Game
In building up the layers of thinking and feeling that make up the gestalt state of *responsibility,* we begin with the primary state experience of *being responsive* to some task, person, or situation.

Q: Why do we not hold rocks and stones "responsible"?

A: Because they do not, and cannot, *respond* at all.

It takes something *living* to be able to *respond* to the environment. Inanimate objects are unresponsive. They do not move themselves, yet they can be moved. A rock may be flung through the air and smack someone in the face, but the rock itself does not fling itself through the air. It does not even react. It does not respond at all.

So first there has to be the ability to respond and to be responsive in a given context. This refers to the *ability* to respond. I might want to give a tourist directions, but, if I don't speak French, Russian, or some other tongue, I will not have the *ability* to respond. Responsibility arises from the foundation of responsiveness. Conversely, this means that the more responses I can produce, and the more responsive I become, the more responsibility I can handle. The less responsive I am mentally, emotionally, and personally, the less able I'll be to take charge in a field.

2. The Control Over Responses Game
Responsibility also necessitates that we *have control over* our responses. What we cannot control, we cannot be held responsible for. We do not hold infants responsible for many of their actions

(for example, throwing food all over the kitchen) because they do not have control over their actions. They are behaviorally incompetent. Actions, events, and processes to which we might like to respond and do respond, but to which or over which we have no influence, describe a whole range of things for which we cannot be responsible.

Can I control my thinking? My speaking? My acting?

3. The "Sensing a Need or Opportunity" Game

With the state of being responsive and able to control our responses, the higher-level state that we call *responsibility* next needs some *reason*. Some responses *need* to be made, *have* to be made, or it *would be great* if they were made. This is where meaning and purpose enter the game.

For example, the sense of responsibility we feel for our newborns not only involves responsiveness, but involves our realization that they *need* to be fed, kept dry, and rocked. Along with our realization of the *necessity* to respond for the sake of some value (such as life, safety, wellbeing), we also may feel a strong *desire* to do so (to be a good parent, for instance, or to be loving).

Responsibilities highlight our values and meanings. We respond *to* the things that we value and that we don't value. We *take action* to attend to the hurting emotions of a friend *because* we care about that person, want him or her to feel better, to feel our support, and to be a good friend. We do not want to neglect or ignore our friend. Values drive *The Responsibility Game.* No valuing of something means no sense of responsibility.

Do you feel responsible for:

- Your work?
- Getting out of bed and get there?
- Giving it your best?
- Investing your mind, body, and soul into the actions and responses that you give?

If so, why? What do you value in such responsiveness?

Does it not come down to your higher frames of mind – those frames that you decide regarding what you will do and then just do it? It might involve being dependable, trustworthy, capable, excellent, achieving, successful.

Being responsible also involves a motivated "propulsion system." Typically, we feel *obligations* that we need to do certain things, that some actions are required, and we feel compelled and attracted to other actions. We *get* to choose. This enables us to take a step toward fulfilling our highest goals and values.

Leslie Cameron-Bandler and Michael Lebeau (1985) argue that *responsibility* as an emotion depends largely upon the words that govern our *modus operandi* in the world, which linguists call "modal operators." These terms control the qualities and effects of how we go about things. It arises from our sense (or frame) that something needs to, should, or must be done, or that you can, should, need to, or must take action to do something. In reflecting our *modus operandi,* our M.O. These terms set up the kinds of games that we play.

4. The Ownership Game

Imagine that something *needs* to be done *and/*or you *desire* to do it, and, further, you have the *ability* to respond. Do those elements, in and of themselves, generate the gestalt sense of responsibility?

We're close, but are not quite there. We still need to add another quality to the mix. In order for you to feel responsible, you have to *own* it. If you don't own it, then you'll probably end up saying,

"*Somebody* needs to clean the toilets!" "Who's going to write that report? Somebody ought to do it because it has to be done by Friday!" "It isn't my fault that the Brown account didn't get processed. Don't blame me."

Without *ownership* (and the willing ability to play *The Ownership Game*), we will more likely take off playing some very different games, games characterized by demanding, blaming, excuse making, and arguing.

Ownership refers to the internal willingness to see oneself "at cause." This refers to a specific attitude and recognition:

"My actions and responses, that is, my responsiveness and *ability* to control my responses, have effects."

Once we step into and use the ownership frame of reference, the frame sets another series of forces and influences into motion so that we play another game. This *mindfulness* about the actions comes out of our power zone and heightens our awareness of our powers. This induces a sense of efficacy and self-efficacy. We now feel something that counteracts the irresponsibility that arises from disempowerment, learned helplessness, and despair:

"I can act and make a difference. What I do can and does influence things."

5. The Competency Game

With *ownership* of our basic controllable responsiveness toward obligations and opportunities, we still need one more thing— actual *ability*.

This explains why you can't be *responsible* for performing brain surgery if you come upon an accident victim on the side of the road. If you lack the training, knowledge, and skills for doing so, you would stand there looking at an open brain, and *not know how* to act, at least not intelligently. You may feel that someone *needs* to open the person's skull. You may strongly desire to help him out. You may even assume ownership that *you* should do it—especially if you caused the accident. Yet if you *cannot* perform the act—you cannot be held accountable for failing to do it.

If we *feel responsible* and at the same time don't believe we *can* do something, then we fall into the emotional pit of feeling inadequate, guilty, bad, and depressed.

6. The Know-How Game

Responsibility also involves awareness of *what* needs to be done. Being capable of responding, a willingness to take ownership of acting, and even having the ability, but *not knowing what to do*, puts us into a place where we cannot be response-able. To such a situation, we would ask, "What do I need to do right now?"

The Sub-Games Add Up to the Big Game

If we combine and sequence these subgames and the frames that drive them, we have the components of the larger-level frame of mind that we call "responsibility." Together they give us the following:

- *Responsiveness:* A sensitivity to the environment, to others, to a given context—"Can I respond? Do I have a sensitivity to and responsiveness to this?"
- *Ability or competence:* Skill, a sense of competence to act, capacity to respond—"I can do this. I have the ability, skills, and know-how to do it."
- *Control:* The ability to influence my own actions—"Can I control my actions?"
- *Need:* The necessity or desirability of the action—"Why must this be done?"
- *Ownership:* Acceptance and acknowledgment that I can act in this situation—"I must do this. This action belongs to me."
- *Knowledge of what to do:* Informed actions—"I see what can be done."

The Full Package

We could say that it takes many ingredients to create the complex and layered state that we call *responsibility*. Or we could say that there are numerous frames of mind that enable us to play this *Responsibility Game*.

The following contrasts what happens when we have *some* of the ingredients, yet lack others. There are many sequences that can fail to result in responsibility. There are lots of ways to experience *"irresponsibility."* That is an easier game to play. It's not as rich and full. Mapping out and building up the meta-level structure of response-ability demands much more. It takes more skill and understanding to play that game.

Figure 9:1

Suppose we have ...	But don't have ...	Result
a sense of need and ownership	ability	irresponsibility
a sense of ownership and ability	a sense of need	irresponsibility
need and ability	ownership	irresponsibility
knowledge about what and how to do something	ownership	irresponsibility

In each case, we do not have enough of the essential ingredients to generate the higher-level state of "responsibility." Once we have all of these pieces together, then we can sequence these frames so that we play the game of *feeling responsible* in a positively powerful way. This higher frame then begins to operate as an *attractor* in a self-organizing system. The feeling of responsibility, in turn, activates our problem-solving thinking. We go into a mode of *figuring out how to fulfill the responsibility*. It energizes our mind–body creativity to take effective action. It initiates a very powerful game. It makes for success and excellence not only in business, but in sports, personal relationships, and more.

Oppositional Qualities
If these components constitute the elements of the game called *Personal Responsibility*, then what mental and emotional states prevent, sabotage, or counteract this game? What states or other games *oppose* the playing of this one? What did you find as you thought about a time when you did *not* take responsibility for something?

- The primary state of feeling incapable, unable, incompetent
- The state of feeling accusatory and blaming
- The meta-state of *fear* about assuming ownership
- A *dread* of responsibility
- A *refusal* to accept responsibility
- A learned sense of helplessness and powerlessness

The Responsibility Game

With all of these various parts that go into the mix, how do we construct the frame game called *Personal Responsibility*? How do we sequence the order of the pieces so that we play out this resourceful state?

First, Recognize Your "Response" Powers
At the primary level, take a moment to feel the *responsiveness* of your entire nervous system, your body, brain and its sensitivity to the world out there as well as to its own self. Use your sense receptors to get in touch with the world: open your eyes and notice what you're seeing; open your ears; take a deep breath; smell, taste, feel your sensations on the inside of your body and use your tactile senses as you touch your environment. *Come to all your senses...* in realizing that it lies in the very essence of nervous tissue, protoplasm, to respond to stimuli.

The height of our *responsiveness* to the world occurs in our brain, our cerebral cortex, and all of the higher functions of our nervous system. Not only do we *sense* the world via our many senses, we also *think about*, *represent*, and *conceptualize* the world. We have incredible powers of mind to do this kind of mental mapping. We use symbols to "stand for" and refer to events, persons, things, and ideas. This allows us to build an entire inner world of representations and ideas, and nobody can *make* us do this in a particular way without our consent.

From these powers of mind arise our emotional powers. An "emotion," after all, involves our basic senses (feelings, sensations, kinesthetics) plus some cognitive content. In *emoting*, we incorporate into our body (soma) our ideas and values. We *somatize* our beliefs, and values. The *motions* (*sensations*) that we feel in our body involve the metabolizing of our thoughts. And here, too, nobody can *make* us have these emotional experiences without our permission.

Second, Fully "Own" Your Powers

As we fully experience these internal and private powers, we own them. Affirm them. Acknowledge them. Claim them as *ours*. "These are *my* mental and emotional responses to things."

While you're at it, claim also your powers of speech and behavior. These public facets of our power enable us to *act upon the world*. This contrasts with our private powers, which mostly give us the ability to *act upon ourselves*. When we think and emote (access process states), we *influence* our nervous system, our mind, our body.

Nothing will empower us as much as this very simple but profound exercise. Do not discount it due to its simplicity. After you've *owned* your powers in the inner recesses of your thoughts (affirmations about your thoughts and emotions), express this out loud. Then tell someone:

"I have some incredible powers innate to my very being—I have powers of mind and emotion that are mine. I can think anything I want to think. I can and do emote in ways unique to my own way of thinking and framing things. These are my inalienable powers."

"I also have incredible powers of languaging and behaving. As a symbol user and meaning-maker, it lies within my powers to represent things and to construct frames of reference. Nothing means anything in and of itself. I attribute meaning. And I also have the power to *act on* the meanings that I create."

Martin Seligman (1975, 1990) says that both what he calls *learned helplessness* and *learned optimism* are ways of thinking about the amount of power or influence we exert in the world. Each describes an *explanatory style* that frames the events and processes that we engage in and experience from others. And however we frame it—in terms of having power to make a difference, or being a victim to the influences of others—it becomes our program, orientation, and life.

Third, Forecast Your Future
Having a sense of our powers and a meta-level *ownership* of the powers, the next move will simply take us to a meta-position so that we can use our conceptual powers to decide what we *need* to do and what we *want* to do. Here we get to build our own programs for experiencing a *sense of obligation and a sense of opportunity.*

- What do you want to *do* given these powers?
- What do you value?
- What do you seek?
- What outcome do you want to attain?

The greater clarity we construct, the greater compulsion and propulsion powers we program into our entire mind–body system. Design some well-formed outcomes of things that we really want to achieve, attain, and experience. Realize that, as you do this, it will become your value system, belief system, ethical system, and the foundations for the "personality." "As you think in your heart, so you will become."

Leslie Cameron-Bandler and Michael Lebeau (1985) write,

> "Remember, to get yourself or someone else to feel responsible in this way, it is important to know the reasons 'it' needs to be done, and those reasons must be experienced as acceptable, or worthy. It is not enough to make someone *be* responsible; that person must *feel* responsible if he is to wholeheartedly fulfill the task." [Page 62.]

To validate and confirm the *importance* of feeling responsible we need *reasons*. Reasons enable us to think *about* it (ah, a meta-level) as important, significant, and meaningful. "I ought to do this *because* it means this or that ..."

Fourth, Develop the Abilities to Achieve Your Outcomes
While the level of actual ability occurs at the primary level, we build up those *potentialities* by engaging in the mapping or modeling process. First, we have to develop understandings, beliefs in our self-capacities, and know-how learnings. We have to develop

mental strategies for how to accomplish things—how to become skilled.

Think about some of your competencies. Riding a bike, roller-skating, skiing, cooking, reading, using a word processor, dressing yourself, driving a car. How did you *learn* to develop such *response-ability* in such areas? Did you not both learn by developing understandings and then practicing such until you honed your responses and they became more and more appropriate, fitting, and refined?

Even the most *experiential types of learnings* involve concepts—understandings, mental models, explanations, reasons, whys. Here coaches and instructors often "teach" the skills by providing lots of succinct direct commands. They *coach* us through the process giving us understandings, ideas, and metaphors, as well as encouragements, to reinforce the learnings.

Fifth, Take Action to Get Physically Involved
This describes the final step. If you do *not activate* the program for taking action, it does not express response-ability. You're just wishing, dreaming, and hoping. You're still not *acting*. So act. Try it out.

Make your dreams come true. You know you *can*. Now with the decision *"I will …"* also specify when and how.

Figure 9:2

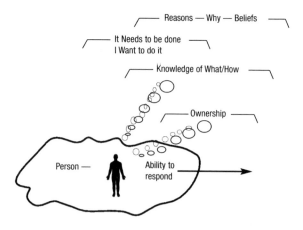

Putting it all Together

The game begins as we *feel our innate responsiveness and powers* and have acknowledged them. We also *feel ourselves as "at cause"* in the world, someone who can make a difference, make things happen, and have internal permission and validation to take effective actions. Then, as we see things, we can say, "That needs to be done"; "I get to do this or that"; "Here's a response I can make that will contribute." And, when you *feel* that ownership, then you can acknowledge your potentialities: "I can do it"; "If I can't pull it off at first, I can learn. I can become more skilled, more efficient, more successful." We can also go further. We can access our highest executive meta-state to say, "I *will* pull this off"; "I *will* take effective action to respond in this situation."

Setting higher frames

To Protect and Support "Responsibility"

Given all of these elements that make up the gestalt state of response-ability, what higher frames do we need to set in order to secure and protect the resourceful meta-state of responsibility? What other higher frames can we set so as to design-engineer it so that it becomes even richer and more powerful?

Permission for Responsibility

How about this? What if you gave yourself total permission to accept and take ownership in your innate powers, and then glory in those powers? Do you have permission to own your powers? Has someone taken permission away? You can now overcome any taboo by giving yourself permission until you *feel that freedom* to totally *affirm and validate* the importance of this.

Valuing its Importance

How much do you value the significance of accessing a sense of response-ability? What ideas about its importance would you like to apply to it? What states would you like to bring to bear upon it? Doing this will enable you to outframe the responsibility state by valuing it for whatever reason or reasons that you create. For example:

- It's good to assume responsibility.
- It contributes to my welfare and that of others.
- It is morally good to own your responsibilities.

Powerful Confirmation
You could simply say a big bold *"Yes!"* to the state by validating and affirming it as true and valid. This highlights the fundamental importance of the Meta-*Yes*-ing Pattern:

- I am a responsible and proactive person.
- I am responsible for what I have and can do.

Frame it as the Ultimate Reality
You could outframe it with thoughts and feelings of "This is real"; "This is ultimate"; "This is just the way it is."

Unquestionable
Another way to set a frame that stabilizes whatever lies below it involves bringing thoughts, images, and metaphors to bear upon it that communicate the message, "This is unquestionable."

Each of these meta-moves enables us to set a higher frame that can stabilize and solidify the lower frames embedded within. In doing this, we can *protect our business expertise*. It provides us the ability to establish long-term and enduring beliefs or attitudes.

An *attitude* operates as a deep, profound, or high level *predisposition of mind and body* that sets up a direction or orientation in life. Even the word "attitude" as a "posture" (a mental posture, social posture, or physical posture) alludes to the original metaphor of how solid a set of ideas can become. When they do, they become our default way of thinking and feeling. And we "carry" them with us as our basic orientation in the world.

Leslie Cameron-Bandler and Michael Lebeau (1985) write:

"Once you feel responsible for something, your thinking becomes oriented toward figuring out just how to fulfill that responsibility—that is, how to do what you need to do ..." [Page 61.]

"Using 'responsibility' as an example, you can bring yourself or someone else to feeling capably responsible by building in the necessary modality components of that emotion—that is, by effectively conveying to someone that:

—"It needs to be done" (in order to avoid negative consequences or to attain positive consequences),

—"It is his to do" (he is the best, only, or proper choice),

—"He can do it" (what needs to be done is possible for him to do). [Page 62.]

After the Structure—Above the Structure
The state of *feeling responsible* describes a complex and meta-level structure. This is *not* a primary state. Check it out. Where in your body do you feel *"responsible"*? It is not primarily a kinesthetic sensation. It refers to a judgment, a mental understanding. It arises as a meta-feeling about a critical human concept—"responsibility."

As such, this raises another crucial concern. Suppose we have gone through the entire process and have built up various layers of states upon states to map out *feeling responsible* for ourselves, our lives, the way we think and feel. How do you feel *about* "being responsible"?

Ah, we have now moved yet another level *above* this entire gestalt. Why would I suggest such? Because, as with every concept that we humans can conceptualize, we develop thoughts and feelings about the concept *as a concept*. What have you attached, or what has someone else attached, to *the idea of being responsible*? Do you experience this as a positive and empowering state? Do you experience it as a burden, a problem, something liable to get you into trouble, or what?

145

Our reflexive consciousness enables us to easily develop *poor relationships to ideas and concepts.* I know that sounds funny. We usually think about relationships as something we have with other people, not to ideas. Yet this uniquely distinguishes our species. We can get into states (meta-states) where we have a *bad relationship with ideas.* We can *hate* the idea of "authority," "manipulation," "relationships!," "success." We can *fear* ideas of "mathematics, " "public speaking," " wealth," " love," "intimacy,"*etc.*

So, again, how do you feel about "being responsible"?

Whatever you answer will tell about the higher frames in which you have this whole domain embedded. Does it serve you well? Does it allow you to step into it and feel empowered? Does it attract you?

Taking Courage to Fully Accept Responsibility
There's no question about it—it takes courage to accept our *response-ability.* Without courage, the fears of the risks can feel overwhelming so that we might cower back in timidity. *Decide,* then, to use your highest executive powers of choice to focus your mind to accept your responsibilities, knowing that it will empower you. And I would not suggest that you build up a tenacious courage to do that—but, of course, you're even free to do that, are you not?

Summary

- To experience and feel the electrical charge of the high-level state of *response-ability* necessitates adding several key ingredients together in your mind–body system. When you do that, you can play *The Games that Business Experts Play,* such as the games of *Responsibility, Proactivity, Initiative, Risk Taking,* and *Efficiency.*

- There's power, energy, and a sense of personal control that comes with *responsibility.* If you don't sense that by just hearing or saying that word, then reframe it until you do.

- Playing this game of the business experts eliminates all the games of disempowerment: "I'm a Victim"; "Yes, but …"; "What if …?"

Chapter 10

Positioning to Play with Excellence

Playing Games of Efficiency

Games in this Chapter
The Frame-Setting Game
The Aim Game
The Solution Game
The Feedback Game
The Relevancy Game
The Discernment Game

Efficiency Frame Games

Once we have powered up with the foundational games, developed the flexibility and mindfulness to recognize the new games in town, and have begun playing *The Personal Responsibility Game*, we're ready to refine these powers and develop the specific high-level efficiency skills that will give form to the particular expertise needed in business.

What frames of mind do we need to succeed in business to tap into the wisdom of a business expert? What frames enable highly skilled people to hone their expertise so that it moves them to excellence in their chosen field? What frames are absolutely essential for developing your own working genius?

The Frame-Setting Game

Whether they know it consciously or just operate from unconscious competence, business experts are skilled players in *The
Frame-Setting Game*. Every day they play the game with such skill
and grace that most people never notice it. They are the frame set-
ters. They set the frames and so they govern the games. This is one
of the secrets of *frame games.*

> *The frames we live within, and work from, completely control our
> destiny, our experiences, our financial and business success. They
> control the games we play and can play. After all, he who sets the
> frame controls the game.*

Frames are inevitable. Even this very moment, you are reading
this page from some frame-of-reference. But which one? Do you
know? It's frame awareness that enables us to play *The Frame
Setting Game.*

- Who set that frame?
- How well does it serve you?
- Does it undermine and sabotage your highest skills and
  expertise?
- What can you do to take charge of the frames that life, your
  family of origin, and your culture have bequeathed to you?

These frame questions explore a dimension of life that typically
lies outside of our daily awareness. Yet our frames and matrix of
frames most crucially govern our experiences. To raise your
awareness about frames and frame setting, consider the following
questions.

- What are the dominate frames in your life?
- What frames of reference do you typically use at work?
- How much do those frames enhance your work?
- What frames have been set in your particular career?
- Who set them?
- For what purpose?
- Do you find them empowering or engendering of your own
  creativity?
- How skilled are you at frame setting?

- How skilled are you at going meta to your own frames in order to make sure that your frames serve you well?
- Do you have the ability to hear *frames* as people set them with you in conversation? Would you like to?
- Do you know how much more resourceful that would make you?
- Do you know in your gut, and at the kinesthetic level, that *frames govern* and that "he who sets the frame will control the experience"?
- Would you like to take charge of your own life and increase your persuasion skills a hundredfold by learning how to work from the top down using meta-levels and frames?

Such questions highlight the domain of frame setting. Frames play that important a role in our communications, experiences, and especially interactions in work. After all, every business has already set many frames.

When we set a frame, we provide a structure for thinking, feeling, or responding. Like an architect designing a building, we think first about form and shape. Like an automobile designer, we think first about the chassis and how its construction affects the car's performance. Like an artist, we think first about how to set a frame regarding the size, borders, and organization of the materials.

The frames we set affect the range of what others consider possible, orients the perceptions and understandings of others. They create a mental-emotional world, a matrix of beliefs. When we live our lives blind to the governing frames, we are played by those frames. They control us. We then become a puppet in the games.

Frame blindness prevents us from truly understanding what our bosses and customers want. It prevents us from understanding our company and our career domain. It hinders us in pacing, matching, and gaining rapport so that we can have some impact and influence. It will be these areas that we will begin to explore in this chapter.

If this is what we mean by frame setting, then how do we play the game and how can we become experts in playing it?

The Frame-Setting Game is simple. Consider the content of *what* you say (verbally and nonverbally) in terms of what these ideas, concepts, and images presuppose. What is the underlying or overarching structure, form, or process implied? An expert in frame setting not only thinks in terms of content, but also in terms of structure.

So if I approach a situation where someone is, say, stuck, upset or angry and set a Problem-Focus Frame, how different if I had asked, "How can we solve this?"

If I ask, "How can I help?" that invites you to play the game inside the frame: "I am the Expert ... Just ask me—the Answer Man." How different if I had asked, "What solutions have you come up with so far? Which one do you think has the greatest possibility of handling this effectively?"

To think in terms of frame setting, question the presuppositions of your statements.

- What am I assuming?
- What state or emotion could this trigger?
- What direction or orientation could this establish?

The payoffs for this game are many. You get to control and manage the overall direction of your life. You establish the overall feel or emotional tone of interactions. You increase your influence and persuasion with others. You avoid getting swept along with toxic and unenhancing games.

Some frames are already set, and set pretty firmly. At the biological level and neurological level, our bodies establish a great many of our frames. Given the kind of bodies that we have and the way they operate in relationship to gravity (up and down), the way we see (straight ahead and some peripheral vision, but not behind), the way we hear, and son on, our very neurological organization sets many of our frames. So does the language of the culture into which we are born, as noted by linguists and research in semantics: Korzybski (1933, 1994) noted that in his work; so did Whorf and Sapir at the beginning of the twentieth century; so do Lakoff and Johnson and others today in the field of cognitive linguistics.

Frames are inevitable. When we set frames, we establish *presuppositional structures*, which will then govern how we think, feel, and act. We set frames by using linguistic formats and non-linguistic rituals.

The Aim Game

A Game for Focus, Purpose, and Direction

Because excellence results from creating and developing *a clear goal* that specifies where you want to go, *The Aim Frame Game* establishes clarity about *why*. By starting with the end clearly in mind, we develop a sense of empowering direction. We do this by first constructing a desired outcome and then embed it in a series of meta-outcomes.

The first why establishes our end game *frame*—the *end* that we're aiming for. The series of outcomes identifies our hierarchy of outcomes that formulate our neuro-semantic levels of meaning. Together this generates clarity and focus in our sense of direction. It enables us to live purposefully.

It also builds *bounce* or *resilience* into our life and neurology. If something then sets us back or upsets our progress, we don't lose our dreams, we just *bounce right back*. Our *Aim Frame* sustains us through the ups and downs, the challenges and difficulties. We know where we are headed, and why!

The Aim Game enables us to handle the everyday details necessary to move in the right direction. When we develop clarity about all of our higher-level outcome frames, we are empowered to determine *which details* to treat as highly important and which to treat as trivial and peripheral to our goals. Then, when we see details balanced inside a clearly articulated set of desired outcomes, we are far more enabled to take care of those details.

I describe this as meta-detailing in *The Structure of Excellence: Unmasking the meta-levels of Submodalities* (1999). I took my cue from the work of Robert Dilts, *Strategies of Genius*, and have designated this element of genius as the ability to go meta, identify the key ideas or principles, and then, from that perspective, detail the specifics.

A precisely articulated *Aim Frame* also assists as we work with others. When we establish and communicate a common understanding about our goals in terms of our aim, this supports team efforts in business. It gives us a sense of a corporate vision or mission. A business plan or a mission statement typically serves to construct an *Aim Frame* that initiates this game. It sets out a direction and a course for the business. This lets people know where they're going; it provides specific directions about how to get there, and the evidence for detecting when we arrive at the destination.

Rules: Much has been written about the elements of good goals and how they instill a sense of direction, the feelings of motivation, and the criteria for evidence. Key eliciting questions to set this frame and initiate the game include:

* What do you want?
* Where are you going?
* What will get you there?
* How will you know when you have arrived there?
* How detailed and precise is the map for getting there?

Once we have established our aim, we can then turn our goals into 3-D holograms in our minds so that we can step into them and more fully use them as life-sized maps as we navigate our way toward that desired future.

Leadership involves the ability to "create worlds to which others want to belong" (Robert Dilts, 1993), so play *The Aim Game* to avoid the disempowering sense of "going nowhere" or "just drifting." Play it when there is dissatisfaction and frustration

The Solution Game

In *Smart Work: The Syntax Guide For Mutual Understanding in the Workplace*, Marshall and Freedman (1995) describe two frames that play a dominant role in any and every business (pages 23–24). These *frames* pop into our minds whenever anything happens at work that we have to deal with—difficulties, complications, set-backs. Let these things cue you about when to play this game.

Description: These frames have also played a central role in terms of our basic perceptual patterns, orientation, and presuppositions about "causation." They summarize two central *perceptual styles* that lead to the two thinking patterns, optimism and pessimism. The first pattern establishes the frame for *The Solution Game*. The second establishes the frame for *The Problem Game*.

Rules: To get a feel for these frames and the games they induce, think about some event or situation at work that you are currently engaged in. Got it? Good. Now, ask yourself the following questions. Begin with the first set. Then break that state. Shake yourself out of the place that those questions put you in. Then go through the second set of questions. Ready? Here we go:

The first set
1.   *What* is the problem?
2.   *Why* do you have this problem?
3.   *How* does it make you feel?
4.   *Who or what* is causing this problem?
5.   Whose *fault* is it?
6.   *Who* or *what* prevents you from getting what you want?

Now break the state. What would you like to have for lunch or supper? Imagine taking an inner-mind vacation on a sunny beach …

The second set
1.   *What* do you want to accomplish as your desired outcome?
2.   *Why* do you feel that this is important?
3.   When you obtain that, *what* will that get you?
4.   *How* will you know when you have achieved this outcome?
5.   *What* resources do you need to reach this outcome? *What* resources could assist you in this?
6.   *How* can you better respond to these challenges, limitations, or constraints?
7.   *How* do you feel about this outcome? *How* do you feel about utilizing these resources?

The first set of questions makes it very easy to step into *The Problem Game.* "Houston; We have a problem!" The questions pull you into thinking about "the problem," and you thought about it as a "problem." And, as you thought in this way, it elicited a certain orientation as well as certain emotions. It set up a game.

What states and meta-states did it evoke in you?

What games did you play or feel like playing by the time you finished?

Did the questions hook you into that state?

The second set of questions established a different frame, did they not? If you took the time to consider the questions, you would have entered into *The Solution Game.* To even consider the second set of questions, and especially *to answer them,* you would have had to use your brain in a very different way from the way you used it with the first questions.

How much more empowering did you find the second set of questions?

To what degree did they orient you toward solution and creativity?

One more thing. To discover just how much more resourceful this makes you, stop—and ask the next set of questions about the two different states or orientations that the two sets of questions evoked. Ask each question for each elicitation.

The third set
1. As you check your *energy level* after asking the first questions that presupposed *The Problem Frame,* how much energy do you feel? How much energy do you feel after asking the second set of questions about *The Solution Frame?*
2. How do you feel about yourself after each?
3. How do you feel about others in the situation?
4. How is your level of optimism?

5. What is your clarity about the situation? How much clarity do you sense that you have?

Having used this process as an exercise in our workshops, *Games Business Experts Play*, most people find it absolutely amazing that *framing-questions* can have that much impact. The questions that we ask, and the presuppositional frames of reference that they evoke powerfully, affect our states, emotions, energy, thinking patterns, and life orientation. This is the amazing power of frame setting and how all *frame games* work. Set a frame by a simple question, and—hey presto!—we're off to the games.

The Feedback Game

A Game for Obtaining Critical Information
Payoffs: Imagine a business *not* open to feedback. Suppose a company or organization, seeking to produce some product or service was not open to customer complaints, questions, and reactions. Would this support *excellence* in quality and service?

Description: The question is rhetorical. To develop and keep moving toward high quality in any field or business, we have to establish a healthy and vigorous relationship to feedback. We have to welcome feedback, listen to it, honor it, and utilize it. This is how we play *The Feedback Game*. We recognize the value of keeping our eyes, ears, and mind open to the results we're getting.

Cues: The cue as to when to play this game occurs whenever we get a response that we don't want and/or didn't expect. It is precisely when the ball misses the basket that we will want to know—where did it go? How far from the basket? To the right or the left?

Payoffs: So what? What's the payoff of the game? Continual improvement of skills, intelligence, awareness, and the power to use every response in a constructive way. It results in greater practical intelligence and an acceleration of learning, since we don't waste time fretting over errors or guilting ourselves about misses.

Imagine trying to learn to shoot a basketball through the hoop without the feedback information that we can gather and use when we see and feel how a given attempt plays out. If we keep shooting without information about how we're doing, we can't improve our skills. The rule of this game is simple: Stay open to feedback.

Yet how many business people, craft people, supervisors, managers, and executives truly operate from a *vigorous relationship to feedback*? How many welcome feedback? How many empower those providing the feedback so that they feel safe and valued in doing so?

The problem with "feedback" is that the majority of us have linked it with numerous negative associations. We think of it as negative, "failure," "blame," "a put-down," "an insult," showing "inadequacies." Given that, who wants information about how we have missed it, erred, or failed? Yet learning, expertise, excellence, improvement, development, and genius all depend upon feedback.

The Relevancy Game

A Game for Staying on Target
Cues: How many times have you engaged in conversations, activities, or meetings that you later discovered were not relevant at all to accomplishing your goals? Irrelevant committees, meetings, actions, processes, and conversations abound in the way business operates. The relevancy frame changes this. It sends our brains to questioning and thinking *in terms of relevancy*. And this describes how we play this game.

- "Is this relevant?"
- "Does this truly contribute to moving us toward our goal?"
- "How does this positively influence what we're seeking to achieve?"
- "We're talking about X, John. How do you see Y as relevant to that?"

Payoffs: By establishing a frame of relevancy, and letting it govern our actions and communications, we establish a criterion by which to judge the value and importance of things. This new game, *The*

Relevancy Game, saves us from irrelevancy, getting lost in details, chasing rabbits about things that do not matter for the issue at hand.

Earlier, I mentioned meta-detailing, which I described *The Structure of Excellence: Unmasking the meta-levels of Submodalities* (1999). It is a key ingredient for business excellence. The *detailing of specifics* in any given domain makes for excellence if it comes out of a larger frame of significance, what we call a "meta" (higher, larger) frame. It is this higher meaning that makes our everyday activities so much more than just the *detailing* of items. With meta-detailing, our focus on specifics is not amorphous. Our higher-level meta-frame enables us become highly focused so that we make that value, understanding, or principle real in everyday terms.

Failing to establish a relevancy frame leaves us open to "the tyranny of the urgent." Then we choose how and what to respond to based upon how much noise and intrusion it makes in our lives, rather than its importance.

Payoffs: When we explore the structure in *ineffective people,* we typically discover very busy people. We find people whose lives and schedules are full. They are busy doing lots of things. What makes them *ineffective* then? They are doing things that really don't count. They are doing things that are not ultimately relevant to their success.

Consider the subject of relevancy in regard to Edwards Deming's fourteen points for making management more effective and focused on quality. He began with vision and focus about the things that do count. The following applies equally well to an individual as it does to a group or organization.

"Create constancy of purpose for improvement and service" (Point 1).

"Improve constantly and forever the system of production and service" (Point 5).

"Institute training, leadership, a vigorous program of education and retraining" (Points 6, 7, and 13).

He then presented some things *irrelevant to business success*. These things do not contribute. Many of them *increase ineffectiveness*. In *The Relevancy Game* we have to address these off-limits subjects.

"Cease dependence on mass inspection" (Point 3).

"End the practice of awarding business on the price tag alone" (Point 4).

"Drive out fear" (Point 8).

"Break down barriers between staff areas" (Point 9).

"Eliminate slogans, exhortations, and targets for the workforce" (Point 10).

"Eliminate numerical quotas" (Point 11).

Do you play *The Relevancy Game* or do you often find yourself playing *The "Being Overly Involved in Irrelevant Details* and *Not Aware of It" Game*? If you want to access your personal work genius, learn to catch it and shift to *The Relevancy Game.*

The Discernment Game

Consider the subject of discernment, or judgment, in business. Without the ability to make discernments by which we make judgments about the quality, excellence, usefulness, and relevance of our product, we would have no way to improve quality. That's the payoff of this game: To continually improve until we master our skills and develop expect knowledge. We play *The Quality-Control Game* as we choose valued criteria to evaluate our products and service. We also need discernment to sort and separate the best person for a job, decide on the best system, and to govern our perspective as we develop wise insights about business decisions.

Yet we do not need a kind of judgment that involves *blame and fault-finding*. That's an entirely different dynamic (mental-and-emotional state) and a dangerous one to the health and sustainability of effective business.

What's the difference between these two kinds of judgments? In *The Blame Game* we attack a person; we seek to find someone or something that we can then punish. People typically do this in order to make themselves feel better or superior, as it seeks to take them off the hook.

In *The Discernment Game* we evaluate a behavior, process, experience, or understanding; we seek to understand a process or pattern. We aim to identify the factors and contributing influences so that we can make things better and use such feedback loops to accelerate our learning.

This has a strong similarity to *The Problem Game* versus *The Solution Game*. In focusing exclusively on problems—especially their source and cause—most people can easily fall into the trap of *The Blame Game*. In focusing on solutions, most people do not even think about "blame" inasmuch as they think about understanding, gaining clarity, creating new response patterns to the challenges in the future.

Summary

- How do we position ourselves to play the *Business Games* that allow us to succeed in the long run? By becoming more empowered in the way we *take* full responsibility for *setting the frames* that govern minds—ours and others'. This facilitates the desired game.

- We have now explored some of the most basic games that business experts play: *The Frame-Setting Game, The Aim Game, The Solution Game, The Feedback Game, The Relevancy Game,* and *The Discernment Game*.

Chapter 11

The Making-Work-Meaningful Game

Games in this Chapter
The "Valuing Work as Important" Game
The Meaning-Making Game
The "I Am So Much More Than My Job" Game
The "I've Got a Sense of Control Over My Work" Game
The "Finding Pleasure In My Work" Game
The "Setting New Meaning Frames" Game

What comes to mind when you think about the following? I'll say the word (well, write it) and you immediately respond to the term without thinking about it. Say aloud whatever comes to mind. It doesn't matter what comes—welcome it and just notice it. Ready? Go.

* Work
* Business
* Career

What thoughts and feelings emerge for you when the idea of work bubbles up into your consciousness? Do you—

* Get all excited and thrilled?
* Imagine all of the wonderful and creative things you'll do?
* Delight yourself in making money, helping people, developing your skills?
* Wish you could do something else?
* Feel stressed and upset about the demands, pressures, dissatisfactions?
* Feel grumpy and negative?

Now that you know about games, you know that these questions enable us to flush out your current *Business Games*. Once you do that you can play *The Quality-Control Game* to see if they enhance or limit you.

This is important because *how you engage in work*, whether from a pleasant, joyful, and enthusiastic attitude or from a grumpy, negative, and demotivated attitude, governs the quality and nature of your work. What state characterizes your *work state*? How enhancing do you find that state? How much control or flexibility do you have over that state?

The *quality* of our life and experiences results from the thoughts-and-feelings that we bring to things and from the higher-level thoughts-and-feelings within which we embed primary experiences. Therefore, to enhance and empower our experiences of work, we have to play *The Quality-Control Game.*

The Problem with Grumpy Workers

Do you ever go to work grumpy?

Do you ever meet grumpiness in those you work with?

Do you believe that disgruntledness will just go away if you ignore it?

- Most of the time such *disgruntledness* simply creates an atmosphere of negativism, stress, irritation, and unpleasantness. Of course, sometimes it grows until a worker blows up in a rage and goes after supervisors and co-workers with a loaded gun. Now that's quite some game to play!

- Statistics indicate that most people do not find their jobs enjoyable or meaningful. In the book *Working*, Studs Terkel asserts that "most people are unhappy with their jobs." I wonder how many people *drag themselves* to work, regretting it, complaining about it, and wishing themselves somewhere else. If you didn't get paid for doing what you do from Monday to Friday, would you do it? So, why do you do what you do? What would you prefer to do as an expression of your creativity, skills, aptitude, and contributing something significant to the world?

- If you don't go to work because of its inherent values and enjoyment, *and yet* you do your work with joy and resourcefulness, then you have discovered the secret of making your work meaningful. You have framed your ideas of work with *meaning*. This speaks about your skill in running your own brain, managing your emotions, and taking charge of your life. Congratulations!

Those who have not yet learned how to do this will suffer from job discontentment, boredom, and a sense of futility. The problem with that is that we don't thrive when we engage in repetitious activities that we consider insignificant. *We must have meaning.* The problem doesn't lie in work itself. It doesn't even lie in menial work. The problem lies in our *attitude* about work.

Setting Meaning Frames in Your Everyday Work

If you feel stagnated by your job *and yet* you don't want to leave it, what can you do? You can explore ways to create meaning and enjoyment about the experience. As a *brain-runner* (you do "run your own brain," don't you?), you know that nothing has meaning in and of itself. We construct meaning. Meaning is an inside job.

So when your work lacks zest and enthusiasm, when your interest wanes, and when disenchantment arises, you have a great opportunity to practice using your brain to set new frames of invigorating thoughts, beliefs, and values. This will give you the power to live affirmatively and vibrantly regardless of your external situations.

If you don't do this, then letting the *conditions of the workplace* determine your state of mind and mood will only recruit you to set and play the game we might call *"I Am a Powerless Victim Who Can Do Nothing!"* Now *there's* a game to tax your spirit and crush your

hope! That could have been true in the early days of industrializa-
tion when children worked fourteen-hour days and when men
and women worked in squalid mills, faced oppressive bosses, and
had very little recourse for mistreatment. Today, while things are
not so gruesome, many people let unsatisfying work do violence
to their spirits.

The New Game in Town

Catching a Powerfully Positive Vision about Working

Wouldn't it feel great to do what you want to do *and* get paid for
it? Many compensate for the lack of this by settling for doing what
they *want* as a hobby, volunteer assignment, or after-hour exploration. Yet we do have another choice. We can *learn to like what we
do*. This means learning to run the higher levels of our brain to
manage the meanings. Doing this allows us to create meanings
that will transform our work experience

The quality of our life arises from *meaning*, from the meanings that
we attribute, not how much or what we possess. It lies in *going
meta* to set frames loaded with rich and significant meanings about
work that empower us to move beyond boredom and
insignificance.

Do you ever feel *bored* with your work? If so, your boredom is a
function of your thinking. Boredom is your state and experience,
it is not what exists "out there." Your work activities undoubtedly
give you many opportunities to cultivate a wide range of skills. Yet
is *that* the frame of reference you typically use? Is that what's in
your mind? Where does your brain go regarding your work activities and tasks? What does your work mean to you? What games
of meaning do you play? When you think about going to work,
what comes to mind? Boredom, tediousness, meaningless?
Bureaucracy, impersonal, incompetence?

Hugh Prather describes boredom in terms of the thinking that
frames it and suggests another kind of thinking to relieve it:

"I don't like what I'm doing and I can't think of anything else to do, or what I do think of seems remote and impractical. My mind races from one unsatisfactory plan to another, and my boredom deepens and I become increasingly frustrated. I am noticing that when I am bored, I think I'm tired of my surroundings, but I'm really tired of my thoughts. It's trite, repetitious, unobserved thinking that produces the *discontent* ... Adopting a quiet awareness, a kind of listening attitude usually *freshens my mind* and brings the situation I'm in to life." [*Notes to Myself*]

Henri J.M. Nouwen writes:

"Boredom is a sentiment of disconnectedness. While we are busy with many things, we wonder if what we do makes any real difference. Life presents itself as a random and unconnected series of activities and events over which we have little or no control. To be bored, therefore does not mean that we have nothing to do, but that we question the value of the things we are so busy doing.

"The great paradox of our time is that many of us are *busy and bored* at the same time. While running from one event to the next, we wonder in our innermost selves if anything is really happening. While we can hardly keep up with our many tasks and obligations, we are not so sure that it would make any difference if we did nothing at all.

"Boredom is often closely linked to resentment. When we are busy, yet wondering if our busyness means anything to anyone, we easily feel used, manipulated, and exploited. We begin to see ourselves as victims pushed around and made to do all sorts of things by people who do not really take us seriously as human beings."

The "Valuing Work as Important" Game

As a valuer, we have tremendous capabilities for both discovering and creating meaning. Doing this falls back to choosing ideas, meanings, and frames of reference that endow our activities with positive and compelling meanings.

What meanings could you add to your job, work, or career? Give your mind some exercise—make a written list of inspiring ideas, great motives, wonder-filled attitudes that you would like to bring to your daily activities. Would you like some priming of ideas?

- To learn, discover something new?
- To expand your skills and expertise?
- To express compassion to customers?
- To develop a greater sense of responsibility?
- To persevere?
- To become more patient, less quick to anger?
- To become more skilled and flexible in communicating?
- To raise your frustration tolerance?
- To develop more centeredness and therefore less reactivity to criticism?

Identify your job expectations, assumptions, beliefs, understandings, and values. What do you seek to get out of your work other than pay? After you identify the semantic features (the frames and definitions that create your meanings) that you use as your way of thinking *about* your work, step back and look at those ideas as frames, knowing that "as you think, so you will experience." "As you frame—so will be your game."

Perhaps the time has come to put some new frames around things.

- Do they serve you well?
- Does feeding your mind with those thoughts nourish your soul?

Ellen Langer of Harvard says that when we get into habits of thinking rigidly, we become *mindless*. We become blind to all of the other possible meanings that we could give things. She says that mindless people burn out when they see their job as "the same old thing." They fall into rote habits of *not*-thinking, "We've always done it this way."

The cure for mindlessness? *Mindfulness*. Being mindful enables us to see the novel even in the familiar. This flexible and creative style of thinking turns "stumbling blocks to productivity into building blocks." To promote this, Langer recommends using *the power of uncertainty.* Now that's a different game! How do we play that one? First, decide that you will keep your mind open to the fact that we can understand information in multiple ways. We only need to keep our mind alive, fresh, and interested. Refuse to let the mind close shop.

The Meaning-Making Game

To play this game, *decide* to *affirm* your powers of *inventing* and *creating* meaning and of attaching meanings to the events and people in your life. Freshly affirming these *creative* powers recognizes and owns your power-to-respond to your daily tasks. It enables you to know that you can view them through any glasses of meaning you choose.

When you step up to play *The Meaning-Making Game* you access the power to take anything and transform it into the *meaning* of your life. You can do it with the greatest of ideas, you can do it with the sickest. The ability to do this is not connected to the quality of the idea. You have to do that. So, just because you can do this with any given idea, that does not necessarily make it productive or healthy. You can invest too much meaning in something. You can invest meaning in things in such a way that they become addictions, idols, and destructive experiences.

What meaning do you give to the experience of making money? Have you over-invested in that idea and treated it as your very purpose and mission in life? Do you frame it as "the solution to everything"? We live in a culture that overinvests in the toxic thought that *having* will somehow make us happy, fulfilled, or important. This frame downplays *The Being and Becoming Games.* We are more than our possessions. Many with a great many possessions have empty and hollow inner lives.

Many with all the external symbols of wealth (possessions, money, status) still don't know *how to be.* That's because *having* is a poor substitute for *richly experiencing.* "Thing" addiction can prevent us from learning the skills and experiences of *being.* How's your skill for warmly absorbing the beauty around you as you move through everyday life? How well do you know how to feel refreshed by a cool breeze, to enjoy a book without owning it, or to walk barefoot in a summer rain?

Kahlil Gibran described work as "love made visible." The Benedictines said, "To work is to pray." As these statements frame work as noble and uplifting, even spiritual, that establishes a new game. What would it feel like for you if you played these games? *The "Work to Contribute Something Significant to the World" Game,* or *The "Loving Extension of Myself" Game?*

Play *The Meaning-Making Game* also by learning to view the short-term activities and goals of everyday tasks *through the lens of long-term mission and purpose.* This will enable you to immerse mundane tasks in a pool of the eternal. So if you view learning as your mission, then every little piece of learning becomes a touch of the eternal in your daily life. If you view becoming more valuable and effective as a person as your mission, then getting a promotion or new responsibilities can then become signs of such.

"Well, I can't see my job as anything but unfulfilling. How else could I view it?"

How about as a way to support your family, as an extension of yourself to provide the necessities of life, as a challenge to becoming more internally referenced instead of a victim of external circumstances.

If you continue to view your job in the old way, what *legacy* will you leave? Will that perspective liberate you from daily irritations? What games does it recruit you to play?

The "I Am So Much More Than My Job" Game

After you expose your *expectations* about your job or career, evaluate the *realistic* level of these expectations. Get rid of every fairytale meaning that you have attached to your work activities. What expectations do you need to release? Which ideas and beliefs undermine your happiness and effectiveness?

By *assuming* that work, career, or job *defines* them, many people play *The Identification Game: "I Am My Job Description."* By overidentifying with their careers, they thereby sell their souls to their jobs. Their game becomes, *"I'm Nothing More Than My Job."* Their job description then defines who they are. Culturally, this is a strong and pervasive trap.

Reframe this old attitude of mind. Know solidly that *you are so much more than your job*. Set the frame that you are a *being* who works rather than a job title. What you do at work only expresses some of the things that you *do*. *Refuse* to allow the work activities to *define* your Self.

Decide to Refuse to Commiserate about Your Job
Do you block yourself from endowing your work with positive meanings by keeping yourself in a miserable state of mind? Have you learned to derive some *joy and pleasure* from commiserating? Consider that as a higher-level frame of mind. Does a higher frame of *pleasure* keep you in the commiserating habit? If so, then it will become your game. Why would you give it up if you get such a kick from it?

The Misery Game is also driven by the belief that your job, boss, and co-workers *make* you discontented, upset, frustrated, angry, or miserable. When you believe that you *are* a victim of their actions and words, that they have power *over* you, you have a self-fulfilling game. And that frame, functioning as an attractor in your self-organizing system (as do ideas in all higher frames or meta-states), will make it so that you will see, hear, and feel precisely what you expect to see, hear, and feel. And that will confirm your worse fears.

Interrupt that game by shifting into a more proactive and responseable state:

"My mental and emotional responses come from me; I create them. No one *makes* me have these thoughts or feelings. I have chosen to have them and I can equally choose to say no to them."

If you still have a *commiserating program* in your as a neuro-linguistic state, what have you programmed into it? What are the rules of this game? Do you create your discontentment by "catastrophizing" and "awfulizing" (blowing things out of proportion), throwing temper tantrums, viewing things egocentrically ("*I* want things to go *my* way!"), bitching and badmouthing, blaming, acting like a victim, passively refusing to take responsibility?

The "I've Got a Sense of Control Over My Work" Game

Do you feel in control of yourself, your thinking and feeling or your responses at work? How much "control" do you feel and perceive in your work? When we feel and act resourcefully, we sense that we are in control of ourselves and our world.

I am using the word *"control"* here very purposefully. Many fear the term. Many feel aversion and hesitation to the very idea of wanting to be or being in control. They seem to think that somehow "control" is a bad thing and to want to be in control of their lives is an immoral thing. Yet even the Bible recognizes the fundamental role of *power*. "God does not give us the spirit of fear, but of *power*, love, and sound mind." It is the fear of control that creates semantic reactions against it as if it represented a bad thing. What thoughts and feelings do you bring to bear on the *idea* or *concept* of "control"?

From 0 to 10, how much *control* do you feel about yourself, your life, your job? When we feel *out of control*, we experience feelings of impotence, helplessness, weakness, being a victim. And that's not a resourceful place to come from! Such thoughts will undermine self-confidence and joy.

To gain a greater sense of control, first determine your areas of control. We can't control everything. That's obvious. So what can we *exercise control over*? This redirects us to our *power zone*, to our basic human powers of state—thinking, emoting, speaking, behaving, relating. This defines our *power-to-respond*. Everything beyond this circle of response describes what we cannot control: the economy, for instance, how people think, feel, and respond, national politics.

De-stress yourself. Grant things beyond your power zone the right to be. Accept what you cannot control so that you can focus with more clarity and power on what you can. If you send your brain out to concern yourself about things beyond your power zone, you *dis-empower* yourself.

Then you will develop *"learned helplessness."* Martin Seligman's research about this demonstrates how devastating this plays out in human consciousness. It creates the *"Three Ps"* of clinical depression: *personal, pervasive, permanent.* It's *The "How to P All Over Yourself" Game.* When you develop a good case of this toxic mental disease, then you'll program yourself with several poisonous ideas: "Nothing I do really makes any difference"; "Whatever happens will happen anyway, so why try?"

To de-stress yourself and sanely adjust yourself to reality, accept and acknowledge that "out there" you can, at best, *influence* and persuade, but not control. This will allow you to play *The Serenity Game.* After all, the serenity prayer creates the magic inside *the game of acceptance*: "God, grant me the courage to change the things that I can, to accept the things that I can't change, and the wisdom to know the difference."

What can you control? At best, your brain and body—your neurolinguistic states. If you take up this challenge, it will occupy most of your time, will it not?

When we feel little or no control at work we typically step into the game of *learned helplessness.* This destructive state eats away at self-confidence, joy, and performance.

Conversely, by setting the *frame game* about our power zone, we learn to focus on running our own brain and managing the higher levels of our mind. This endows us with a sense of *being in control* of our states and supports our sense of being able to trust ourselves, and operate from a state of confidence in our thinking, emoting, speaking, behaving, and relating.

Thinking about the Meta-Levels of your Job

Just as you have an "inner executive"—the higher mental frames that govern and regulate your everyday primary states—so you probably work in a system that also has people higher up in the hierarchy (managers and executives). Many times the stresses and strains, the discontentment, and misery of work involve getting along inside a work system—especially when you work within a toxic or dehumanizing system. Here again, recognition and acceptance enable us to avoid dis-empowering ourselves over things we cannot control.

Given your job, what "world" do you work in? As you develop a clear and unmistakable understanding of the world you live in, this will empower your orientation to that world. It will empower you to work in a smart way. Once you have this clarity, then turn up your own states of serenity, joy, humor, and playfulness. As you so sweeten your insides, the misery of grumpy and crabby people around you will weaken. Then, like Victor Frankl in the death camp, you will be able to say,

"The one thing they can't take away from me is my freedom to choose my own response!"

The "Finding Pleasure In My Work" Game

Job enjoyment occurs as an "inside job" just as it does with all meaning-making. It comes from the ability to run your own brain and to not give all your power away to external events to determine your state. So, when you go off to work, make sure that you take along with you all of your *pleasure-creating skills*. Then, from your repertoire of skills, you can take delight in anything that happens. This will give you time to play, reflect, see humor, and so forth. So, doggedly determine to keep your sense of fun and ludicrousness when you go to work.

By deciding to adopt a positive mindset, you can make the best of your situations and not fall into the mistake of getting serious or stupid. Once you set up quality optimism as your game, and it becomes your frame, then it will also work in a self-organizing way to magnetize good things to you. It thereby becomes a self-fulfilling prophecy.

"But I can't take optimism into the job I have," you might argue. "People are far too negative there!" Great, what an excellent opportunity for the highest quality of optimism training! This means that it will really blow the socks off of the entrenched pessimists there when you don't buy their toxic ideas! How surprised or blown away do you think they will be when they find that they can't brainwash you into the stupidity of their seriousness? And how much of a sweet torture would you like to give them with your skills of swishing their brains to positive resources?

From a *frame games* point of view, we can *stubbornly* decide to adopt a happy attitude no matter what. Then, just as "misery loves company," or so the proverb says, so does *happiness*.

The "Setting New Meaning Frames" Game

This is a game for your everyday working states.

1. Access your typical work state
We will use this as your reference point. As you now imagine going to work tomorrow, just let the typical thoughts and feelings that you generally experience arise. Just notice the attitude or mood that your thoughts put you in. Experience it and notice your typical everyday working states.

2. Quality-control your typical work state
Ask yourself these questions:

- Do your everyday thoughts put you in the best kind of state?
- How well does that state serve you?
- How much fun and enjoyment does it enable you to experience?
- How creative and playful do you become?
- How respectful and compassionate do you become?
- How excited and passionate do you become?

- How effective and productive do you become?
- Do you want to keep that everyday state and the game that it initiates?

3. Design-engineer some higher-level qualities for your work state
What *quality* or state (for instance, joy, relaxed, alert, confident) would you want to experience as your everyday work state? Identify the qualities that would enhance your experience.

4. Access the frame, apply, then embed your work state in higher levels of meaning
One by one, take the ideas that feed each quality and state and access them fully. When you have done that, amplify that state, as a mind–body state, to your referent experience. Bring it to bear on your work.

Continue this process until you have embedded your everyday work states into several higher-level frames-of-reference so that you have created entirely new *frame games*.

5. Set the frame of control over these new work frame games
Embed these new thoughts and feelings that create the new games within an even higher frame. Namely, "I have the *ability* to respond to things effectively, and to take charge of my responses and to play my everyday work state the way I want to."

6. Vow to continue
Finally, commission that part of your mind that makes decisions, that executive level of mind, to take complete responsibility to continue to do this as you move into your future days and weeks. Will that part of your mind take full responsibility for this new game?

Summary

- The first frame setting to do with regard to work, business, and your career involves using your meaning-making powers to ensure that you refuse to let "the job" set the frame for your thinking and emoting.

- If you hate your job, find it meaningless and tedious, insignificant or frustrating, then *own* your neuro-semantic powers and set out to enrich your job with all kinds of invigorating meanings.

- Know that you do not *have to choose* to play a victim to your job, but that you can make an empowering decision today to be at your best, to take on life's challenges from an attitude of curiosity and playfulness, to *power up*. This enables you to create as much joy and fun and vitality at work as you want to. How much fun and joy and vitality do you want to experience?

- Will you begin today or tomorrow to start to live much more *on the edge* of this excitement than you have ever before now? And, when you give yourself to such invigorating ideas, do you want to do so from an attitude of passion, love, adventure, wonder, spirituality, or a combination of all of them?

Chapter 12

When the Game of Business Gets Tough

Games in this Chapter
The Resilience Game
The Persistence Game
The "Defusing Hotheads" Game
The Calm Eustress Games
The Stress Game
The Cool Alertness Game

Anyone can succeed in business when they have an excellent product or service, when they offer a special skill or service, when the economy is booming, when there's plenty of money and opportunities all around them, when there is good team support, when they're in good health, when things are going well with their personal life.

The challenge occurs when things are *not* going so well. Stress, problems, angry customers, sabotaging employees, grumpy bosses, financial setbacks, a recession in the economy, bankruptcy, creditors hounding us—these are the things that put our work genius to the test. These are the times when we need some additional games that will support our spirit and enable us to win in these situations.

Games For Hard Times

- What gives you a hard time at work?

- What kind of people make it hard for you?

- What circumstances challenge your attitude or determination?

- What problems knock you down or get you off track?

For some it will be putting up with customers, bosses, or employees who are stressed, angry, upset, or insulting. What games can I play when I'm up against "difficult" people? Or stubborn and resistive people? Or those who are rigid, closed-minded, and who have to be right?

For others, "hard times" have more to do with the kind of challenges or situations that they have to face: financial pressure, deadlines, legal paperwork, union issues, management issues—the list goes on. What is it for you?

We will undoubtedly need the ability to defuse stressed-out hotheads whom we encounter so that they don't suck the life out of us. We also need the ability to be firmly persistent in pursuing our goals. We need the ability to be *resilient* no matter what setbacks occur. So these are but a few of the games that business experts play.

The Resilience Game

Description: Would you like to play *The Resilience Game?* Then know this: it is driven by a very special frame of mind, the frame of determination, the attitude that says, "I always bounce back!" This is a frame with an attitude, "Nothing can knock me down for good. Knock me down and I'll be up again, and *in your face!*"

The frames that allow us to play the game of resilience involve the frames that enable us to see ourselves as internally motivated and oriented. We operate from our own center—a center of values and visions. When we have our "locus of control" focused on things *outside* of ourselves, we're always looking outward for validation, affirmation, confirmation, and approval. We play *The "I Need to be Validated" Game*. Of course, that puts motivation, determination, decision making, responsibility, and flexibility on authorities and experiences "out there."

Conversely, when we operate from an *internal* locus of control, we live **beyond** external dependency. People who quickly recover from a setback so that they bounce back into the fray of life and activity do so because they have a captivating vision and they refuse to let external factors (people, events, circumstances) throw cold water on their passions.

What is it that causes those who get knocked down to stay down, to wallow in their emotional pit, and not to rally back immediately? What causes that? They lack or lose an invigorating frame. Because their vision has been darkened, because they have lost hope in what they valued, and because they have released their grip on feeling empowered and able to take effective action, they continually experience the "down."

What happens that allows them to eventually *come back*? The opposite. They come back when they recover their vision. They come back when they renew and refresh a compelling vision for life after the setback. When they do that, they can play *The Resilience Game*.

What's your script for being a resilient person? What frames support that game in your life? Take a moment to write out the rules for this game: "Never say die"; "Never stay down"; "Bounce-back power comes from an invigorating vision." As you articulate the game setup, rules, and payoff, do so with clarity. Expressing your vision and values, refreshes your source of energy and vitality. Make your vision and dream big enough and exciting enough so you experience it as a truly invigorating frame of mind, one that will keep you in the game.

Something special will happen to you when you have your game plan for resilience. You will develop a fire in your belly. You will have a passion big enough to put real "bounce" into your heart and soul. You can begin to develop that now by simply exploring what qualities put "bounce" into you. What other supporting frames of mind about yourself, your life, your goals would enrich and texture *The Resilience Game*? As you find them, add them to the mix. (See *Meta-States* (2000) or *Dragon Slaying* (2000).)

Benefits and cues: Playing this game means that you'll never stay down, but will bounce back, respond more intelligently, and fulfill your highest objectives.

The Persistence Game

Description: Those who succeed dramatically in business and who achieve their lifetime goals play another game—*The Persistence Game*. They just never give up. They go after their goals in a multitude of ways and, if something knocks them down, they learn, they become smarter. They develop richer knowledge, which they use to respond more effectively. This is part of their game plan. They are always learning, always improving, always strategizing, always moving toward their goal. To a great extent, this describes their genius. They keep after it until they succeed. They develop an open feedback loop to mistakes, errors, misjudgments, and things that fail. This openness to learning from mistakes makes them formidable opponents.

What a game! Do you play that one? What would it take in terms of great ideas, understandings, beliefs, and values to get you to step right up to the plate and play *The Persistence Game*? What typically tempts you to give up and not use persistence as one of the key factors in your strategy?

Rules and payoffs: The rules of *The Persistence Game* do not require or expect instant gratification. Conversely, the persistence game is framed in such a way that it views mastery as something that involves growth, development, and improvement over time. The persistent player recognizes the value of investing and of continuous improvement, and knows that, if it really counts, there will be a price. Persistent players welcome such.

By way of contrast, those who are impatient, who think short-term, and who can't play the process game, become suckers for every quick-fix scheme that comes down the road. The impatience frame undermines them every time they attempt to play *The Persistence Game.*

The "Defusing Hotheads" Game

Description: We all know that people get "hot" and angry and stressed. The more stress, pressure, and demands, and the more important something is, the more likely that we will interpret upsets and distresses as threats. Yet when we do we enter into a new game. We enter into the primitive *Fight/Flight Game.* It's then that we become reactive, defensive, hot, and irrational, and we stop playing well with others. The strange thing about this is that the reactiveness is not about true threats and dangers, but about meanings, about what things mean to us.

It happens when we interpret things as a threat—as a psychological threat to our goals, image, reputation, or finances. In turn, this elicits the general arousal syndrome (*The Fight/Flight Game*) and explains how we go into such states of distress. During the twentieth century, stress and the stress diseases have become a new phenomenon in the world of work.

Those who don't know how to play *The "Defusing Hotheads" Game* will play out a defensive maneuver in *The Escalation Game,* "You can't talk to me that way!" Because this game deploys challenging, it typically escalates things until both persons play *"So's Your Old Man!"* It never makes things better.

Rules: Several frames drive *The "Defusing Hotheads" Game:* the acceptance of emotions, acknowledgment that people can get into unresourceful states, separating behavior from person, compassion for the limited states of others, staying centered and refusing to take the interactions personally, the willingness to graciously defuse another, and so on. Defusing is counter-intuitive. As an interpersonal game, it's quite an advanced one, one that only people who know how to master themselves, run their own brains, and control their own states can play. It takes a lot of "uninsultability," holding onto a much greater vision, staying centered and focused, truly caring about people, and being able to see beyond obnoxious behavior (see "Defusing Hotheads" under "Trainings Available").

Payoffs: When we learn how to effectively defuse hotheads, we develop a higher-level sense of confidence so that we're not put off, afraid of, or intimated by stressful situations. We know that we can maintain presence of mind, our highest skills, and can effectively turn even a hot and stressful person around.

The Calm Eustress Games

Description: Business experts play it cool under pressure. That's their game. And they get paid well for it. They know that by managing their states and transforming stress and pressure into excitement, fun, and adventure, they become much more successful. *How* do we calm ourselves in times and situations of stress and translate those mental-and-emotional energies into eustress (good stress)?

Cues: Unquestionably, the stresses and strains of work, the demands, pressures, fears, worries, and schedules can recruit us for the stress games where we become reactive, defensive, angry, or fearful. We all know that this will not serve us well. We know that chronically living in stress will exact a toll from us mentally, emotionally, personally, and physically. We know that, as it reduces our higher problem-solving skills, creativity, and presence of mind, it prevents us from playing more resourceful games. It can also set off psychosomatic aches and pains and create all kinds of dis-ease within us that then spill over into other areas of life.

Cool Games for Dealing with Pressure
What stresses do you face with your job activities? Make a full list of all the things that you do in your work that demand mental, emotional, personal, and spiritual energy. After you do that, look at the ideas, beliefs, and understandings that you use to frame your thinking. What do you find *stressful* at work? Here are some possibilities:

- Authority and red tape
- Bureaucracy
- Company policy
- Customers
- Deadlines
- Demands
- Difficult people
- Diversity
- Downsizing
- Employees
- Internal politics
- Management
- Re-engineering
- Schedules
- Speed of change
- Technology

"Stress is in the Eye of the Beholder"

Stress, like beauty, lies in the eye of the beholder. Neither "stress" nor "beauty" refers to the brute facts of the world inasmuch as we cannot put these intangible things on a table. Both words refer to a higher-level (or meta-level) evaluative phenomenon that occurs exclusively *in the mind*.

When we take a verb (such as "worry") and turn it into a noun, we give it the illusion of substance. Linguistically, while this makes it easier to "handle" these concepts, it also seduces us into thinking that "stress" (or any similar noun) is externally *real*. It is not. It is an entity of the *mind*, not of the world. It is just a way of thinking and framing experiences.

What, then, do we mean by the term "stress"? What does this concept refer to?

The word "stress" has been around as a scientific term since the sixteenth century, and was used a lot in the late 1900s in the field of bridge building. Engineers used it to refer to the amount of pressure and strain on a bridge from the forces of gravity, earth movement, winds, earth shifting, weight, use, or whatever. They measured the pulls and pushes and talked about the amount of *stress* on a bridge, and how much *stress* a bridge could take.

A stress researcher, Dr Hans Selye, applied this term to the amount of mental and emotional pressures that we can take. He studied and wrote about mental, emotional, financial, and sensory pressures and about the emotional states of stress, distress (destructive stress), and eustress (good stress).

Because *stress* refers to the amount of perceived pressure that we experience in the face of various situations, challenges, and tasks, stress depends upon the amount of perceived resourcefulness that we bring to each situation. The lower our sense of perceived efficacy and empowerment, the more stress we feel. The higher our sense of personal confidence, the lower the stress.

Stress arises as a *relationship* between the situation and what we bring to each situation—our expectations, desires, objectives, and resources. We bring our frames and *frame games* to external situations. This explains why we experience a situation as distress at times and as excitement (eustress) at other times.

Stress does not exist "out there." Stress is always an inside experience—the result of our frames. This game has a structure, it has roles that we can model and replicate. So does the game of eustress, by which we can play out motivation, excitement, risk taking, and challenge.

To excel in any field we have to manage and control our states from *stress reactions*. Stress management and states of excellence go together. Most of us know that. If we get into a reactive stress reaction (fighting, fleeing, freezing), we will not function at our best. We will lose the presence of mind necessary to have ready access to our most developed skills and understandings.

The Stress Game

Cues: Neurologically, the emotion of stress operates in a very special way. We cue it in one of two central ways.

- Whenever we send any cognitive message to our cortex of *"Danger!"*
- Whenever we send any message of *"Enough! Overload! Too much!"*

Either of these two messages cues the cortex to signal the thalamus to activate the Fight/Flight response of the autonomic nervous system. When that happens, *the general arousal syndrome* occurs neurologically: blood is withdrawn from the brain and stomach and sent to the larger muscle groups, adrenaline is released into the blood, the heart beats faster, eyes dilate, skin sweats, fats, cholesterol, and sugar in your bloodstream increase, the stomach secretes more acid, the immune system slows down, thinking shifts to a more black-and-white, survivalistic mode. We then start sorting for one thing: "Should I fight or flee or freeze?"

Out of this mix of stress come two central emotions that encode this state and two central directions or orientations. This gives us two subgames. We go into *The "Go At" Game* or *The "Go Away From" Game* or mode of operation. These show up in our bodies emotionally as anger or fear. Because most of us have a favorite style and direction, this creates two nonassertive communication games: *The Passive and Aggressive Games.*

- What's your "stress style"?

- Do you have a predominant one?

- Do you have a preferred style at work? In relationships?

- During sports?

Rules: *The Passivity Game* is played by moving away from stressors and taking actions to make the stress and/or stressor go away. Stuff emotions. Constantly remain on the lookout for dangers, problems, things that could go wrong. Take counsel of your fears and let it dominate you. Desperately long for peace, tranquillity, pleasantness, resolution. Care about what others say and do. Refuse to find value in conflict, confrontation, disagreement, arguments.

The Aggressive Game is played by moving toward stressors and taking actions to take on the stress and/or stressor. Turn your negative emotions outward and let others experience your distress. Constantly look out for opportunities and challenges. Think more about what could go right, what you could do, what adventures or risks might make life more exciting. Long for directness, forthrightness, things out on the table. Care more about getting things done than what people say or think. Don't care very much at all what people think. Love a good challenge, especially a good debate.

When we learn to become *assertive* (and it does take learning and practice), then we react neither passively nor aggressively. In the literature on stress, the passive style has been designated the *Type B* response pattern. This contrasts with the aggressive *Type A* response pattern and *frame game.* In the 1980s, *Type C* came to describe the assertive response style. This describes the ability to think and talk out one's internal stressors rather than act them out in fight or flight (see *Speak Up, Speak Clear, Speak Kind: Assertive Communication Skills*, 1987).

With all of that in mind, imagine putting together a team with half playing *The Passive Game* and half playing *The Aggressive Game.* Turn up the pressure and then ask them to "do business" as a team.

The Stress Response
Once we send the *"Danger!"* or *"Overload!"* message to the brain so that it cues the autonomic nervous system, be prepared for a wild *Game of Fight/Flight!* A neurological stress response will explode. All *communications, behaviors, perceptions, memories, and learnings* will become dependent upon the stress state. State dependency will take over. We will then play "fight or flight" and see the world through those frames. That frame will govern what we remember and communicate, and how we act.

Although *state dependency* happens with all states, when we experience an intense level of a state, the dynamics of state dependency dominates. When that happens, it will then take some time for all of the neurotransmitters, adrenaline, and the activation of the autonomic nervous system to run their course. At best we can develop some good ways to *interrupt* the state, add some calmers (count to ten, lower the voice), and suggest some larger frames (you don't want to go to jail). Among other calming techniques are deep-breathing exercises, shifts in postures, focus, affirmations, visualizations, and pattern interrupts.

At that point, the best we can do in terms of stress management is to use the human technology that can help us hold down the responses so that we don't kill each other.

The time to learn state management skills is *not* during the emotional stress storm. We don't learn navigation skills when the whole ship is tossing and turning in the midst of hundred-foot waves in the open sea. To do that is only to ask to be ineffective. To play *The State Management Game* effectively, we have to learn the game during more quiet times.

We can also learn how to avoid sending *"Danger!"* and *"Overload!"* messages unless there is an actual physical threat. By *not* going into the stress response game in the first place, then we don't have to exert such mental and emotional energy to get out of that intensity. The strategy to do this? Learn to set entirely new frames of reference in the first place. Then, when disappointments, frustrations, setbacks, and resistance occur, we will give them meanings that allow us to access our most resourceful states, not our primal Fight/Flight states.

To play *The Stress Management Game* well, access and install your most resourceful frames. Connect them to things that would otherwise send you into a primitive and unthinking reactiveness. Differentiate between true physical dangers and psychological ones. Formulate your game plans for how to maintain a calm and thoughtful state when facing stresses in business. You will then be able to maintain presence of mind, calmness of spirit, non-defensiveness, and full access to your creativity and problem-solving skills (see *Instant Relaxation*, 1999).

Stress at Different Levels

At the primary level, stress shows up somatically as muscle tension, tightness, soreness, inflexibility, headaches, backaches, and various other symptoms. Such stress plays a significant role in most diseases that afflict the body, significantly contributing to and exacerbating heart disease, ulcers, cancer, and others.

Stress management and relaxation skills at the primary level work with and address these symptoms. Some stress management skills aim to make us more productive by giving us better ways for managing our schedules ("time" management). In this way, we can juggle more activities and work more efficiently. Those who use drugs and alcohol to relieve the effects of stress will find that this works only to a limited extent. Merely medicating the problem with drugs and alcohol will *not* solve or stop the problem that causes the stress. It does not address the *cause* of the stress and, in the long run, can create all kinds of counter-productive problems.

More useful primary-level (or physical) stress reduction skills involve learning how to recognize signs and symptoms of stress in the body. We can learn how to breathe more fully and deeply, how to relax tight muscles or stretch. Yoga exercises provide an excellent training for identifying stress in the body.

The management and reduction of stress at meta-levels essentially involves deframing and reframing the conceptual meanings that create the stress in the first place. Here we learn to perceive things in new ways, to recognize our limits, to comfortably say *"Yes"* and *"No"* to our highest values, to take pleasure in what truly serves our wellbeing, and to bring higher level resources to bear in our everyday experiences.

The Cool Alertness Game

How can we become truly masterful in coping with and handling the demands, threats, fears, and other challenges of everyday life at work and at home? How does this game work? How do we set it up?

1. Recognize the presence of stress
Since we cannot effectively manage anything *outside of awareness,* our first task is to make our stress conscious. Do this by granting yourself permission to notice the presence of stress in your life and its symptoms.

Begin with your body. At the primary level, stress shows up in the body as such things as tightness, muscle tension, inflexibility, fatigue, aches and pains, ulcers, shallow breathing, and tired dry eyes. How are you doing?

Enter into the tension or fatigue and let it teach you. Quiet yourself and establish communication with that part of you. You might ask your stiff neck or sore back or racing heart,

- "What message do you have for me?"

- "If you were to speak to me, what would you say?"

- "Is the tiredness physical or mental?"

Then use various breathing, stretching, and moving exercises in order to come to your (body) senses.

One day a good friend of mine who definitely operates from the "go at it" mode and is a veteran player of *The Aggressive Game* arrived home and decided to walk down three houses to the group mailbox in the subdivision. On the way to get her mail, she met her neighbor, who said, "Where are you marching to so fast?"

"Marching? Who's marching?" she responded.

"You are... Look at yourself."

And she did, and she discovered that, sure enough, she was marching. Some would call it "rushing." Yet until it was brought to her attention she had no awareness of it. Stress is like that. It can operate outside of our awareness.

2. Detail your current stress strategy
There is order and structure to how you stress yourself. How do you do it? Begin with the stimuli that you use to go into the state of stress?

- What induces a stress experience in you (schedules, people, activities, places)?
- What things do you hate, can't stand, rattle your cage?
- When do you typically feel stress?
- What do you say to yourself that increases the stress?
- How do you express these thoughts in your mind?
- What tonality, pitch, and volume of voice do you use?
- What is the quality of your pictures when you stress?

As a subjective experience, stress does have a game plan. This magic doesn't just occur without the casting of some "spell." So, how do you do it? What *stress language* do you use?

- "I *have to* get this job done!"
- "*Nobody ever* helps me."
- "*Why* can't anything ever go right for me?"
- "I *hate* it when she uses that tone of voice."

What *thinking patterns* do you use to crank up your stress?

- *Personalizing:* interpreting things as being about you, taking it personal?
- *Awfulizing and Catastrophizing:* blowing things way out of proportion?
- *Emotionalizing:* treating your emotions as the final word from heaven?
- *Minimizing or Discounting:* rejecting positive frames and solutions?
- *Maximizing or Exaggerating:* responding in an extreme way?
- *All-or-nothing Thinking:* creating a dichotomy, allowing no grays?
- *Perfectionism:* treating everything as never good enough?

What *physical elements* add to your stress or prevent you from operating from a calm alertness:

- Shallow breathing?
- Hunched shoulders?
- Poor posture?
- Contracted abdomen?
- Lack of focus: constant eye shifting?
- Tightening and holding neck or jaw muscles?

Seek out a skilled practitioner to assist you in the discovery process. Almost everybody finds it much easier to have their strategy elicited by someone else. When we attempt to do it on ourselves, we can sometimes put ourselves into the recursive loops that put us into a spin.

Once you know the game plan, you will have lots of ways to mess it up and to prevent the old program from working automatically. Then you can play around to change the game plan until it serves you well.

To flush out the frames that create your *stress game*, that qualify and texture your particular type and kind of stress, ask:

- What qualities characterize my stress?
- What would others say about the properties of my stress?
- Which of the following kinds of thinking/believing describe me?
  - I must perform, achieve, produce!
  - I have to be liked and approved of.
  - I must be in control at all times.
  - Who's ahead? How do I compare with X?
  - Things must be done right.
  - You can't trust others to do it right; you've got to just jump in and make it happen.
  - What would happen to this place without me?
  - I want things to happen *now*!
  - I should not be frustrated or disappointed. It's not fair.
  - How can I alter my physiology so that it serves me better?
  - How can I breathe in a calmer way?
  - What tone of voice do I use in my self-talk?
  - How do I use my posture? How can I?

These are the kinds of frames that ran *The Stress Game.* They create or play off various pressures and needs: needs for achievement, approval, control, competition, perfection, impatience, anger.

Does your stress have a feel of anger in it? Or perhaps impatience? Or perhaps you have competitive, must-be-better-than stress? Do you experience stress as a make-or-break feeling? How much do you have your identity and self-definition wrapped up in such things as achievement, approval, control?

When we think and believe in toxic ways, thinking that our very *being* is dependent upon what others think, the job we hold, status symbols, and so forth, we create fire-breathing dragons in our mind. And the games they will play there will consume a lot of psychic energy.

3. Develop relaxation resources

Almost everybody I know can easily "fly into a rage." If you can do that, you have all the neurological equipment you need for learning how to "fly into a calm." This makes flying into a calm, and accessing a state of instant relaxation, a very real possibility. Actually, it is more than a possibility: it is an actuality. You already can do it. You already play that game. I know you can. After all, you have a "telephone voice," don't you?

You know the scenario. You're in the living room or kitchen and having a fight with a loved one. You're saying things that you'd never say to a stranger—you save those kinds of things for the people that you love most. Perhaps it's your way of testing to see if they can keep on loving you! So you really get into it. You raise your voice. You feel really, really angry, upset, frustrated—and then the phone rings.

Shucks. You'll have to get back to this game later.

You take a breath, and then politely answer it, "Hello …?"

That's your "telephone voice"! See, you *can* fly into a calm!

Go ahead. Develop this skill as your game. Orchestrate it so that it becomes stronger, more powerful, and so that you have ready access to it in a split second. Since it's already a resource, you need only to develop it further and put it at your disposal.

Amplify it. Think about a time when you really demonstrated the power of your telephone voice. Be there again, seeing what you saw, hearing what you heard, and feeling what you felt.

What enabled you to step out of the angry and yelling state to the calm and cool state where you said, "Hello"? What ideas, beliefs, values, and decisions empowered that response? Why didn't you answer the phone with your angry voice? Why didn't you yell at the person calling in?

The answers that you find to these questions will help you to flush out your natural *"flying into a calm" frames.* As you make these clear, amplify them, give yourself even more reasons for doing this and then set up a trigger to cue yourself that you can *step back into this place of mind and emotion* whenever you choose.

- What would be a good symbol of your "flying into a calm" state?
- What sound, sight, and *sensation* could remind you of this state?
- Let that be your trigger.

Now practice stepping into it, setting that anchor, breaking state, and then firing the anchor to *step back into that place of self-management.*

4. Set the relaxation state as your frame

Access your best representation of a relaxed state by thinking of a time when you were really relaxed in a calm and centered way. Recall it fully so that you can make snapshots of this state. That will allow you to step back into it very quickly and efficiently.

After you have fully accessed and amplified this primary resource state, step back from it and examine it.

- What is the nature and quality of *this* relaxed state?

- What qualities and factors make up this state?

- What other qualities would you like to edit into this state?

Frequently, the relaxed state that we access is appropriate for a sunny beach, but not for the work environment. So we assume that we cannot use it there. What then?

What if you tempered and textured your relaxed state so that it became a highly resourceful state even at work? What if you qualified it with the kind of qualities, resources, and distinctions that would give you the kind of mastery you need at work? That's what meta-stating is all about—setting the higher frames that establish the new game.

This highlights how a meta-state differs from a primary state. In the primary state of relaxation, you feel relaxed. Muscles are limp, breathing is slow and easy, calmness and comfort predominate your mind, everything feels at ease. It's a great state. But hardly the state you need at work, when you want to produce creative products, when you want to delight and wow your customers, or when you want to perform at peak performance. We need a special kind of relaxed state for such occasions. We need a higher state of

- Alert relaxation, or relaxed alertness
- Calm confidence in our skills
- Relaxed attentive listening
- Relaxed readiness energy
- Acceptance of everyday frustrations

What *kind* of relaxation do you need or want? When I train, I want an excited relaxation that cares very much about communicating with clarity and enabling everybody to feel a part of the discovery process. When I run (even in a race), I need a *confident relaxation* that knows how to measure my energy output so that I can stay in for the duration without burning out. When I model the structure of someone's expertise, I want the calm relaxed mind that allows me to stay clear without contaminating it with my assumptions, but simply discovering what's there. I need the relaxed mind of confidence that trusts in the process.

What kind of a relaxed mind and emotions do you want or need in a given situation?

Play *The Cool Alertness Game.* Set the frames that you will need to feel relaxed with yourself so that you can play with confidence, assurance, and centeredness in your values. That meta-state structure will enable you to operate from a sense of safety and security. It prevents *"Danger!"* and *"Overload!"* messages from triggering reactiveness.

When we play with this kind of centered sense of self, we have a platform of comfort and security from which we can sally out to the adventures of life. This gives life balance. We shuttle out to a challenge, then we retreat to our relaxation zone to recuperate and replenish our strength. We move out to perform and do things as achievers, then we move back and just be and enjoy ourselves as persons.

5. Access your Cool Alertness Game
Imagine what it would look, sound, and feel like when you completely and thoroughly step into your *Cool Alertness Game.* Float back in your imagination to capture bits and pieces of anything that will enrich your construction and edit your self-image. Allow these pieces to come together to create a powerful sense of a core self: relaxed, confident, assured..., comfortable in your own skin, breathing fully and completely, taking charge of your thinking, emoting, speaking, and behaving... Just imagine what that would feel like and how that would transform your life...

And, when you have edited it to your liking and it feels compelling, step into it and be there. And enjoy it..., so that you experience it as a joyful, relaxed core state. And now, as you *translate it from mind to muscle,* imagine breathing with this and seeing out of the eyes of your core relaxed state. And hear the voice of this state—speaking with a calm confidence that radiates a sense of your inner power.

Is there any part of you that would object to living this way? And would you like this as your way of being in the world?

6. Keep refining and texturing this game

Nor does this process end with the first design-engineering of this highly resourceful state. With the tools for modeling excellence, you can now maintain a creative attitude about all of the other resources that you can find and incorporate in that *Cool Alertness Game*.

For instance, why not add a big dose of healthy humor to the mix? The ability to lighten up, to not take yourself so seriously, to enjoy people and experiences tremendously enriches relaxation. We can explode most fears by using the humor power of exaggeration. Exaggerate the fear until it starts to become ridiculous. Then exaggerate it some more. Eventually, it becomes funny and then your humorous perspective enables you to operate in a more human and delightful way.

Or how about *appreciation*? What if you moved through the world with an appreciation of things, people, experiences? How would that *texture the quality of your stress*?

Magnanimity is another resource. It enables you to operate from a sense of having a big heart and thereby prevents you from becoming mentally ruffled. How would that enhance your life?

Then there is openness to reality, flexibility, forgiveness, playfulness, balance, and the list goes on and on. Dr Suzanne Kobasa, who co-authored *The Hardy Executive: Health Under Stress*, quoted the research about the Three Cs that prevent a person from spiraling in stress to illness. The Three Cs are: *commitment* to self, work, family and other values; a sense of personal *control* over one's life; and the ability to see change in one's life as a positive *challenge*.

Summary

- Stress is not a "thing," but a response—a mental-emotional and body response. It's a process the mind–body plays when it has "threat" frames. Stress emerges from the way we frame things, from the meaning we give, the expectations we bring to life, and our coping skills. As we frame, so we play the game.

- While we can only partially change the world and environment in which we live, we have nearly total control over *how* we think and emote—our framing powers. Herein lies the realm of magic, of renewal, of transformation.

- It takes only the power of framing and reframing to transform old attitudes and beliefs that create distress so that we can operate from more functional maps that endow life with lots of eustress—excitement.

- Knowing now how to establish the game rules for your own personalized *Cool Alertness Game,* you will only become increasingly more stress-resistant and effective under pressure. Imagine that!

Chapter 13

Learning to Be Your Own Best Boss

Effective Self-Bossing: The Magic Art of Getting Yourself to Do What It Takes

> "Genius is 10 percent inspiration and 90 percent perspiration."
> —Edison

Games in this Chapter
The Discipline Game
The "Getting Yourself to Act" Game
The "Willingness to be Trained for Excellence" Game
The Discipline inside the Competence Game

The Discipline Game

Experts in every field play one game that really sets them apart. On the surface it seems like a hard game, a distasteful game, and even an unpleasant game. This surface impression of the game itself causes it to work as a barrier to most people. It puts most people off. They won't go there. To them, it just seems to high a price to pay.

Yet the experts have a secret. By living from a different frame, and so in a different world, they experience this game very differently. For them, the game isn't difficult, distasteful, or unpleasant at all. For them it is fun and exciting. They love it. They can't wait to get out of bed in the morning so that they can get to it.

What is this boundary-like *frame game* of the experts that enables them to succeed fabulously and separates them from those who do not? I hesitate even to mention it. Most people find the word itself negative. Edison's famous quote, "Genius is 10 percent inspiration and 90 percent perspiration," hints at this secret.

After modeling Einstein's strategy for creativity, Robert Dilts suggested that with Einstein we have to turn those statistics around. His studies led him to suggest that genius primarily takes inspiration and vision and afterwards just a *little* sweat to make it happen.

Whatever the ratio of inspiration to sweat, the game of business excellence typically calls upon us to produce *both*. Both play an essential role in this game. No matter how great, insightful, or outstanding an idea, product, or service is, if somebody does not actually *apply* these things and turn them into practical applications, the inspiration will not hit pay dirt. We have to get ourselves to take effective action if we want to turn our dreams into actualities. To get something done, to accomplish something, to bring something new and useful into everyday life, we have to play *The Discipline Game.*

There, I said it, "Discipline."

Conversely, you can run yourself ragged busily doing things, meeting with people, talking, planning, running statistics, creating promotions. Yet if there's nothing of substance, no real brilliance, no truly creative inspiration behind all of the busy work, nothing lasting will come of it. You could brilliantly produce and market junk—but it is still junk.

In business, we need both games. We need a *great idea* (*The Creativity Game* and *The Inspiration Game*) and we need *the ability to implement* that idea (*The Discipline Game*). We need vision, skill, ability, expertise, *and* we need the everyday practical *discipline* to make something happen. In fact, the problem most people struggle with is the latter one.

If you want to truly succeed, do you *know* what to do? At this very moment, do you *know* more than you *do*? Are you able to get yourself to actually *do* what you know you ought to do and even want to do? Can you get yourself to do it?

Not only in business, but also in personal health and well-being, if you cannot manage yourself—your states, emotions, mind, and behavior—if you cannot get yourself to come through with your plans and to stay focused, you will never develop your personal excellence at work. That much is obvious. What is not so obvious is this: *just how do we learn to get ourselves to actually do what we know and want to do?* This is where we encounter another game ...

The "Getting Yourself to Act" Game

How easy is it to get yourself to actually *do* what you know to do? What you want to do? What you have to do to reach your goals? Or, perhaps I should ask, how hard is it?

The idea of *training* yourself to take action is what we mean by that word "discipline," which tends to hold so many negative connotations. In this context, discipline means to *train* the mind and character so that we enter into a mode of life where following the rules or principles of an expertise is natural. Discipline means having order and control so built into our life that we easily manage ourselves and our states—in other words, we have self-control. These don't sound like negative things, do they?

Ah, but many people (perhaps most) think of "punishment" when they hear "discipline." They think about whippings. They think about being castigated, chastised, and corrected. They recall harsh images of being forced to follow the rules, and taken to task for violations.

The original image behind the term pictures a *disciple* who is wanting to follow a new way of life and learn a *discipline*. Even today we call a field of study a discipline. So at the heart of the term is the idea of being a learner or discoverer in a field of study. It also speaks about "a training that corrects and perfects mental faculties or moral character." It speaks about a learning that brings order to a person's mind and control to a person's

201

actions, hence "self-control." It identifies a learner or *disciple* who studies and gets in shape for an adventure.

Yet this term sounds much too mundane and uninspiring to make a game of it. It certainly does not sell many books. It never packs training seminars. What does? What does sell these days and pack training seminars? Ah, yes, ease, quickness, immediate results, comfort. No wonder "discipline" lacks P.R. appeal. It bears no mystique, no excitement, no wonder. It comes to us in blue jeans and sweats. Who wakes up in the morning feeling compelled to delightfully enjoy an experience of "discipline"? It sounds like something to avoid, not to set as an attraction.

And yet there are those images of Rocky Balboa in the *Rocky* movies, going through his drills, taking effective action to get in shape, welcoming the discipline of exercise, training, and mental preparation so that he can be at his best, and worthy of the opportunity. So we do know, somewhere inside, that *personal discipline* does beat at the heart of excellence. How then can we reframe "discipline" and attach more positive feelings and exciting images to it?

The "Willingness to be Trained for Excellence" Game

Earlier, I mentioned that playing The Discipline Game is one of the secrets of success in every field. Experts in the field of wealth building and financial independence know this and so play this game. Long-term success depends on it. Consider the following quotations in terms of the *frames* and *frame games*.

Stanley and Danko in *The Millionaire Next Door* (1996) writes:

"How do you become wealthy? Here, too, most people have it wrong. It is seldom luck or inheritance or advanced degrees or even intelligence that enables people to amass fortunes. Wealth is more often the result of a lifestyle of hard work, perseverance, planning, and most of all, self-discipline ..." [Pages 1–2.]

"What have we discovered in all our research? Mainly, that building wealth takes discipline, sacrifice, and hard work ..." [Page 5.]

"Have you ever noticed those people whom you see jogging day after day? They are the ones who seem not to need to jog. But that's why they are fit. Those who are wealthy work at staying financially fit. But those who are not financially fit do little to change their status.

"Most people want to be physically fit. And the majority know what is required to achieve this. But despite that knowledge, most people never become well conditioned physically. Why not? Because they don't have the discipline to just do it. They don't budget their time to just do it. It is like becoming wealthy in America ..." [Page 40.]

"Could I live on the equivalent of 6.7% of my wealth? It takes much discipline to become affluent. We have interviewed many people worth $2 or $3 million who have total realized annual household incomes of less than $80,000." [Page 56.]

Have you ever met anybody who wanted to be successful and wealthy and *not* have to work for it? Consider that thought for a moment as a frame of reference. Suppose you woke up in the morning and moved through the world organizing your thoughts, emotions, and behaviors inside that idea. As a way of mapping how to be and function in the world, how far would it take you in the direction of succeeding and accumulating wealth? What behaviors would it generate? How would you think and talk if you used that idea as your way of framing things?

As a *frame*, it would probably create a lot of high expectations, sense of entitlement, passivity, frustration, disappointment, reactivity, and depression. The person afflicted with that frame would be thinking:

- If I want something bad enough I should get it. In fact, I *will* get it.
- If I want something, *it will just come to me.*
- I don't have to work for it; that's crazy. Just wishing and hoping and affirming that I'll get it is enough.
- I'm entitled to get what I want.

- I want success and wealth *now*. Why doesn't my boss (the world, God, the system, my family) *just give me* what I want? It's my right!

Frames, as layers of our *conceptual frameworks*, govern our mapping of the way the world works and so refer to the dominating ideas that set up our games.

Ingredients of the Discipline Game

What are the elements of *The Discipline Game* that makes so much of a difference? What are the component mental and emotional pieces of this thing that we call "discipline"? Suppose we wanted to build up an empowering strategy or game plan for the kind of personal discipline to get ourselves to actually do the things we know would increase and support our success. What ingredients would we toss into the mix?

- A willingness to learn and to be trained for competence
- Saying *"Yes!"* to all of the essential facets of business
- Developing empowering and supporting reasons and under-standings for our *"Yes!"*
- Saying *"No!"* to everything that interrupts, interferes, and that does not contribute to our business
- Making an empowering definitive decision to cut off the alter-natives that interfere with our *"Yes!"*
- Willingness to accept appropriate effort, discomfort, stress and strain, and challenge
- Apprenticeship to learning and adjusting to the reality con-straints in a given business
- Prioritizing our valuing, scheduling, devotion, energies
- Owning our response-abilities

The Discipline of Success

A tempting and seductive idea dances before the minds of many people. It entertains them with the alluring song that it sings:

- "Success ought to come easy."
- "If I could only win the lottery!"
- "If only power, fame, and wealth would drop into my lap!"

Do those tapes run in your head? Do you dance and sing to those lines? Is that the game you're looking for?

Yet the temptress called Ease speaks falsely and delusionally. Success too easily won will not bring long-term pleasure or enjoyment, or even maintenance of the success. Mihaly Csikszentmihalyi demonstrated this in *Flow: The Psychology of Optimal Experience* (1990). Without the *effort* to utilize our best skills, to stretch to new levels of personal achievement, to overcome challenges, we do not *own* the success, and so it doesn't "make soul grow." It doesn't make us more complex, rich, or full.

> "The best moments usually occur when a person's body or mind is stretched to its limits in a voluntary effort to accomplish something difficult and worthwhile. Optimal experience is thus something that we *make* happen." [Page 3.]

Figure 13:1

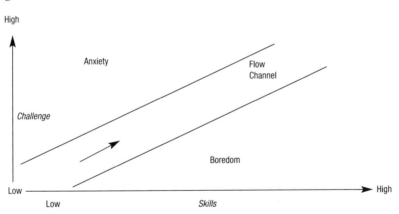

"The most enjoyable activities are not natural; they demand an effort that initially one is reluctant to make. But once the interaction starts to provide feedback to the person's skills, it usually begins to be intrinsically rewarding." [Page 68.]

Flow experiences occur through developing skills in a context of challenge. Yet two threats rise to stand against flow. As our skills develop, we get *bored* with the current level of activity. We need something more. We need some challenge. Yet, as challenge increases, so does anxiety. So the "flow channel" occurs between two axes (challenge and skills) and between two territories (anxiety and boredom).

> "It is this dynamic feature that explains why flow activities lead to growth and discovery. One cannot enjoy doing the same thing at the same level for long. We grow either bored or frustrated; and then the desire to enjoy ourselves again pushes us to stretch our skills, or to discover new opportunities for using them." [Page 75.]

The training for success (i.e. discipline) in business (or in fitness, healthy eating, relationships, study, or whatever) arises from mental clarity. We become clear about what we want and learn what it takes. We play *The Aim Game* (see Chapter 10). We develop an intelligence and so enter an apprenticeship to that discipline. Only then can we make a definitive decision to say *"Yes!"* to those things that we desire and *"No!"* to all those things that interfere. This describes an ordering of consciousness that focuses our mind. We learn the discipline and so become disciplined. This "discipline" is not the pain of being made wrong: it's the joy of becoming ever more competent. As we learn to run our own brain, we develop the kind of *state management skills* that will carry us through. Then we can get ourselves do *what* we want to do and *when* we choose to do it. That's true self-control.

Discipling (being a disciple to) our field of study, area of business, or domain of expertise specifies the specific "work" or *effort* that has to be endured, learned, and reframed in order to become successful. And at first, it may feel "hard." At first, it often feels like work. And so it should. We have to learn how to discipline our mind and emotions, our speech and our actions so that we become skillfully competent. This holds true for whatever task or business we have in mind: rollerblading, skiing, and biking; graduating from school, interviewing, and selling; programming a computer, and creating your own small business.

None of these come "easy" or "natural." We have to learn. We have to be trained. This explains why, if we set frames that learning and training are fun, we will find it easy and natural even through the awareness of our incompetence stage.

Another thing may make it seem easy at times. If we have caught a vision of something big and exciting, and have uttered a thunderous *"Yes!"* to go for it, then we may experience the effort we expend in the learning curve as pure fun and delight. If we have not framed it as "work," it may feel more like an exciting exploration. Our *"Yes!"* will carry us forward. And when we have a big enough *"Yes!"* even the *"Nos"* that we have to say along the way do not have the feel of "self-denial," "going against the grain," or "making a sacrifice." It rather feels like part of the fun.

Checking the Ingredients
If these are the items or ingredients in *The Discipline Game*, then check to see if you have them as part of your game plan.

1. A willingness to learn and be trained for competence
Are you willing to learn the expert game? Are you willing to go through the drills to train yourself mentally, emotionally, linguistically, and behaviorally? Are you willing to put in your time practicing, rehearsing, and role-playing?

2. Have you uttered a thunderous *"Yes!"* to your business?
What parts and facets of your work do you simply love to do? When I work with people to install that "propulsion system" we spoke of in Chapter 9, I usually begin by finding out what they have already said an empowering *"Yes!"* to. That gives me the information about how they utter an empowering *"Yes!"* to something. Saying *"Yes!"* to something makes you a disciple to that discipline. Have you become a disciple to your area of expertise? Do you study it? Constantly seek to improve your skills? Does it capture and captivate your attention?

What are the essential activities that make up your business? Which ones have you not made a definite *"Yes!"* to? How much more of a *"Yes!"* do you need to develop in order to propel you forward?

3. Have you developed supporting reasons, beliefs, and understandings for your "Yes!"?
The power, stability, and consistency of your empowering *"Yes!"* depends upon the meta-level frames that support it. This moves us up a level—to a higher level of mind, to your beliefs, reasons, and understandings, to the frame that governs your game. Do you have some supporting beliefs for your *"Yes!"*? What beliefs support you in this? Why do you want and need to do this? How is this valuable to you? What do you get from it? What meaning do you give to it?

4. Have you uttered an in-your-face "No!" to the opposite?
What is the opposite of your *"Yes!"*? If you've said yes to developing a charming rapport with people, then the opposite would entail ignoring people, not thinking and speaking empathetically, not paying attention to them, those kinds of things. The opposite would also entail telling people off, letting them have the brunt of your anger, letting insulting words fly out of your mouth.

What do you have to say *"No!"* to in order to succeed in your line of work? Athletes have to say *"No!"* to missing workouts, for example, failing to eat properly, letting discouragement get a grip on them.

How do you need to utter your *"No!"* so that it "cuts off" (hence, *de-cision*) the alternatives that would undermine your success? How much more of a strong and definitive *"No!"* do you need? Can you say *"No!"* to yourself?

I remember asking that of a person in a demonstration in a training session. We were exploring some facet of his accessing his own "personal genius."

I inquired, "What gets in the way, or could get in the way, of your reaching this desired outcome?"

"Several things could get in my way and sabotage my efforts," he replied.

I inquired about specifics, and he began enumerating a list of things.

"Sounds like you'll need to have the ability to say a strong and powerful 'No!' to these things," I told him, "so that you demonstrate that you run your own brain, and that you don't give all your power away to these things."

"Yeah, I guess so."

"So tell me, how skillful are you in saying 'No!' to yourself so that you can utter the much greater 'Yes!' with full conviction?"

That stopped him. He had never thought of that.

"Say 'No!' to myself? I never thought of doing that!"

"How can you utter a powerful and resounding 'Yes!' to your goals without saying 'No!' to all of the other things that get in your way?"

Yet he knew that he needed to develop that skill if he would step up into the domain of excellence.

5. Have you made an empowering definitive decision to cut off the alternatives that would interfere with your "Yes!"?
This may indeed be the decision point where you win or lose your success. Are you willing to say "No" to these things? Are you willing to "pay that price" for the development of your excellence? High achievers do not get there without effort and struggle. They pay a price.

6. Are you willing to accept appropriate effort, discomfort, stress and strain, and challenge to succeed?
How well have you adjusted yourself to the fact that it will probably take work, effort, extension of yourself, problem solving, creativity, frustration tolerance, patience, development of skills, and more? What supporting ideas, beliefs, and understandings would assist you in creating this transformation of meaning? What

frames have you developed so that you can patiently accept these facts?

Stephen Covey writes in *Principle Centered Leadership* (1990):

> "Highly effective people carry their agenda with them. Their schedule is their servant, not their master. They organize weekly, adapt daily. However, they are not capricious in changing their plans. *They exercise discipline and concentration* and do not submit to moods and circumstances [this describes their game]. They schedule blocks of prime time for important planning, projects, and creative work. They work on less important and less demanding activities when their fatigue level is higher. They avoid handling paper more than once and avoid touching paperwork unless they plan to take action on it."

7. Have you entered into an apprenticeship to the discipline of adjusting to the reality constraints of the business?
How much study do you put in on a daily basis in your commitment to become more knowledgeable, mindful, and up-to-date regarding your area of expertise? How much training will you give yourself this month, this year? What quality of training will you devote time, energy, and money to? Whom will you model? How will you go about the modeling? Apprenticeship is the key to developing the necessary discipline. Success comes to those who plan to succeed—to those who *study* to succeed.

8. Have you prioritized your valuing, scheduling, devotion, and energies to make it happen?
Have you identified the key ingredients to your business success? Have you made these items your first priority? What stops you? When will you do this? Have you sat down to write out your objectives and goals as well as drawing up an action plan for getting there? Which one thing can you do today that, if you did it regularly and consistently, would definitely move you out into the direction of the future that you want to build for yourself?

9. Have you owned your response-ability for your business success?
How do you answer the question, "Who is totally and absolutely responsible for my success?" Do you accept and take full responsibility for your thinking, emoting, speaking, behaving, and relating? How much more response-ability do you need to own and accept? How will you do this so that it begins to build a positive attitude toward responsibility?

Earlier, I described "responsibility" as literally speaking about our *response-power*. We have the power to initiate responses and to own them. Responsibility refers to my *ownership of my ability to choose my responses.*

Have you accepted and owned your *power zone*? To what degree have you recognized your four ultimate powers of mind (thinking, believing, valuing, conceptualizing), emotion (feeling), talk (languaging), and behavior (doing, gesturing, acting)? How well have you integrated the realization that nobody can *make* you think or feel anything without your permission?

Sequencing the Structure of the Discipline Game
How do we put all of these ingredients together to create the empowering *Discipline Game* so that we can actually *get ourselves to do things*? In what order? How much? To what extent?

It depends. It depends upon whether you have a preference for *first going toward* what you want or *first moving away from* what you want to avoid. Do you first perceive things in terms of *moving away from* or in terms of *moving toward*? How does your motivational direction work? If you feel that both forces seem equally balanced in you, then it doesn't make any difference. But, if you have a clear-cut, definite preference, then start with that preference. That is, start either with your "Yes, I want that!" or your "No, I will no longer put up with or tolerate that!"

Do you feel that you do not have a *strong and intense enough "Yes!"* or *"No!"*? Then let's move up to the frames that embrace and engulf those responses.

Figure 13.2

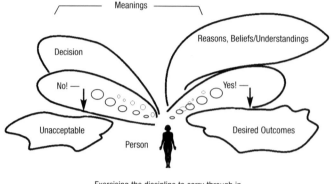

Exercising the discipline to carry through in
the activities that support success

Why must you go for *this*? Why must you get away from and avoid *that*? Gather as many higher-level reasons, motives, beliefs, understandings, memories, and imaginations, and make sure you represent them in vivid and dramatic ways so that it empowers and juices up your *"Yes"* and *"No."*

The higher frame will govern, so, as you *set* these higher frames, establish the directions you want your brain top go in. Once you have gone up, in your mind, then make an empowering *decision* for your *"Yes"* and away from your *"No."* A decision cuts off alternatives as it taps into the power of your intention to go for your *"Yes."*

Here also you may need to make explicit the fact that, as you *"Yes"* your objective, outcome, goals, and direction, you are simultaneously *"No-ing"* the things that you might otherwise let interfere with or sabotage you. Look those things in the face and utter a strong and compelling *"No!"* (or, better, a *"Hell, No!"*) to them. Here you get to *refuse to allow* these interferences *power* to govern your life. Did you notice that that statement involves several meta-levels? It speaks about how high, in your mind, you need to go to *set that frame*. But you can, if you so choose. It's your brain.

Feel Free to Reframe at Meta-Levels
Suppose at those levels you recognize that the *meaning* that you give to some of those interferences (for example, ease, comfort, effort, work, challenge, time elements, what others will think) still exercise too strong an influence? What then? Easy. Reframe.

That's right. Reframe the meaning of those items so that *the way you think about them shifts in a way that supports you.* Your new frame will lead to a new game. As the game master, you can choose the game you want. Create *mind-lines* (statements that you find succinct and meaningful and that *grab* your mind and won't let it go), which you can use conversationally to reframe the old meanings.

- What does "ease" mean to you?
- What else could it mean?
- What meanings do those who seem skilled in getting themselves to take effective actions give to it?
- What does "effort" mean to you?
- Does that meaning serve you?
- Does it support you in the development of your own self-discipline?
- Does it enable you to discipline your mind, emotions, tongue, behavior, skills, etc. for excellence?

You know that meaning does not exist externally. You know that meaning does not exist "out there." You know that meaning is not "real" in that way. The *reality* of meaning occurs at the level of mind since it is a product of your mind.

At the first level of *meaning-making*, we simply *associate* or *link* things together. This creates our sense of "cause-effect." At the next level up, we create meaning by putting our experiences, memories, and understandings into various conceptual *contexts*. Doing this creates conceptual and semantic meanings—our frames of beliefs, values, identifications. (See Bibliography: *Communication Magic* (2001) and *Mind-Lines* (1997).)

Self-Apprenticing
In transforming the meanings of your life, you apprentice yourself to the particular area in which you want to become an expert. You

begin by filling your mind with it and letting it capture your heart. As you construct your meanings, the frames then support the discipline. It gives you the eyes to perceive your discipline as valuable, positive, and enriching. This creates a stable frame that will support you through the days in which you have to persist, use the feedback of unsuccessful attempts, hone and polish your skills, and practice your trade until you become really good at it.

This also supports your ability to prioritize your schedule so that you *put first things first*. How well do you currently prioritize so that you come through with doing the things of importance to you? Obviously, you have to *see the value* of something to put it first. Beyond that you also have to overcome the temptation to merely respond to things that *feel urgent*. When we respond to doing *only* the things that *feel* urgent, we become reactive. We run around putting out fires. We answer any and every bell that rings. We salivate at the sound of all the phones, beepers, e-mails, and invitations that pass our consciousness.

Yet there are many important things in life, perhaps even *most* of the things that we recognize as important, and yet they *do not feel urgent*. Check this out for yourself. Put a check mark by all of the things in the following list that actually *feel urgent* to you.

- Exercising
- Calling friends
- Writing letters
- Taking time off to relax
- Studying
- Meditating on high values
- Bonding with loved ones
- Spiritual development
- Watching a sunset
- Doing some sit-ups

A great many of the truly valuable and important things in life *do not feel very urgent*. So, if we depend upon *urgency* to get our attention or get us to act, we will end up running around just doing "urgent" things—and this typically means "urgent" in terms of what others want from us. Make your own list of things that you have decided are really important to you. When you finish that list of highly significant actions, just notice how much urgency they evoke.

Most of us have no problem with doing things that we recognize and feel as both important *and* urgent. But what about things important and *not* urgent?

Most of us also have little problem getting around to doing things *urgent* and *not important*. The phone rings and we answer it. By default we treat the *urgencies* that others put upon us as things we have to do. Here we really need consciousness or *mindfulness*. Is this really important? How much value does this really hold for me? What does it mean to do this or *not* to do this?

Things that fall into the category of not urgent *and* not important are the worst of time wasters. A great prototype for this is mindlessly watching TV, program after program, hour after hour.

The Discipline inside The Competence Game
Whenever we apprentice ourselves as disciples to a discipline, we move through a set of developmental stages. I'm not sure who first articulated these stages—it may have been Abraham Maslow. The stages begin with being incompetent and not knowing it. Ah, the blissful state of ignorance! The *unconsciously* incompetent stage. At this stage we have no discipline, no learning, no skill, no challenge. Here we live in a Garden of Eden—blissful, happy, and ignorant. Like infants, we're also unskilled, unchallenged, and unable to play any *Expert Game*.

Then we become conscious. The light appears. Suddenly or slowly we begin to recognize a whole new world of excitement, skill, expertise, and knowledge. So, we bite into the forbidden fruit of the "Tree of the Knowledge of Good and Evil." But, instead of being instantly transported to the paradise of Expertise, it creates the anxiety, pressure, distress, and unpleasantness of recognizing all that we don't know. We become *consciously* incompetent. We face, for the first time, the challenges of the reality constraints regarding what it takes to become competent. We face the work, the process, the struggle, the challenge. Typically, we now feel confused, inadequate, incomplete, "dumb," and incapable of handling things. And, sure enough, we are incompetent.

Many people are tempted to run back to the Garden of their Ignorance and Innocence when they first encounter the stage of conscious incompetence. We don't like feeling incompetent. Who does? And, if we run any mental program of comparison, perfectionism, or impatience in our head, we will go into a state of self-judgment. "I hate being put down like this." "What's wrong with me that I can't get this?" "Why does it have to be so hard?" "I'll never get this."

Of course those *frame games* will recruit us for depression, self-pity, fearfulness, timidity, or procrastination. At this stage, it seems as if the "discipline" of apprenticing ourselves to the new domain is hard and uncomfortable, perhaps even overwhelming. Here many turn back and refuse to go on. Why? Because they don't have a good relationship with *learning* itself, with unsuccessful attempts, with using so-called "failure" as just feedback. They don't know how to play those games to get through the process. They don't know how to give themselves a chance—an opportunity to grow and develop their skills. They impatiently judge and evaluate themselves harshly. If only they would take a kinder and gentler approach, validating and celebrating every little step of progress.

Yet if we work through this stage we will find ourselves in the marvelous and wonderful place of the third stage. This is the stage of *conscious* competence. In this stage we feel great! Here the discipline (the learning, the training) seems easy and delightful. We like it so much we even show the "discipline" off. Here we have attained a level of competence and so enjoy it as a skill and enjoy confidence it brings. Here we have become a practitioner of the art. We know our business, and we do it well. And, though we know that we have many more things that we can develop, we delight in the level of mastery that we have attained.

Then something strange happens. It habituates. And when that happens we lose awareness of *how* we do the things that we do. It drops out of awareness, and we now perform at the expert level *intuitively* (it is an in-knowing, *in-tuit*). We have just stepped up into a new level of development. We are now *unconsciously* competent! The discipline now seems like a piece of cake. We experience it as "no problem." We can do it without our conscious mind, with our eyes closed. It's that exalted feeling we experienced as children when we shouted, "Look, Mom, no hands!"

Our knowledge and skills have become higher invisible frames that make up the Domain of Knowledge that we just intuitively live in and operate from. And the derivative skills have become installed in our muscles, in our very neurology. Now the expertise operates at a completely intuitive level. The mastery has now become quite pronounced. This is the level where experts operate and do things that seem so "magical." It's their *unconscious* competence. This also means that the expert, typically, will *not* be able to explain their expertise. They just *do* it. They have lost awareness of how they do it.

So to move beyond that, and up to a newer and more complex level of *conscious* competence, we have to bring back into awareness the structure, form, and process for the excellence in order to train others in it. This represents the fifth stage in the development of competence, when we can teach it to others.

Figure 13:3

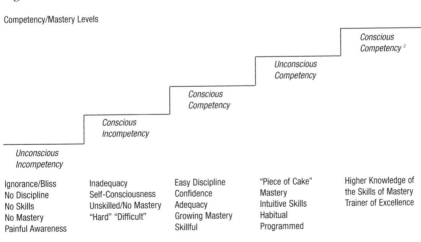

Competency/Mastery Levels

217

Summary

- If we want to play *The Game of Excellence* in business, or in any other realm, if we want to step into mastery level of skill and expertise, we have to play *The Discipline Game.*

- Success in business necessitates a committed discipline by which we apprentice ourselves to the necessary understandings and skills. This will not happen overnight, but takes time. It takes time to gain a clarity of vision that enables us to utter a strong and resounding *"Yes!"* to the things of value and a similar resounding *"No!"* to the things opposite to our objectives and to the things that get in our way.

- Are you ready to play *The Discipline Game*?

Chapter 14

Business Games that Enrich the Lives of Others

"If a customer leaves feeling 'sold' rather than 'serviced,'
somebody goofed in a major way."
—Scott T. Gross

Games in this Chapter
The "If it Weren't for the Customers" Game
The "Positive Outrageous Service" Game
The Customer Service Game
The "Sick and Tired of Dealing with People" Game
The Human Touch Game
The "CEO Customer" Game
The Delighting Customers Game
The Ongoing Learner Game
The Giving Game

Business experts know that to play in the new *people-intensive* field of business today we have to develop some radically new attitudes about customers. In a changing market where customers and clients no longer *have* to do business with us, or take our offerings as they are, where they have many more options, they will (and do) vote with their feet and will do so more often than ever before.

As the new marketplace emerges, this means that succeeding in business will require giving more attention to customers. It means learning how to really listen to customers, attend them, and give them the royal treatment. It means even treating them as we would treat the CEO Why? Because, after all, they are the ones who pay the bills and determine what succeeds.

Business experts know the importance of treating customers as if they were royalty. They know that, as technology improves and establishes quality of products, attention will shift from *what* we create, produce, and sell to *how we relate* to people. This will make *customer service* increasingly important all over the world. It will make delighting and charming clients and customers more critical to success.

Lee Iacocca succinctly described the critical importance of high quality customer service.

> *"When* product and price are inseparable, people will buy from the company that provides *the best service."*

Yet knowing that we need to consider how we treat our customers and improve our relationships and service with them is very different from knowing how to do that and shifting to play that game. We have known for a long time that out of top-level customer service come all kinds of great payoffs: superb-quality products and services, financial success, happy employees, and loyal customers. We know that. We know that this represents a key secret for business success. Treating our customers well is very important.

The problem lies not in *knowing* this, it occurs in actually producing top-notch and high-quality customer service. As front-line people find that quite challenging, so supervisors and managers find it equally challenging to so treat the people below them.

The "If it Weren't for the Customers" Game

If business success, especially in the new marketplace, is as simple as delighting the customers, why don't more business owners and managers follow that principle and simply shift to playing this new game? Don't most companies and business leaders realize the importance of customer service? Yes, I think they do.

What, then, is the problem? There are several. One is the prevalence of the old games and how deeply entrenched they are in our minds and practices. Old business models put success entirely and exclusively on the product, virtually ignoring customers and how we treat them. This highlights another problem: the lack of training in how to give people "the royal treatment."

Think about the last time you went into a store to shop, or into a restaurant for a meal, or dealt with someone on the phone, at the post office or when you checked into a hotel. Did you get *the royal treatment*? Did the people "waiting on you" make it a delightful and honorable experience? Did they play *The "Give Them Outrageously Positive Service" Game* with you?

Or, did they give the impression that their business would be much better if it weren't for your bothering them? Did they make the experience a pleasant one, or, better, a warm and fun one? Or did they seem to be operating from some other frames of mind? "Hey, it's just a job." "Don't ask me, I just work here." "What do you want? I need to get back to work." "People are a pain in the rear end."

The "Positive Outrageous Service" Game

In his book on selling, Scott T. Gross calls the key secret of business excellence "positive outrageous service." Indeed, the title of the book reflects that: *Positive Outrageous Service* (1996). Similarly, in *Customer Satisfaction is Worthless: Customer Loyalty is Priceless* (1998), Jeffrey Gitomer describes high-quality service as the secret pathway to riches and success. But Forler Massnick gets the prize for the most compelling title that highlights this game that business experts play: *The Customer is the CEO* (1997).

Each of these works (and many others) highlights the very structure and essence of *excellence* in business—*truly serving the customer* in providing high-quality products and services. When we play that game, the experience we give our customers and clients will stand out as positive, honoring, respectful, satisfying, and memorable. *The "CEO Customer" Game* will even affect our motivations. We create products and services to *contribute something of value* to the world. If what we have to offer has no value or benefit to people—then the business has outlived its usefulness or never had one.

The Customer Service Game

Let's begin by clarifying what we mean, think, and feel about this arena of "customer service."

- When you hear the phrase, "customer service," what do you think or feel?
- Do you have a different set of references, feelings, or thoughts when you think about *giving* customer service from when you *receive* customer service?
- In what ways does your business serve customers? Do you have an operational definition of what "the best performance" of customer service would be like?
- How well do you provide *top-notch service* for your customers?
- Does your customer service reach the level of making the customer feel like your CEO? Does it reach the height of positive outrageous service? Does it automatically create intense customer loyalty?
- How would your thinking, attitude, and actions change if you gave *that* kind of service? How much would that cost you?

The game of "customer service" begins with the things we say and do to our customers. It involves the level of our friendliness, pleasantness, interactions, attention, and the extent to which we make it easy for customers to do business with us. It involves such skills as effectively handling complaints and problems by attentive listening, remaining nondefensive, seeking to understand, and wanting to create a win/win arrangement for all. Customer service, also involves something else: it involves a conceptual frame of reference about people, service, time, and effort.

- What do you think about the idea of *serving* customers?
- Does the idea of giving customers an exceptionally positive experience excite you?
- Does that idea seem silly, unnecessary, and a bother?
- Do you have an attitude that you could get a lot more done if it weren't for the customers?

These are the factors that establish how we play the game.

The "Sick and Tired of Dealing with People" Game

While business experts know of the importance of giving customers good value, high-quality products and service, and a warm
pleasant experience, many others play a different game. The attitude of many people about dealing with the public makes it nearly
impossible to give high-quality customer service. Then there are
those negative experiences with stressed-out, angry, and disgruntled customers that can lead some employees to "cop an attitude,"
so that they don't try to be pleasant. Lacking the skills for handling
grumpy people and for defusing hot and stressed-out customers,
they take it personally, and gave up *The Warm and Pleasant Game*
entirely.

Obviously, work stresses can overwhelm and interfere with the
interpersonal nature of the new workplace. Stress does that.
Perhaps we have far too much to do, are way behind, under pressure to produce, etc. No wonder we don't feel up to wanting to
extend ourselves to "make the day" for a customer. When we're
not feeling valued, resourceful, calm, and confident, it's going to
be nearly impossible to delight and please others. Here is a factor
in playing *The Delighting Customers Game*, when we do not *feel good*
or resourceful, it's difficult to manage our own states to pull off
high-quality service. At such times it is hard to get our own ego
out of our way. And whenever our ego gets in the way, it's nearly
impossible to attend to making a customer feel good. This not only
underscores the importance of top-quality state management
skills, but the states and frames of mind we have to be in to effectively *extend ourselves for the benefit of another*. It suggests the kind
of empowerment training we need in order to play *The "Customer
First" Game* with any delight or warmth.

Those who work on the front line with the public are actually an
internal "customer" of the business, at least the "customer" of the
overseeing supervisor or manager. From a systems point of view,
the front line employees are the customers of the all those higher
up in the business or organization. This poses questions for that
management: How well are you treating your internal customers
(your employees)? Are you giving them *the royal treatment?* Are
you making their day with your charm, delight, and respect? If

management expect them to extend themselves to the *public* customers, should they not model it to them, the *internal* customers?

When management fail to treat the first-line people as highly valued customers, they will eventually receive the same in kind: a lack of loyalty, disgruntledness, less than quality work, anger and disappointment, and resentment. What goes around comes around. It belongs to the higher-paid management to set the pace, to model the excellence. Conversely, if they treat their internal customers *royally*, they show the kind of business genius that will lead to financial success, high-quality products and services, and long-term success. Since it is all a system, the interactions at one level will influence interactions at other levels. The treatment that the leaders give at their level will be the treatment that emerges at the other levels. This is the way leadership and organizations work.

The Human Touch Game

The task of any business obviously involves creating high-quality products that fill a need in the market. Yet it involves more. To do business in an effective way that succeeds financially, we also have to communicate, influence, sell, and relate to people in such a way that *the experience itself of delivering the product* (tangible or intangible) enriches and delights their perceptions. Certainly, you can recall experiences like that—when the *way* someone did business made it extremely valuable and enriching.

Business success involves both *tasks* (product creation) and *people* (service, communication, experience).

- The *business task* involves what we do in our business. This is what we make, produce, or supply.
- The *business context* involves how we treat people (be they employees, peers, management or outside customers).

When we think systemically, it's clear that it is not the company that actually pays our salaries: it's the customers. The company merely distributes the money that the customers spend for the products and services. No customers, no business. Thinking this way reorients us to the true function of business. In the long-run, we succeed in business only to the extent that we provide something that our customers value. Enough to invest in. A market dries up when people no longer want our products or services. When that happens, there is no more business.

Forler Massnick (1997) writes:

"The customer decides what quality is. Something like 80% of dissatisfaction voiced by customers has nothing to do with product. It has to do with *service, attitude, relationships—the human aspects of doing business.*" (Page 5, my italics).

The "CEO Customer" Game

With all of this in mind, what frames do we need in order to play this game effectively? What states do we need in order to give our customers service, a service that's charming and personal? To give them an outstanding service experience? What *states* do we find customers in that we need to deal with to bring the best out in them?

Gross writes: "The size of the transaction is often not so much a measure of your ability to sell as it is a measure of your willingness to serve." (Page 41.)

Figure 14:1

Receiving "Service" *Customers* Needs	Giving "Service" *Employees* Gifts
To know and understand	Attention
To clarify confusions	Empathy
To make a decision	Seeking first to understand
To place an order	Friendly pleasantness
To fix a problem	Delightful charm
To deal with frustrations	Warmth, thoughtful
To deal with angers	Flexible
To deal with negative emotions	

Imagine turning the experience of dealing with the public into a game—the game of surprising people in delightful and charming ways. Then what states would you need to be at your best? To be warm, friendly, and pleasant? Explore this from the position of *being* a customer. When you are buying and/or calling, shopping, or whatever in order to satisfy a need or want, *what kind of interactions* do you want from those who show up to "serve" you?

Understanding the "Giving Service" world

As with every domain, area, or field, certain principles govern that arena. What are the *principles* that govern business success in terms of *quality and excellence* in the field of customer service?

1. The customer is the reason for the business.

When we do not have any customers for our business, we go "*out of business.*" Businesses come into existence because customers need or want something. We organize business to produce and supply that want or need. This means, as we've seen, that *the customers pay the bills.* Customers' wants and demands create the business. Isn't that great? Every demand from a customer creates your business! This leads to the frame that the customer is the Chief Executive Officer. The customers ultimately utter the final and decisive "*Yes*" and/or "*No*" to our products and services.

Given this, suppose that you treated your customer as *your boss.* Play with that idea for a moment. Would that transform the way you act, speak, or relate?

Peter Drucker has said:

> "There is only one valid definition of business purpose: *to create a customer.*"

Forler Massnick writes:

> "A company that identifies customers as the driving force has a clarity of purpose that cuts through a lot of strategic planning complexity. Such a company taps a wellspring of ideas for new products and services, opens up new territories and alliances, stimulates innovation, encourages flexibility, and keeps the company on its toes." [Page 63.]

Jack Smith, CEO of General Motors, put it even more succinctly:

> "Focus everything—all assets, all decisions—on your customers. They are the ultimate arbiters of success or failure."

2. Business involves two levels of experience
In "doing business," we first of all create a product and/or a service. We can think of this as the hard science of the business—the brute facts of *what* we have to offer at the primary level. At yet a higher level, we bring an *attitude* with us as we engage in the business. Our attitude reflects the frames that we bring to the job and the frames that we operate from. In establishing the game that we play with our customers this comprises the soft part of the business—*how* we give our products and services. So now we can ask: "What attitude do you bathe your customers in?" "What emotions do you set as the contextual frame when you do business?"

Figure 14:2

3. The business lies in the hands of the service givers
Would you like to hear something sober enough to scare and terrify a business owner? Above and beyond the products or services created by a business, the interface between the business and the public or customer lies in the hands of the company's front-line people. When the service reps are out on calls, they *represent* the business. When the sales force are face to face with buyers, they represent the company. What we think of any company depends on *the way we are treated* by those who answer the phones, take the orders, handle returns, resolve conflicts, ship products, deliver services. At that point work style becomes exceedingly important. The games they play, or attempt to pay, and the warmth—or lack of it—that they bring to their interactions are everything for the business.

4. The quality and nature of the service giver's attitude governs the customer's experience

Above and beyond the products and services, we can count on and expect that our customers will be profoundly affected by the *attitude* of those on the front line who serve them. This attitude will be conveyed by, among other things, the way they talk, act, smile, etc.

So,

- How well are the front-line people trained in providing charming and delightful service?
- Have they been personally empowered to play such games?
- Have they been officially empowered by the company to give customers the royal treatment?

Given this importance of employee attitude here is yet another hard psychological fact. It is impossible to satisfy the external customers with top-quality service if employees feel dispirited, disgruntled, unappreciated, taken advantage of, or stressed out. If we want employees to treat customers with a quality attitude, we have to get management to start that game. They have to listen to, reward, and appreciate employees with delight and charm if they want them to pass it on to the external customers.

5. To thrive, a business must aim to create customer loyalty, not mere satisfaction

Actually, to merely "satisfy" a customer means very little. Satisfying a customer means that they received what they wanted, but nothing more. Does that create any commitment? Any provider can give them that. And customers will easily change if they hear of a better price or service. So, give them a charming and delightful experience that exceeds expectations, communicates a sense of care and appreciation, validates them, affirms their uniqueness, transforms them into *loyal* customers who will not easily switch. Then they will fight rather than switch. They are loyal to a business that treats them as special and valuable.

To elicit loyalty we need only to model our customers. We need to discover *what* our customers want and *how* they would like it provided. This involves a moving target. What delights and satisfies customers continually changes. So we will need to continually monitor what they need, want, and expect. Such attentive monitoring will elicit a wealth of information.

6. Keeping a customer costs less than creating one
How much does it cost you or your business to obtain a new customer? Add up all of the costs that go into advertising, marketing, research, and development. Now, if it costs a considerable amount to create new customers, wouldn't it be wiser to set a game plan for keeping current ones? Would it be wise to treat the current customers with special care?

Suppose we made it our game plan to delight our clients and customers to keep them returning and bringing others. What frame would you need to adopt in order to think this way? Do you know what elicits loyalty in you? When customers become loyal, they provide free and extremely effective marketing for your business. You couldn't buy better public-relations messages. That's the big *payoff* for playing this game.

7. The best job security you can create comes from delighting your current customers
If you want to make yourself invaluable to your business or want to secure your business, make it your strategy to keep your customers returning. How do you do that? All you have to do is provide them high-quality products and services within an attitude context of appreciation, respect, delight, and charm. Sometimes fun, too, depending on the kind of business you're in. That's all.

How to play The "CEO Customer" Game
1. Establish the business frames for delighting customers with high-quality service
What's your game? What game do you intend to play regarding how you treat your customers? Is your game plan to delightfully treat your customers? This is not rocket science. It requires only that you develop a focus and a willingness to serve and then an inspiration to go one step further than expected.

What would you have to think-and-feel, believe, and understand in order to step up into the top ten service states? How would this be important to you? How would it be a value to the business? What is the current orientation and frame of the business? What current games might get in the way? "Just do business, attitude is not that important"? "You know how 'the public' is"?

How would you like to enrich the quality of your own states when you do business so that it adds more charm and effectiveness to your customer-service skills? Positive outrageous service, according to Scott T. Gross, is all about having many people *feel really good* about doing business with you.

2. Discover and use the language of delight with your customers

How do you talk to customers? What kinds of lines do you use with buyers during various scenarios: when they need more information, ask questions, make complaints, express displeasure, try to make a decision?

How many times do you communicate a *"No,"* or an attitude that's not seen to be helping or seeking to understand? How many times in a day do you quote company policy? How much of your talk could we say is the *language of helpfulness*? Do you also convey that by your tone of voice?

What language of rapport do you use? Do you know how to pace and match the states of your buyers so that you can pace them? How often do you engage in the persuasion of charm with your customers? What does that look and sound like?

To get off on the best foot with a customer, demonstrate from the very beginning that you respect them. Ask permission to ask them questions that will help you to serve them. Avoid the hard-sell approach. Avoid the goofy Either/Or questions: today most customers are more sophisticated than that. Simply being remembered and recognized is a great big stroke for most people. It communicates respect.

3. Continually monitor the process of delighting

If you have set *delighting* and *charming* as part of the attitude that you want to bathe your customers in so that you give them something to notice about you and talk about, then you will need to learn how to effectively access the delight state. This will mean interrupting yourself when you get into another state. It will mean monitoring your own stages of states.

What is your delight factor? Move beyond delight to *"Wow!"* Gross (1996) writes,

> "Positively Outrageous Service is all about wrapping an experience around a service transaction. It is a WOW on a random basis." (Page 106.)

How do you do this? Keep inventing new opening lines that people find fun and engaging. Look for new ways to say *"Yes"* to your customers. Enjoy what you are doing yourself so that your customers will pick up on that attitude easily and naturally.

4. Refuse to be recruited to any nondelightful games or states

When a product or service has not lived up to expectations or when there have been problems in the process of doing business, customers will get into negative states. They want things fixed. This will lead to complaining.

Typically, most complaints are handled poorly. Why? Because we fear confrontation, facing negative emotions, being taken advantage of, being wrong. This puts *us* to the test.

"Can I access an uninsultable, centered, strong state that will allow me to hear the complaint as a complaint, gather information, and enter into a seeking-to-help relationship with the complainer?"

We have to have some pretty strong and robust frames to do that. Our customers will not always be in the most positive states. We can expect unpleasant "negative" emotional states at times. We can expect the Fight/Flight emotions of fear and anger to arise and put buyers or potential buyers into states of stress. Now we have to shift to the defusing strategy and game.

Gross writes,

> "If you have a policy to do whatever it takes to make things right when things go wrong, simply asking the customer what it would take to make things right often yields surprising results." (Page 50.)

"I'm really angry about this ..."

"Yes, I can see that. And I agree. I also get angry when I feel poorly treated. Let's get this straightened out the best we can."

We need to adopt an attitude of curiosity: "I wonder what kind of problem he's trying to solve?"

If you can't solve the problem or undo something, you can at least give the customer compassion and understanding. Don't hold back on giving these gifts. They will often work magic right before your eyes. You can at least give the customer the sense that you are on their side. This builds loyalty. So does apologizing without making excuses.

5. Give customers a delightful story
People talk about things out of the ordinary, whether extraordinarily good or bad, positive or negative. So aim to give your customers a story of delight so that they can then tell their friends about how you went out of your way, you made their experience pleasant, you worked to understand and attempted to accommodate.

To give Gross's *positive outrageous service,* aim to provide one that's out of proportion to the circumstances, that's random and unexpected. This will engage the customer and it will create compelling word-of-mouth advertising. Surprise people in pleasant ways. Once you do this, you set up a halo effect for your business. People will begin to see it as highly desirable, the best, or of high quality.

6. Meta-detail your services

I first introduced *The Meta-Detailing Game* in the book *The Structure of Excellence: Unmasking the meta-levels of Submodalities* (1999) as I related it to the structure of genius. This introduced a new distinction in modeling the strategy of genius. *Meta-detailing* refers to setting a high-level (or meta) frame about something significant or important and then employing that frame so that it operates as a self-organizing attractor in the mind–body system. When that happens, the higher frame modulates all other perceptions, communications, and behaviors and directs focus in a strong and powerful way.

This applies to the game of *Delighting Customers*. I have found numerous descriptions of meta-detailing for customer service in Gross's book. When you have established high-level frames of value, understanding, and decision, then you view the so-called "details" as values. Gross writes:

"What's the difference between the amateur and the pro? *The details*. Pros handle the little stuff. Amateurs do not. 'Don't panic, but do watch the details.' The professional is a master of details." [Page 163.]

"The pro is able to look into the very face of chaos and pick out the first thing. First things first. Handle it, and then get the next 'first thing.' Then the next."

"Pros at any job have the ability to decide not just what is important. They also have the ability to see in a heartbeat those things that don't need to be done at all." [Page 165.]

"Another thing that marks out a pro: the ability to see more "first things." What is the difference between the best in the business and the also-rans? It's the details. Little, itty-bitty differences that add up to the big differences." [Page 166.]

"The leaders are those who sweat the small stuff. Amateurs cannot tell what is big stuff and what is simply stuff. Worse, amateurs sometimes can't recognize stuff when they see, smell, hear, touch, or taste it. Pros are master sniffers. To get people interested in handling the details, they have to be shown the beauty in the details." [Page 170.]

"Attention to details inspires great confidence. What do you think when a mechanic keeps the work area spotless? All that is required for great customer service is for us to pay attention. Great servers are great noticers. They notice the small details. They anticipate problems and fix them before anyone else knows that there's a problem." [Page 188.]

Summary

*   Are you ready to "do business"? Do you feel ready to make your business a happy, delightful, and charming place? Would you like to play that game?

*   Establish your game plan and frames for getting into a deep and profound appreciation of the value of serving with charm, of delighting people, and making others feel really good. Do this in the growing realization that this will secure your professional financial future, and your enjoyment of everyday life.

*   Access every resourceful thought, idea, feeling, and belief that will help you to *set this kind of frame* for yourself and others. Let it become a self-organizing attitude to elicit your business excellence.

Chapter 15

Getting to Resolution:
The Welcoming and
Resolving Conflict Game

"Their game was resolution and getting people back to their lives."

Games in this Chapter
The Conflict Resolution Game
The Resolutionary Frame Game
The "Stuck Without Resolution" Game
The Meta-Thinking Game
The Dialogue Game
The Agreement Frame Game
The Win/Win Game

The Conflict Resolution Game

There's another game that business experts play, a game that's essential for long-term success in the new marketplace. It's The game of *quickly embracing conflict and resolving it.* This contrasts with the way the great majority of us typically handle "conflict" as we grow up. We usually play *The Passive Game* and *The Aggressive Game* (see Chapter 12). In the presence of conflict, we opt for games of avoidance, denial, pretension, attacking, smoothing over, distracting. Business experts do not do this. They roll up their sleeves and treat conflict as a valuable and important opportunity for creating alliance, finding new solutions, understanding others more thoroughly, and enriching their lives.

The "Getting to Resolution" Game

Expertise, or even excellence in any area, doesn't make *conflict* irrelevant. Not at all. In fact, if anything, the more we passionately go after our goals and seek to do something powerful and important in the world, the more conflict we'll have to deal with. The more our expertise increases, the more likely we'll conflict with others. All too often it's an occupational hazard of success.

Does that surprise you? Does that violate any expectations you have about finally becoming so skilled that you can easily get along with everybody? At this level, conflict doesn't necessarily mean that we're doing something wrong or that we've got problems. It means we are standing out and affecting our world, and upsetting things in the process. It means that our understandings, models, skills, hopes, dreams, plans, and processes *conflict* with those of others. It means the presence of different maps of the world, differing styles, understandings, intentions, etc. It means that our uniqueness and individuality is standing out and calling for some frame that can create unity and harmonize the two.

As such, conflict is a pervasive force in all of life, personal and business. So we have to learn to deal with it. We have to learn to play a new game with it. Steward Levine, an attorney, or as he says, "a repentant lawyer," writes in *Getting To Resolution: Turning Conflict Into Collaboration* (1998), that he "saw the light" about conflict and so developed the frames for a model to effectively resolve it. He set out to do this when he recognized that the more "successful" he became as a lawyer, the less effective he became at "resolving matters." *The Lawyer Game* apparently didn't serve *The Resolution Game.*

So he just quit. "I stopped practicing law," he wrote. In place of that he set out to *model* the how effective experts resolve conflict.

> "I was fascinated with *how* the most effective judges and lawyers understood people's real concerns. They knew what to honor and what to respect. They knew how to frame situations and condition people's expectations. They embodied a tradition that accommodated competing concerns and built consensus. Winning or losing was not the point of their work. Their game was resolution and getting people back to their lives." [Page xii.]

Detecting your Default "Conflict" Frame

Our ideas, emotions, or concepts about conflict inevitably establish frames, and so *frame games*. What frames have you set in your mind about conflict? Do you access positive or negative frames? Do you frame it as a useful opportunity or as the possibility of hurt? Here are some explorative questions to detect the games you play around conflict. As you think about some recent conflicts that you have experienced, consider these questions:

- Do you *like* or *enjoy* conflict?
- Do you *fear* and *dread* it?
- Do you find conflict *distasteful, obnoxious,* and *terrible*?
- Do you revel in conflict?
- Do you *appreciate* conflict as providing valuable "information"?
- Do you *respect* it as a call for attending a relationship?
- What frame of reference do you use when you approach the subject of "conflict"?
- *How* do you think about it; *how* do you feel about it?
- Does that game serve you well? Does it enhance your life?

You already have some *frame game* that you play when it comes to conflict and to your ideas about "conflict."

Conflict is inevitable. The simple fact that we move through the world as unique individuals with our own sense of destiny, mission, values, desires, and experiences necessitates that we will come into *conflict* with others. We can count on this and expect it. We can also celebrate it. Of course, *how* we understand our differences contributes to conflicting or collaborating. Our attitudes and frames can put us at odds with others or in alliance. *How* we conflict (the actual game that we play) also affects whether we experience "conflict" as a resource or an enemy.

Typically, most of us play a negative game. We attach lots of *pain* to the experience and the idea of conflict with the result that it feels negative. Unpleasant experiences support this attitude. We don't like it, so we seek to avoid it. Yet, paradoxically, this very attitude actually contributes to our inability to handle conflict effectively. Why? Because it leaves us less prepared to deal with this pervasive aspect of life. It orients us to play various conflict-avoidance games, and that makes things worse. This frame leads to denying, pretending, covering-up, rationalizing, and fearing opposition, criticism, and rejection. It leads to neglecting conflicts when they are small and manageable and letting them "pop out of nowhere" after they have simmered and festered and become large and unmanageable.

Obviously, *we need a new game about conflict.* We need a new perspective for thinking about conflict. We need one that enables us to move toward it with faith, hope, and even love. We need a game that allows us to encounter it with playfulness, curiosity, and exploration. We need a game that allows us to move toward the at-odds relating (conflict) while seeking to make things better while they are "small and manageable" and to do so in a warm, charming, and defenseless way.

The old maps get us into trouble and make interactions worse and increase the possibility of conflict. These include the following frames:

Scarcity
"There's only so much. You have to fight for and compete for the goodies. There's not enough for everybody!"

Competition
"Only the competitive win. Good guys finish last. Nice guys get the shift."

Win/Lose
"In the world, somebody will win and somebody will lose."

Manipulation
"If you want to win, win by manipulation. Use persuasive techniques to win over people to your point of view. Take advantage of every influential tool you can and refuse to play on an even playing field. Manipulate by hoarding and controlling information."

Distrust
"Behind every behavior you'll find hidden agendas, lies, and attempts to trick you. Don't trust people. Expect the worst."

Short-term opportunistic winning
"A sucker is born every minute. Grab all the gusto (or gold) you can—while you can."

Blaming
"Others 'make' me feel the way I do. If something goes wrong, someone is to blame. Defer responsibility to others when you can."

Only winning counts
"He who dies with the most toys, wins!"

Invulnerability
"Show no weaknesses. Don't let anybody have a chance at your soft underbelly."

Logic
"The only thing that counts is 'the facts.' Forget emotions, relationships, and ethics. They are overrated and don't need to interfere with business. After all, business is business."

These are the frames that get us to either greatly *dislike* conflict or to play on the fears of others who *can't stand conflict* and *push their buttons*. The ideas and cognitive schemas in these frames inadequately map how to deal with differences, the fact that we want different things, that we use different values in evaluating things, and that we bring unique perspectives to things. Such frames lead to such unproductive and even destructive games.

The Resolutionary Frame Game

Steward Levine speaks about the new game. He calls for a new attitude which he calls a *"resolutionary"* attitude. This frame looks for a fair outcome, one that satisfies everyone's intentions and perspectives. It has number inherent presuppositions involved in it. As a way of thinking it implies the following:

Abundance
"There's enough for everybody! As we interact, we create all kinds of new sources of income, wealth, richness, etc. Synergy arises so that we have more together than competing against others. A mind-set of abundance wherein all win means that we do not need for anyone to lose."

Cooperation
"We'll get more by working together than by working apart. Efficient collaboration shows up as teamwork, community, partnership, etc."

Win/Win or no game
"We can let go of ego concerns and move to community concerns. If I win at the expense of your loss, I will have to begin to watch my backside, operate by more distrust, expect resentment, anger, and more conflict."

Nonmanipulative dialoguing and advocating
"In the Win/Win abundance model, we dialogue in order to get the highest kind of information and then we advocate (even strongly and intensely) our point of view—while inviting and empowering the other to also advocate his or her point of view. We seek to persuade and influence—in an above-board and open way."

Trust, authenticity
"I expect people to be people—human beings with wants, desires, emotions, understandings, ideas, etc. I will trust their humanity and invite their authenticity by demonstrating such myself. I will disclose openly and honestly in order to receive the same."

Vulnerability with firmness of boundaries
"I will operate by vulnerability to invite it and do so out of the strength of my own identity, values, beliefs, and choices. I will embrace the strength of vulnerability, and honestly disclose information."

Response-ability
"I will assume and own full responsibility for my own thoughts, emotions, language, and behavior."

Long-term learning
"I will aim to learn through the process. If I have learned something that makes me better, that contributes to the world, I have won. I will avoid looking for a quick fix in situations where I don't have clarity. I will 'learn my way through' without having to know the outcome in advance. I will trust myself and the universe for it."

Psycho-logical reality
"I will recognize and honor that in human experience and relationships, emotions, needs, intentions, desires, dreams, and other facets of our psyche count as well as ideas and logic."

Do the values and ideas in these frames present a new and empowering mental map? Do they offer a new game? You bet they do! They provide us the foundation for *The Resolutionary Frame Game.*

The "Stuck Without Resolution" Game

Consider the converse game. Without resolution we get *stuck* at various impasses in conflict so that we can't get on with life or fully participate in an experience. We become past-oriented and begin to reference past hurts as our guiding principle. That's how the game is played. It creates other problems that then accumulate.

Levine writes,

> "In today's world of 'knowledge work,' focus and creativity are essential. It's impossible to be fully productive when you are angry. That's why getting resolved about the situation that's sapping your strength and attention is very important." (Page 5.)

The Meta-Thinking Game

How do we get resolution? How do we more fully step into the resolutionary frame and then act that way in the world in a wise and balanced way?

The Getting to Resolution Game most essentially involves making a meta-move to our position in a conflict, then to the position of the other (or others), and then to the position of our environment, culture, desires, positive intentions and so forth. From these moves to various higher positions we can then co-construct an *agreement frame*. As this highest meta-position includes multiple perspectives it invites us into the wisdom of the whole so that we are able to work out a broad understanding that involves a mutually satisfying resolution.

When we *go meta*, we are able to see the bigger picture, to see more systemically and to recognize the contributing factors that play into the conflict. When we don't utilize the power of multiple perceptual positions, we operate deaf and blind to any perspective that can include other views than just our own. This causes us to lose perspective. We develop a tunnel vision that locks us into the *self* position only. Levine writes:

"You want to become 'meta' to the situation, which means to be outside or above it. I do it all the time, and you can too." [Page 10.]

"Most of us avoid taking personal responsibility for conflict resolution. Although litigious, we often lack the courage to deeply connect with others. We personally avoid confrontation. If we have a disagreement in a business transaction or with a neighbor, we may let a lawyer take care of it. If we have emotional conflict, we may visit a therapist or counselor who we hope will tell us what to do."

"Conflict is usually recognized by pain and discomfort. When you take personal responsibility, you get to the root of the pain much faster than if you ask someone else to resolve the situation for you. This requires being vulnerable. If you are unwilling or unable to be authentic about your feelings, you may be quick to give up responsibility, and instead take false safety and security behind a more sterile, professional process. In doing that, you give up the possibility of discovering your real concerns, getting to the core of the conflict, and reaching resolution." [Pages 8–9.]

There are many *resources* mentioned or alluded to in these paragraphs, resources that result from taking a *meta*-position to all of the individual positions. Stepping back in our mind and taking a meta-position enables us to more easily accept personal responsibility, develop the courage to confront when things are smaller and manageable, step into a vulnerable role with others, and not fear deeply connecting or recognizing the core of problems. By stepping back (or up) and operating from a higher perspective, we can stay calmer, cooler, and more reasonable.

Playing the Conflict Resolution Game

The Conflict Resolution Game offers us a road map for finding good resolutions. The design of the following process is to provide the frame, position, safety, resourcefulness, and skill for more effectively handling conflict and building up valued and lasting resolutions.

1. *Access a Resolution Frame of Mind*

This attitude step means thinking in ways that support resolution. It means developing the frameworks for believing, valuing, and deciding *for* resolution. It means fanning our passion for agreement, Win/Win arrangements, beliefs in abundance and personal responsibility.

- What frames of beliefs and values excite you so that you vibrate with a sense of power and courage?

- What frame puts you into a state of curiously wondering about just how the resolution will specifically emerge in you?

When you find the *magical* frame that can drive everything in your pursuit of resolution, then strengthen and solidify that frame. Adopt it as your way of looking at the conflict:

> "Resolution is just around the corner—it will emerge in the next round of communication." (Levine, Page 99.)

When we adopt and operate from that kind of abundance thinking, it will help us to sit down together to talk. How different it is from the first step that lawyers typically request, namely, "I want you to stop talking to the other party!"

A strong, vigorous, and healthy resolution state operates from lightness, fun, humor, and curiosity.

> "Laugh at yourself as you disarm people committed to a fight. Watch their faces drop and their bodies relax when you listen and speak from a mood of resolution." (Levine, Page 101.)

A healthy resolution state also knows that "the truth" of the situation involves *multiple perspectives* and will not be a simple construct. Things are "true" according to some frame of reference. After all, when we consider the word "truth," what kind of a word do we have? A verb? An adjective? No. A simple noun, then? Not exactly. What we have is a special kind of noun: a *nominalization*. We have a process (holding something as true) turned into a noun and treated like a thing. Yet "truth" is not a thing. It refers to a mental evaluation, as in, "I hold this as true and accurate given my understandings, criteria, values, and standards." "Truth" depends on the standard used for the evaluating. Thus: "True to whom?" "True according to what values?"

We nowhere find disembodied "truths" lying around in the world as things. "Truth" is always based on "understanding" and a domain of knowledge. And understanding is obviously a personal and subjective state of mind. Specifically, it emerges as an evaluative (meta-level) frame from some particular person's (or group's) understandings, and therefore upon some model of the world. "Truth" arises and exists as a *human construct* about some conceptual understanding. Since we cannot see, hear, feel, smell or taste "truth" we need to acknowledge its nonempirical nature, that it exists as a human state of awareness. Recognizing this helps us temper our advocating so that we don't get into the Deity Mode of saying, "And that's the truth!"

2. Dialogue and Advocate

We next move to the *vulnerability step* in this game. Playing *The Conflict Resolution Game* enables us to openly disclose our stories and to attentively hear the stories of others. This opens up each person in a conflict to *tell his or her story*. In this disclosure, we reveal not only "the facts," but also our emotions, intentions, desires, and dreams from our model of the world. In dialoguing and advocating, we continually shift from first and second perceptual positions as we extend and expand our wisdom about the situation.

It's in this second step that we co-author *a well-formed conversation* or dialogue—one that involves pacing and attending each other, seeking to understand each other, and disclosing ourselves. Here we tell our stories and disclose our intentions. This provides catharsis, "downloading," and the clearing that we typically find necessary to get to the underlying (or overarching) factors—the real issues.

Here, listening to the full story is essential to this step of the game. Such attending provides *validation* of the other person even if we do not share his or her viewpoint. It confirms the person. It gives the person a sense that we understand. Stay as long as you need to in step two to *patiently* and *compassionately* seek first to understand.

If you don't? If you don't, you won't get the other's person true or full story. And, without adequate and accurate information, how can you resolve anything that will really satisfy both parties? This explains why, when we resort to secrecy, maneuvering, posturing, or stalling, we undermine the possibility for resolution.

3. Co-author a Meta-Agreement Frame
The next step in this game is the meta-step of framing. Here we move to the third and fourth perceptual positions to gain the wisdom that results from getting a larger-system point of view. We begin to wonder about what each person really wants, what they have in common, and what can benefit each person; we explore the things that each deems truly important and valuable. Doing this enables each to align with the other's highest positive intentions.

We move into this stage by creating a well-formed and satisfying *desired outcome* of the future that we want to experience with the other person. Here we *collaborate* until we find the resolution—a higher-level-agreement frame of reference. "What do we both want that we can agree upon?"

The dawning and full development of this vision will not usually occur all at once, but in stages. First will come the *preliminary vision for resolution*. Frequently, it will arise by intuition—some inward knowing or glimpse of some possibility. Then comes the filling in of the details as the rounds of communicating and exploring and understanding continue. Here each person who plays *The Conflict Resolution Game* will be alert to an emergent vision. It typically arises best when we engage in dispassionate listening, which refers not so much to caring about the specific details, but caring about working toward a resolution that satisfies all.

Actually, once we have a general agreement frame, the rest becomes fairly easy. It becomes a matter of filling in the details. At this stage we can utilize the *irresistibility principle*. Levine describes this:

"... frame the desired outcome in a way that people in the situation will find irresistible; they have to say 'Yes.'" (Page 139.)

In other words, reframe the essential part of the resolution from being the perceived "problem" to being something irresistibly attractive.

"We have been through too much, our friendship means too much to accept anything other than an honorable separation. Otherwise it would demean the previous years. Surely it's better to preserve our dignity, than rub each other in the mud in order to get some fleeting pleasure of revenge, don't you think?"

"Breakdowns are not a cause for alarm": we expect them. They are "an opportunity for creativity." (Page 145.)

4. Continue to Loop Between Inquiry and Reflection

The perseverance step of the game enables us to simply keep at it. To get an updated and complete description of each person's state and story, we have to continue gathering and testing information until each person feels fully heard, validated, and understood. This seldom occurs on the first cycle. Sometimes it may take multiple, even dozens of, cycles to complete it.

Refuse to settle for inadequate and spotty information. If you do, you will jump to conclusions and create inadequate arrangements. Let this step in the game be driven by *The Resolution Frame*—the passion for a resolution that honors all.

In handling the feedback loop of messages sent and received and enriched and fed back again, we have to have a vigorous relationship to feedback as *information*, not as failure. This calls for patience, willingness to keep adjusting the co-created vision, updating our mental maps, and tentativeness. It calls for a frame of *acceptance* of feedback, *welcoming* of feedback, and *wanting to use* feedback to improve performance and outcome.

5. Bring Closure to Past Concerns

This is the closure step of the game. Frequently, in negotiating an adequate agreement frame, we first need to bring closure to various old hurts and frustrations that would otherwise get in the way. If we don't do this, these old maps (understandings, beliefs, experiences, emotions) will sabotage resolution. Mental and emotional prisons can keep people locked into past hurts.

Figure 15:1
Meta-Levels

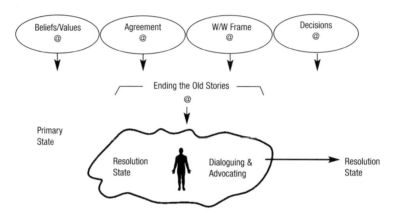

By means of the vulnerable disclosures of our stories, and especially of our old stories of hurt and disappointment, we "download" a lot of feelings: fears, apprehensions, disappointments, frustrations, expectations, anger. Such *emotional* disclosure of information differs from *factual* disclosure. It doesn't need to get addressed so much as simply recognized and validated:

"That must have been hard"; "That sounds like it must have taken a lot out of you."

In 'the alchemy of emotion' we primarily need to discharge the highly charged emotion, get validated and affirmed, and feel understood. Most people find that sufficient in order for them to *let go* of the grievance. To facilitate the stage of emotional completion, use such questions as:

•   What worked about the relationship, partnership, or venture?

- What didn't work?
- Whom do you need to forgive, and for what?
- Whom do you need to thank, and for what?
- What else do you need to say so that you feel complete enough to say, "Today is a good day to die"?
- Do you have any requests?
- Declare that the conflict is current in the moment and complete.
- What's the new era? The new era is …

In the psycho-logical step we seek to bring closure to old hurts, grievances, "bitter roots," and resentments. We are not trying to solve anything, fix anything, deny, explain, or defend. We let the accusation be. We let the other *express* it. We let the person express it fully and completely, saying nothing, but expressions of validation. It simply needs ventilating.

6. Committing to the Resolution

The commitment or action step of the game enables us to begin acting on the resolution. Once we have an *agreement frame* that formulates a resolution that honors everybody and that creates a mutual Win/Win arrangement, we are ready to ask for a specific decision of commitment to it:

"Will you do this?"

"Will we agree to move forward from this agreement?"

This allows us to *real-ize* the resolution. It empowers us to make the agreed-upon vision become our road map for maximizing our potentials.

Summary

- *The Conflict Resolution Game* has various steps to it, various rules by which to play the game. It also has a nice payoff, to deal with difficulties and conflicts when they are small and manageable.

- *The Resolutionary Game* is a new game in town to play when conflict occurs. What would it look, sound, and feel like if tomorrow you moved out into the world as a "resolutionary"? How would it affect the way you relate, communicate, do business, or question?

- When we model the process of *effective conflict resolution* from the experts, we discover its structure. This enables us to replicate the experience—to play that game.

Chapter 16

The Game of Inventing Even Better Games

Games in this Chapter
The Modeling Business Game
The Modeling Excellence Game
The Benchmarking Game
The Theoretical Modeling Game
The "Modeling by Meta-Detailing" Game
The Strategic Planning Game
The "Modeling the Modeling" Game
The "Modeling Dynamic Structures" Game

There's another game that business experts play. It's a game of creativity that seeks to continually reinvent business itself. It's a game of flexibility that is ever ready to adjust to changing circumstances. It's a meta-game of awarenesses that is able to take the best advantages of experts, expertise, and profound knowledge. It is *The Game of Modeling Excellence*.

The Modeling Business Game

To stay in business these days, we have to have several things in place and working really well.

First, we need a *vision or dream* that moves us to produce something of value that contributes to the world. This serves as our guiding principles and meta-frames, keeping us committed, excited, passionate, and motivated. It brings out our genius to the extent that it allows us to focus on something that we care about. It gives us a *great big why*.

We also need the practical, everyday skills for producing our goods and services, and the business sense for managing product, customer service, finances, and other aspects of our work. This translates the vision into practical actions and gives our ideas *hands and feet* in the real world. Specificity and precision at this level enable us to measure and control the quality of our products and service.

Further, we need the learning skills that allow us to synergize our customers' needs and wants with our creativity so that we keep innovating the kinds of products and services that will meet and exceed our customers' expectations—not only for today, but also for the future. This enables us to stay *on the cutting edge* of value and quality. We create and learn. We feed our learning back into our system (business) so that we continue to improve and delight our customers. This creates the security of a solid business foundation and feeds growth and expansion into the things not yet invented, not even yet needed.

We need the modeling skills so that, as we create, learn, produce, improve, and tweak, we develop the orientation and focus of *continual improvement* in the search for excellence. This enables us to keep refining the skills that make us competent and confident in what we do. It empowers us also with a higher level of intelligence and wisdom about what works and why.

Edwards Deming, who almost single-handedly initiated the quality-control movement in Japan and the USA, called this level of excellence, *"profound knowledge."* This means keeping our intellectual methods (theories, principles, frames) in mind and using them in constantly gathering information on how things are working, why they seem to work, what use we can make of them, and how we can refine, tweak, and redesign things to increase the performance and quality.

The "Modeling Excellence" Game

Business experts have learned to stay ahead of the game by playing a higher game, *The Modeling Game.* This shows up today in the passionate search for excellence, quality control, re-engineering, and benchmarking the best. Since these processes tap into the very heart of *modeling,* they operate as a *Modeling Excellence Game.* These processes, among many others, aim simply and directly to increase productivity and profit by improving *behavioral performance.* They aim for greater quality and higher expressions of excellence. The ideology behind this? Create a higher-quality performance and the business will grow and profit. It's as simple as that.

To become a genius at work, there's nothing quicker and, in many ways, more powerful than simply modeling excellence and installing it in ourselves and others. For business excellence, this is an idea whose time has come. Yet, the *processes* for managing, understanding, and developing *modeling skill and excellence* is not so simple.

Modeling (NLP style) begins with a flowchart of the mental and emotional responses that a person makes from initial stimulus to final response. The early cognitive thinkers created a simple model that they called the TOTE (Test, Operate, Test, Exit). George Miller, Karl Pribram, and Eugene Gallanter invented this as a process for tracking what goes on in the "black box" of the mind. View the TOTE model as a flowchart on human responses and as a model for providing more specificity to the older S-R (Stimulus-Response) model.

What happens after someone fires off a *stimulus*? What does the employee, manager, supervisor, or customer do? What kind of *responses* in the business context empower the processes and make everybody more effective, confident, richer, and happier? Those are the *responses* that we need to replicate.

But the S-R model of behaviorism regarding the *functioning* of people contributed very little except its descriptions about the macro-level reactions. From original stimulus to final response, they posited that while there exists a "black box" (mind, emotions, thoughts, values, beliefs, frames of reference), they could say nothing about what went on in there or what it contributed to the final response. They posited that there was no way to offer anything scientific about it. That's why they called it a "black box." It offered nothing to them for their model.

Miller and his associates changed all of that. They posited that, as we process *information* in the form of ideas, thoughts, and representations, these do affect and influence things. So they set out to model some of the things that went on in the black box. One of the things they said went on in the black box was the *testing* of current information. In the black box we compared information stored in the brain with information being input at the time. "Mind" *tests* current world information with remembered data. If what we *want* does not accord with what we are *getting*, we go into action and *operate*.

This introduced the second thing that goes on in the black box. We *operate*. We can operate in one of two ways. We can operate on the outside world by our actions and behaviors to make it conform to our internal information. Or, we can operate on the inside world by adjusting our expectations, beliefs, and representations so that they conform to our experiences in the world. After this *operating*, we test again.

- Has anything changed?
- Is anything different or better?
- How much has it changed?
- For better or for worse?
- How much more is needed?

If things have not changed sufficiently, we loop back to *operate* some more. If things have changed sufficiently, we *exit* the program.

The founders of NLP took the TOTE model and enriched it with numerous models in the field of neuro-linguistics: representational systems, strategy steps, meta-programs, and submodalities. As they then set forth the strategy model for modeling, they gave us strategy unpacking, elicitation, design, installation, interruption, and more. (See *Neuro-Linguistic Programming, Volume I*, 1980.)

We go further in Neuro-Semantics as we add other enrichments: the self-reflexivity of the meta-move, the layering of the levels of mind, the coalescing of those levels, the self-organizing nature of higher frames. This makes modeling more systemic and driven by feedback loops and feed-forward loops. (See *NLP: Going Meta— Advanced Modeling Using Meta-Levels*, 2001.) I offer that description of the field of modeling to provide an idea of this area.

The Benchmarking Game

The first stage in modeling involves the most natural thing in the world—copying, mimicking, imitating, and replicating the resemblance of something that works.

"Who is the best salesperson that we have? Jane. Okay, watch her closely, and do what she does! Now get out there!"

"Who really knows how to manage this process or this division? Fred. Okay, let's get him in here and find out what he does and then we can use his pattern as our benchmark."

Mimicking what is highly successful in the best examples offers a natural and intuitive way to model. It's something we can all do. Because it is how we all originally learned language and a great many of our patterns; it's one of our original games. We simply replicated and copied what others did. We did not study theory. We did not become experts in grammar textbooks. We just listened to what they said and how they spoke and then we began to *pick up on it*. It took lots of practice. And because we were cute, most of our trainers made the learning playful and fun. In the end, we learned the same foreign language that they spoke, even with their particular dialect, accent, and peculiarities.

When we do that in business, it's called *benchmarking*. This popular management practice means looking for the best in the company or field and intentionally copying it. This game has several valuable effects. For one thing, it prevents management from needing to reinvent the wheel. It sets a frame among employees whereby everybody (management included) begins looking for *best examples of effectiveness*. With that frame of mind, the focus ceases to be on tradition, history, and "but we've never done it that way." A new focus develops.

- What's the best and most efficient way to get this task accomplished?
- Who is producing the kind of results that we want here?
- How can we put together these pieces of effectiveness to obtain even higher results?

Modeling by benchmarking also creates a more democratic atmosphere. It assumes that quality performance can arise from anyone, and that, when it emerges, there's a learnable structure to it.

An NLP enrichment to mimicking, copying, and hence benchmarking involves learning *the matching and pacing skills*. Matching a person's tone and volume, energy and rhythm, breathing and other nonverbal outputs provides a powerful way to *enter into another person's "reality" of life experience*. This not only becomes the basis for rapport, but for *identification* as well. Matching a person's sensory predicates (visual, auditory, kinesthetic words), language patterns, emotional and value words, metaphors, and so on further deepens this experience. It enables us to more fully take the empathy position that we call "second perceptual position." Doing this in a relaxed trance state enables us to *deep-trance identify with* someone who has demonstrated high level competence and skill.

Downsides of The Benchmarking Game
A weakness lurks in *The Benchmarking Game*. As with any kind of *mere* mimicking and copying, there's little to guide or control the imitating except *immediate* results. This, unfortunately, sets the frame that overvalues *what works in the short term* and in the here and now. In doing so, it leads to the unfortunate result of eliminating long-term thinking, which takes systemic processes into account.

Further, as this kind of modeling can lead to copying something without understanding how it works or the theoretical formulations, it lacks the quality control that a testable theory provides. Obviously, knowing *what* works and having a precise *description of how* it works puts into our hands a very valuable technology for improving performance. Yet without understanding why and how it works we can't model at the higher conceptual level. That creates other kinds of limitations. It prevents us from having a fuller understanding of the restraints and constraints built into the behavior itself.

- When and where does it work best?
- When and where will it not work at all?
- What conditions, constraints, circumstances, etc. effect it and in what way?

Edwards Deming did not like benchmarking.

> "An example teaches nothing, unless studied with the aid of theory; otherwise people merely copy. They get into trouble ... because they did not understand why something was good or why something was bad." (Dobyns and Crawford-Mason, 1994, pages 130–31.)

Yet, *The Modeling Game* does begin with benchmarking, copying, and mimicking. NLP began this way. The first modeling that Richard Bandler, one of the founders of NLP, engaged in arose from his natural skill in mimicking the auditory expressions and patterns that he heard from Fritz Perls and then from Virginia Satir.

The Theoretical Modeling Game

"Theoretical modeling" describes another facet of *modeling* in the business world. We can also design and engineer processes, patterns, and guidelines by starting with an *idea*, a concept, a desire, a goal, or a theory and then working down. This gives us a deductive approach to improving behavioral performance.

By way of contrast, benchmarking begins with the details at the primary level and then works *inductively*. It copies and replicates; then it "chunks up" the scale from specificity to abstraction. While it does not start with theory, we can use it to arrive at theory eventually. When we use it this way, we ask:

- What does this mean?
- What have we learned?
- What principles, laws, and theoretical explanations does this imply?

It works up (or goes meta) *after* it first experiences and develops the behavioral skills. People who like *details first* and/or use *an experiential learning* style will tend to opt for this approach. It begins by scanning the environment for things that could be copied.

Those who like the *global* or *gestalt* understanding first prefer to start high and then work down. Such persons begin with theory and then move to application. By understanding the *mechanisms* and *laws* or principles involved, whether the field is aerodynamics, physics, mind-and-emotions, or relationships, the modeler first creates a "working model" along with educated guesses about what will happen if he or she does this or that.

Modeling by conceptualization has its strengths and weaknesses as well. On the positive side, it provides a greater sense of direction and focus. It enables us to more systematically follow a principle through to its results and then track those processes and productions on to the subsequent results. This keeps it cleaner and more controlled. Of course, it can also lead to "paradigm blindness"—the inability to see factors and even results that do not fit with the theory. The theory itself can get in a person's eyes. It can eliminate from awareness the emergence of new and unexpected elements.

Conceptual modeling focuses on explanation and, when overdone, it can cause one to become so abstract that the modeler becomes paralyzed from taking action. In spite of these weaknesses, this generally describes the dominant scientific model that has bequeathed to us the majority of the advances that we enjoy today.

The "Modeling by Meta-Detailing" Game

A Synergistic Approach to Modeling Behavioral Excellence

To combine benchmarking *and* theorizing, we find high-quality performance, use the power of copying, mimicking, and pacing it in all of its detailed components, and then work up a conceptual model about *how* and *why* it works as it does. In that way, we put together the *details* at the experiential level with the *meta-frame* at the conceptual level. This game enables us to use the distinction of genius that we discovered in numerous experts. We call this *meta-detailing*.

A meta-detailer is a person who has lots of mental flexibility and so can continually and quickly shift back and forth between the *global perspective* of the forest and the *detail perspective* of the trees. The person who plays *The Meta-Detailing Game* as a modeler is one who can step back from the high-quality performance and not just see "more trees," nor see it all blending into a vague sense of "good stuff." Something new and more and different emerges. In meta-detailing, we can maintain *both* the global conceptual understanding of principles and theory while seeing supporting details.

Meta-detailing in our modeling saves us from two dangers. It prevents us from "getting lost in the details," which can overwhelm and confuse. "Detail complexity" is what most of us suffer from when we know a field really well, but do not have an organizing structure (a frame or meta-level principle) for controlling and managing the details. Sometimes we become obsessive about the details, fearful of losing details, and then unable to sort out crucial details from trivial ones. While it is often true that "the devil is in the detail," *mere* details do not make for excellence. *"Modeling elegance"* refers to simplifying a process to the smallest number of details and distinctions necessary and providing a meta-frame that holds one's focus.

Meta-detailing also saves us from the vagueness of the global perspective when it becomes too abstract and loses critical distinctions. We don't have to read or talk very long with mid-level managers or high-level executives to discover the mind-numbing obscure business and management jargon that seems all so meaningful but actually says nothing. This just gets us stuck in theory, concepts, explanations, and reasons and becomes an indistinguishable haze, lacking perspective.

By learning the skill and art of meta-detailing, we keep testing our theories as we look to see how they interface with the hard-nosed facts of everyday life. Then we feed back the results from that and the things we have learned into our meta-level principles. This *systemic thinking and perceiving* of meta-detailing translates principles into actions, and applications into principles. It allows us to function well in a system of interactive elements. It empowers us to use both feedback and feed-forward loops for ongoing and continual improvement.

We engage in meta-detailing thinking when we ask such questions as:

- How do the parts fit together into the structure?
- What relationship occurs between this part and that?
- What effect will a change at this level have on the whole?
- What details support this frame?
- What thematic principle governs these elements?

Robert Fritz, in *The Path of Least Resistance for Managers* (1999), describes meta-detailing as telescoping, hence *The Telescoping Game.* What is telescoping and what does it produce?

> "Telescoping is just what it sounds: something smaller is contained within something larger, and we can pull it out or leave it tucked in ..." [Page 59.]

> "This process provides everyone with an overview so no one gets lost in obsessive detail. People can see trees and know that they are part of a whole forest. This is a profound change of thinking, especially on the team level." [Page 60.]

In meta-detailing we learn to think systemically because we learn to see how the elements, factors, components, and organization fit together. These connections generate the type of relationships that make up the system itself.

The "Strategic Planning" Game

In business jargon, we speak about *strategies* and *strategic planning*. These terms refer to how we aim to take effective action to create better and/or more products and services, how to enter and capture a market, to gain recognition over the competition, to improve the skills of our people in making this happen, and how to plan for the future. Thinking *strategically* means thinking in terms of such things as:

- Where we stand in the market
- Where we stand in relation to our competition
- Where we stand in terms of our skills, quality control, communication effectiveness, management of personnel, compensation, market presence
- Where we stand presently and where we want to go
- The processes (steps, stages, actions) that will move us from present state to desired state

Strategic planning begins with a focus on *what* we want in terms of our goals and objectives. Yet it does not end there. It also focuses on *how* we seek to get there.

- How do we treat our people and customers in moving toward our objectives?
- What values and principles do we follow in the process?
- What states and qualities govern the process?
- How do we treat feedback, criticism, failure, difficulties, and challenges?
- How do we think about change itself? Creativity? Innovation?

The "Modeling the Modeling" Game

In this process of *business modeling* (which also holds true for all modeling), we eventually become aware of ourselves and what we are doing (seeking to find and replicate high-quality performances, pieces of excellence). Reflexively, we then *meta*-model ourselves as we look at, and explore, the quality of our modeling efforts.

- How well are we modeling excellence and experts?
- What skills, theories, principles, and states do we bring to the modeling process itself?
- What strengths and weaknesses do we have in mimicking, copying, understanding, replicating, and reproducing excellence?

In this game of modeling and outframing our own modeling experiences, we turn back to observe our own insights and skills. Peter Senge, author of the bestselling management book, *The Fifth Discipline* (1990), described this as "meta-learning." Meta-learning turns an organization or business into a *learning organization*, which, in turn, gives us the ability to keep learning, growing, and developing.

The "Modeling Dynamic Structures" Game

Seeing *structure* is easy when it comes to skeletons, the metal girders of a high-rise building, the framing of a wood house, and other forms and expressions of static and stable systems. Seeing the *structure* of a dynamic system, however, is a very different matter. Imagine the things involved in learning to see the dynamic structure in:

- How we generate a mind–body state
- The production of a piece of music by an orchestra
- The functioning of the immune system in fending off toxic elements
- Communicating effectively to influence someone

What kind of a perspective do we need to operate from so that we can *see dynamic structure* and *ongoing processes*? A *systemic perspective*.

The foundational work of Korzybski in the field of General Semantics concerned this kind of systemic thinking. Beginning with the realization that we live in a *process world* where everything changes, where nothing ultimately "stays the same," Korzybski set out to track the changes and to create a process and functional language for mapping such.

The modeling that emerged from General Semantic involved a nonstatic accounting of dynamic structures and of "change" itself. He invented a *Theory of the Levels of Abstraction* (the Structural Differential) for accounting for the ongoing change that occurs as we think, then think about that thinking, and so on. To that he added another theoretical model, the *Theory of Multiordinality.* He designed that to account for how the same term could convey different meanings depending on its context and level of abstraction.

An illustration of *dynamic structure* might be the presentation of a concert by an orchestra. Music emerges from the ongoing movement of sound which flows from a structure—the score being followed by all of the members of the orchestra. There's structure in the air. Yet it is not a static structure: it moves, flows, changes.

To model it we have to detect, recognize, and understand dynamic structure—how it works, how it breathes, the things that affect it. We have to search out the formatting and structuring influence—the score as well as the disciplined skills involved in the members of the orchestra, as well as in the leading influence of the conductor, the acoustics of the building, as well as many other contributing influences.

In terms of human neuro-linguistics, dynamic structure arises from our frames of references and conceptual associations. These generate our "meanings" at many levels about many different things. And it never stays the same. It is forever in flux. Mapping this dynamic structure involves primary-level perception and representation and then all of the meta-level conceptual maps.

We have been doing this in *frame games* as we identify and work with our frames and frames within frames, our matrix of frames that comprise our higher-level structures and rules for the games.

How to Play The "Modeling Excellence" Game

In your business, what specific pieces of behavioral or state excellence would you like to model that, if you did—and *installed* them in yourself—would greatly increase your effectiveness, enjoyment, and wealth.

1. List these behaviors and experiences.
2. Whom do you know who already achieves this?
3. Pretend for a while that you have stepped into that person's skill and imagine what it would be like to experience the world through that person's eyes, ears, and states.
4. As you do, begin breathing, moving, gesturing as they do. Temporarily become that person as you identify with their way of thinking, emoting, and speaking. Mimic them fully.
5. Notice how this transforms your experience.
6. What frames of reference in terms of beliefs, values, understandings, decisions, and identification would you need in order to model this excellence more fully?

And so the adventure begins ...

Summary

-   We can copy, mimic, model, and replicate excellence. We can find experts and replicate the games they play that give them their advantage.

-   We have so much more to learn and develop about modeling as a science and art. As a meta-discipline, modeling is still in its formative stages of development. Yet, we have enough distinctions to begin the process.

-   There is *structure* to the experiences that seem so magical. There is rhyme and reason above and beyond the experience and it lies in the structuring and organizing mind–body (neuro-linguistic) system that produces the maps that govern the experience.

-   When we play *The Modeling Games* with Meta-States we track the circular looping of self-reflexive consciousness. This enables us to discover the higher levels of "mind" that build various reality structures that then set up our neuro-linguistics and Neuro-Semantics to become *self-organizing*.

"The Un-End Game":

Let The Games
~~Begin!~~ Continue!

The Staying Ever Fresh Game

To keep ourselves challenged, we need a new attitude about our goals and outcomes. We need an outcome vision that values unending progress. We need to learn how to play an *Infinite Game.*

We also need an attitude of *feeling thrilled about being challenged.* If, indeed, we play *The "No Failure, Only Feedback" Game,* then the challenges that arise when things get tough or when we don't know how we will turn things around becomes the point at which we need a game that allows us to feel even more alive, excited, turned on, and committed. How would you like to operate from *that* perspective? How much of an attitude adjustment would you need in order to set that as your frame of reference for moving through life?

Typically, most business experts who create excellence come from that place. When the going gets tough—they get even more motivated and turned on. They step up to the plate at their best. They love a challenge. They get aroused and excited about something they don't know how to do. They do not look for the "path of least resistance." They look for the mountain peaks that haven't been climbed. They look for the problems that seem to have no answer—yet.

How do you take to *problems*? How do you respond when things get tough? Do you move through life looking for ease and comfort? Or do you move through with another kind of orientation? Do you look for challenge?

Mihaly Csikszentmihalyi, author of *Flow*, says:

> "High achievers invent ways to challenge themselves, whether they are studying, working, or mowing the lawn. Workers who enjoy what they are doing spend more time working than adults who don't seem to enjoy their jobs. These people are going to be more productive."

How do we keep ourselves challenged? One obvious way involves setting goals that force us to stretch and grow. Refusing to settle for present levels of productivity and quality and constantly pushing the envelope a little bit more forces us to dig deeper within and to stretch out to new and more adaptive behaviors. So look at your goals for the next year. Do you have big, bold, bright, dramatic, challenging goals? Or, do you have little weak, so-so goals? Or, did you decide to sit this one out and try to move through life goalless?

Go for it ...

So, with your eyes wide open now to the games that are afoot in the world, may you move out as a *frame-game master*—fully able to detect games and the frames that drive them. As you do, may you find yourself able to clearly and powerfully respond with a definitive *"Yes!"* and/or *"No!"* to the games that seek to recruit you. May you choose only those that will fit with your values and visions, those that enhance your life and empower you as a person. May you have outrageous fun as you play and may you live long and play well!

More About Frames, Framing, Reframing and Frames of Mind

If you liked this work on *Games Business Experts Play*, and would like to explore the literature that supports the *frame-games* model (NLP, Meta-States, and Neuro-Semantics), then you might like to check out some more in-depth materials on frames, framing, reframing, and frames of mind.

Time-Lining: Patterns For Adventuring In "Time"
A book about the concept of "time" and numerous patterns for thinking about how to code, represent, and play with "time" so that it enhances our lives. *Time-lining* describes how to engage in empowering time travel and use the time-lining patterns of NLP for fun and profit.

Dragon Slaying: Dragons to Princes
The first book to popularize the Meta-States model, *Dragon Slaying* applies it to identifying those higher states or frames of mind that create limitations to our resourcefulness.

Figuring Out People: Design Engineering With Meta-Programs
A book about the frames of mind that become our perceptual or attentional filters, called Meta-Programs in NLP This work presents an encyclopedia approach, identifying 51 Meta-Programs as well as describing how to detect and work with them to increase your language elegance.

Frame Games: Persuasion Elegance
The first book in the *Frame Games* series, which sets forth the frame-games model, a simplified and user-friendly version of

Meta-States. This book describes the frames and games that make up the content of our life.

Meta-States: Reflexivity in Human States of Consciousness
A more scholarly book that sets forth the domain of states-about-states and how each higher state *sets a frame of reference* that then becomes the "attractor," controller, or executive function of mind.

Mind-Lines: Lines for Changing Minds
A book about conversational reframing that presents a model for *the structure of meaning* and how to intentionally shift and change meaning in more than twenty ways. Based originally on the NLP "sleight of mouth" patterns, *Mind-Lines* goes much further as it uses the Meta-States model for analyzing and playfully transforming meaning.

Secrets of Personal Mastery: Advanced Techniques for Accessing Your Higher Levels of Consciousness
A book that popularizes Meta-States with a focus on personal empowerment and mastery. meta-levels and frames are described extensively in this work.

The Structure of Excellence: Unmasking the Meta-Levels of Submodalities
An advanced book about the NLP "submodality" model and how it actually operates as meta-frames. This reorganization of the NLP model highlights the importance of frames with special chapters on, among other things, frames for negation, backgrounding and foregrounding, and transforming beliefs.

Frame Game Secrets

(*From* **Frame Games, 2000**)

Not only does every game have rules by which it operates, but those who know those rules and master them also learn something more important than the basic rules—they learn *secrets* about how to use the rules to play with skill, finesse, and elegance. Similarly the "mind" games that we play with ourselves and others have "rules." They operate according to the way our brains and neurology work. Once you know those rules, you can also learn some of the higher-level principles or *secrets* for making the rules work for you. The following summarizes the *secrets about these rules*—how these rules operate and what you can do when you know the rules of the game.

#1: Frames Rule
Frames govern experience. The frames that we set, that are set for us, and that we buy into *control* our whole mind–body experience and usually do so *outside of our awareness*. The more outside of awareness the frame, the more it *plays* us. The more awareness we develop, the more control we have over the game.

#2: Whoever Sets the Frame Controls The Game
Someone always sets a frame and whoever sets a frame for a context, area, domain, field, interaction, etc. governs or exercises the most influence over that area. Awareness of frames empowers us for frame setting, changing, and rejecting. If someone is playing a mind game with you, look for the governing frame.

#3: The Problem is Never the Person, it's Always the Frame
"It's the frame, stupid!"

To think symptomatically is to become focused on the person, behaviors, and emotions that result from the *frame game.* Yet the person and the expressions of the frame are never really the prob-lem, not the ultimate problem. That arises from *the frame.*

#4: Frame Creates Focus
Frames control the shift and concentration of focus. The structural for-mat of a frame of reference calls attention to the *cognitive content* inside of the frame as it *foregrounds* some ideas, and at the same time, *backgrounds* the shape and form of the frame itself, making it less and less conscious. In this way frames *magically* foreground content and background structure.

#5: Frame Detection Skills Enable You to Master Frame Games
Awareness of the frame exposes the *frame game* itself. By shifting from *content* to *structure*, from the thoughts *within* the frame of ref-erence to the shape and form of the higher-level *thoughts* we are given the power to shape and control frame games. This power involves moving *above* and *beyond* the content to the structure that operates the higher thoughts *about* the lower thoughts. [The term *"meta"* refers to this "above, beyond, and about" relationship.]

#6: The Name of the Game is to Name the Game
When we *name* the game, we expose *the frame* and it typically changes everything. Generally, it's very difficult to continue a toxic game when it's been exposed. So the name of the game regarding sick, toxic, and dis-empowering games is to name the game. Doing so exposes the dragon.

#7: Where there's a Frame—There's a Game Nearby ... and a Neuro-Linguistic State
Frames create the mental and emotional states that we *feel.* The thought-and-felt experience of a *state* of consciousness operates from governing frames. A *state* of mind, emotion, or body as an attitude or mood functions as a holistic mental-emotional energy field. And as an *energy field*, it creates a self-reinforcing dynamic. This "state dependency" means the state influences what we see, hear, feel, remember, act, imagine, talk, etc. When *in state*, we see

the world *from the frame and perspective* of that state. States have *energies*. And we can learn to see, hear, feel, smell, and taste them.

#8: Frame Brains Play Frame Games *with the "Stuff" of Thoughts*
There's nothing mystical about frames. Frames are made out of the "stuff" of "thoughts." The *material* out of which we *construct* our world of meaning, communication, significance, etc. consists of the fairly fluid and malleable "thoughts" or representations that we entertain. Your *frame-brain* frames, and it frames at multiple levels.

#9: People Come with Frame Brains
Our brains do their *work* by referencing and creating *frames of reference* at every higher logical level. This generates our frames and our higher frames of mind. This simply arises from the way we think and feel.

#10: Frame Brains Thrive on Symbols
What do you feed a *frame brain*? As a semantic class of life, we set frames in our brain and body by using symbols (both linguistic and nonlinguistic symbols). This means that even the tiniest little word can sometimes fully establish and set powerful frames of reference and frames of mind that control perception, memory, experience, behavior, emotion and even skills. The *secret of Word Magic* is that as we represent, we encode our mind and neurology.

#11: Frame Magic *involves Detection and Transformation of Thoughts*
A *Word Magician* can make frames magically appear, disappear, and reappear. Since neuro-linguistic "thinking" governs setting frames in the first place, we can use the same for tearing down frames, loosening frames, switching to better frames, and setting higher frames, etc. This means the very *Word Magic* (magic of symbols in neurology) that creates frames can also deframe, reframe, and outframe. This enables us to tap into the neuro-semantic levels of meaning making to enhance them, modify them or dissolve them.

271

#12: *Frame Game Magic Increases with the Intensity of Vividness and Drama*
If you want to get *an idea* into your mind–body, into the fibers of your muscles, make the idea dance and move, give it rhythm, a compelling voice, and let it make a memorable impression upon you. What we "hold in mind" becomes our higher *meanings* or *frames of mind*. Make the ideas memorable through drama and vividness.

#13: *To Set a Frame, Frame-Game Masters use Repetition, Questions, and "Matter-Minding" Processes.*
How do you *set* a frame? All you have to do is repeat something long enough and it will tend to get in, wear a groove in neurology, and become a reference point—even if you don't believe it, like it, or want it. For things you do like, want, and believe in—welcome them in with lots of repetitions and ask lots of questions that pre-suppose it. We breach the mind–muscle connection by emotional-izing thoughts. *Activating the body* with a strong primary emotion (fear, anger, aversion/attraction, joy/sadness, lust/revulsion, stress/relaxation, etc.) typically creates a strong association to cor-responding ideas, concepts, or beliefs and so establishes a frame of reference.

#14: *Play flows where the Game Goes—as Sayeth the Frame*
This engages the Meta-State principle that says, *Energy flows where attention goes—as determined by intention*. The higher frame of *intention and structure* formats, organizes, and controls the flow of energy and attention. It creates pathways for consciousness to flow more easily.

#15: *Frames and Frame Games create a Personal Matrix*
The "world" you live in emerges from the frames you inherit, absorb, and construct. By our conversations and thinking, we enter into the "universes" that we then inhabit. Make sure you have a good one. No, make that a wonderful and magical one.

Bibliography

Bandler R. (1985). *Using Your Brain for a Change* (Connirae and Steve Andreas, eds). Moab, UT: Real People Press.

Bandler R, Grinder J. (1976). *The Structure of Magic, Volume II*. Palo Alto, CA: Science & Behavior Books.

Bandler R, Grinder J. (1982). *Reframing: Neuro-Linguistic Programming and the Transformation of Meaning*. Moab, UT: Real People Press.

Barker, Joel A. (1992). *Future Edge: Discovering the New Paradigms of Success*. New York: William Morrow.

Bateson G. (1972). *Steps to an Ecology of Mind*. New York: Ballantine Books.

Bellman G. (2000). *The Beauty of the Beast: Breathing New Life Into Organizations*. San Francisco, California: Berrett-Koehler Publishers.

Berne E. (1964). *Games People Play: The Psychology of Human Relationships*. New York: Ballantine Books.

Blanchard K, Johnson S. (1991). *The One Minute Manager*. New York: William Morrow and Co. Inc.

Bodenhamer BG, Hall LM. (1997). *Time-Lining: Patterns for Adventuring in Time*. Carmarthen, Wales: Crown House Publishing.

Bodenhamer BG, Hall LM. (1999). *The User's Manual for the Brain: A Comprehensive Manual for Neuro-Linguistic Programming Practitioner Certification*. Carmarthen, Wales: Crown House Publishing.

Bradbury A. (1998). *NLP for Business Success*. London: Kogan Page.

Cameron-Bandler L, Labeau M, Gordon D. (1985). *Know How: Guided Programs for Inventing Your Own Best Future*. Moab, UT: Real People Press.

Covey, Stephen R. *Principle-Centred Leadership*. (1992). NY: Fireside.

Csikszentmihalyi M. (1990). *Flow: The Psychology of Optimal Experience*. New York: HarperCollins.

Dennett DC. (1996). *Kinds of Minds: Toward an Understanding of Consciousness.* New York: Basic Books.

Dilts R, Grinder J, Bandler R, DeLozier J. (1980). *Neuro-Linguistic Programming, Volume I: The Study of the Structure of Subjective Experience.* Capitola, CA: Meta Publications.

Dilts R. (1993). *Skills for the Future.* Capitola, CA: Meta Publications.

Dilts R. (1995). *Strategies of Genius, Volume 1.* Capitola, CA: Meta Publications.

English G. (1998). *Phoenix Without the Ashes: Achieving Organizational Excellence Through Common Sense Management.* Boca Raton, FL: St. Lucie Press.

Fritz R. (1999). *The Path of Least Resistance for Managers: Designing Organizations to Succeed.* San Francisco, CA: Berrett-Koehler Publishers.

Gitomer J. (1998). *Customer Satisfaction is Worthless: Customer Loyalty is Priceless.* Austin, Texas: Bard Press.

Gross ST. (1996). *Positive Outrageous Service—Guilt-Free Selling.* New York: AMACOM, American Management Association.

Hall LM. (1987). *Speak Up, Speak Clear, Speak Kind.* Grand Jct. CO: Empowerment Technologies.

Hall LM. (1995, 2000). *Meta-States: Managing the Higher Levels of Your Mind.* Grand Jct., CO: Neuro-Semantics Publications.

Hall, LM. (1998). *The Secrets of Magic: Communicational Excellence for the 21st Century.* Carmarthen, Wales: Crown House Publishing.

Hall LM. (2000). *Frame Games: Persuasion Elegance.* Grand Jct. CO: Neuro-Semantics Publications.

Hall LM, Belnap B. (1999). *The Sourcebook of Magic: A Comprehensive Guide to the Technology of NLP.* Carmarthen, Wales: Crown House Publishing.

Hall LM, Bodenhamer B. (1997). *Figuring Out People: Design Engineering Using Meta-Programs.* Carmarthen, Wales: Crown House Publishing.

Hall LM, Bodenhamer Bob. (1997, 2000). *Mind-lines: Lines for Changing Minds.* Grand Jct. CO: Neuro-Semantics Publications.

Hall LM, Bodenhamer B. (1999). *The Structure of Excellence: Unmasking the meta-levels of Submodalities*. Grand Jct. CO: Empowerment Technologies.

Herron T, Bohan G, Meyer R. (1997). *People Make the Difference: Prescriptions and Profiles of High Performance*. New York: Oakhill Press.

Hersey P, Blanchard KH. (1998). *Management of Organizational Behavior: Utilizing Human Resources*. (5th ed.) Englewood Cliffs, NJ: Prentice Hall.

Holman P, Devane T (eds). (1999). *The Change Handbook: Group Methods for Changing the Future*. San Francisco, California: Berrett-Koehler Publishes, Inc.

Korzybski A. (1933/1994). *Science and Sanity: An Introduction to Non-Aristotelian Systems and General Semantics*. Lakeville, Connecticut: Institute of General Semantics.

Lederer D, Hall LM. (1999). *Instant Relaxation: How to Reduce Stress at Work, at Home, and in Your Daily Life*. Carmarthen, Wales: Crown House Publishing.

Levine S. (1988). *Getting to Resolution: Turning Conflict Into Collaboration*. San Francisco, California: Berrett-Koehler Publications.

McCormack M. (1984). *What They Don't Teach You at Harvard Business School*. New York: Bantam Books.

Marshall L, Freedman L. (1995). *Smart Work: The Syntax Guide for Mutual Understanding in the Workplace*. Dubuque, IA: Kendall/Hunt Publishing Co.

Maslow A. (1968). *Toward a Psychology of Being*. New York: Van Nostrand Co.

Massnick F. (1997). *The Customer is the C.E.O.: How to Measure What Your Customers Want—and Make Sure They Get It*. New York: AMACOM, American Management Association.

Mayer R. (1996). *Power Plays: How to Negotiate, Persuade, and Finesse Your Way to Success in Any Situation*. New York: Random House, Times Business.

Miller G, Galanter E, Pribram C. (1960). *Plans and the Structure of Behavior*. New York: Henry Holt & Co. Inc.

Peters, T, Austin N. (1985). *A Passion for Excellence: The Leadership Difference.* New York: Random House.

Pine, J, Gilmore J. (1999). *The Experience Economy: Work is Theatre and Every Business a Stage.* Boston, Massachusetts: Harvard Business School Press.

Prather, Hugh. (1983) *Notes to Myself.* New York: Bantam Books.

Roberts M. (1999). *Change Management Excellence: Putting NLP to Work in the 21st Century.* Carmarthen, Wales: Crown House Publishing.

Rossi E. (1988). *Mind–Body Therapy: Ideodynamic Healing in Hypnosis.* New York: W. W. Norton & Co..

Seligman MEP. (1975). *Helplessness: On Depression, Development, and Death.* San Francisco, California: Freeman.

Seligman MEP. (1990). *Learned Optimism.* New York: Alfred A. Knopf.

Selye H. (1976). *The Stress of Life.* New York: McGraw-Hill Book Co..

Senge PM. (1990). *The Fifth Discipline: The Art and Practice of the Learning Organization.* New York: Doubleday Currency.

Stanley TJ, Danko, WD. (1996). *The Millionaire Next Door: The Surprising Secrets of America's Wealthy.* Atlanta, Georgia: Longstreet Press.

Terkel, Studs. (1997). *Working: People Talk About What They Do All Day And How They Feel About What They Do.* New York: New Press.

Thomas D. (1993). *Business Sense: Exercising Management's Five Freedoms.* New York: The Free Press.

Thomas K. (2000). *Intrinsic Motivation at Work: Building Energy and Commitment.* San Francisco, CA: Berrett-Koehler Publishers.

Tracy B. (2000). *The 100 Absolutely Unbreakable Laws of Business Success.* San Francisco, CA: Berrett-Koehler Publishers.

Walton M. (1985). *The Deming Management Method.* New York: Perigee.

Glossary

Association: stepping into an experience to see, hear, and feel as if from inside it.

Attractor: in the process of framing, we set up classifications, categories, concepts, and thus the *frames that create our neuro-semantic* states (or Meta-States). Then the frames become self-organizing systems that are *attractors*—attracting experiences, ideas, and emotions that support them.

Belief: a thought *confirmed* at a meta-level, a conscious or unconscious generalization about some concept (e.g., causality, meaning, self, others, behaviors, identity).

Calibration: tuning in to a person's state by reading nonverbal signals previously observed.

Chunking: changing perception by going up or down levels and/or logical levels. "Chunking up" refers to going up a level (inducing up, induction). It leads to higher abstractions. "Chunking down" refers to going down a level (deducing, deduction). It leads to more specific examples or cases.

Content: the specifics and details of an event, in contrast with process or structure.

Context: the setting, frame or process in which events occur; provides meaning for content.

Dissociation: stepping back from an experience and representing it from an *outside* position, seeing and/or hearing it as if being a spectator or from another very different perspective.

Ecology: examining the overall relationship between idea, skill, response and larger environment or system; the dynamic balance of elements in a system.

Frame: short for frame of reference. We frame things; we frame people, ideas, events, experiences, and so on; a mental, cognitive, or linguistic context for something.

Frame ambiguity: the fuzzy edges of a frame, the lack of clear bracketing of a frame. It may lead to frame failure.

Frame analysis: the process of analyzing our frames, detecting them, identifying the leverage points for shifting them; the processes for transforming them, the games that they engender. Frame analysis provides a way to clearly articulate the levels of mind and the influence they exert over life's experiences.

Frame argumentation: the argument that a frame makes in defense of itself, or from out of its perspective. Frames argue for themselves when they feel threatened. This is a function of what cognitive psychology calls state or mood dependency.

Frame break: breaking a frame, interrupting it.

Frame clearing: deframing, dissolving, or busting up a frame—we clear out mental and emotional room in a person's model of the world for a new frame.

Frame confusion, frame clearing: the quality of confusion/clarity within a frame.

Frame cues: the signals, indicators, clues, linguistic markers that indicate the presence of a frame.

Frame of mind: via the process of repeating and habituating a frame of reference, we send our mind and emotions out to a particular referent again and again. Over time this leads to turning the referent that we merely represented and thought about occasionally into something always on our mind—in fact, the frame of mind that we operate from. The referent "gets in our eyes," so to speak, so that we view the world and all of our experiences through the lens of that experience or idea. This turns the referent experience into a perceptual filter.

Frame of reference: the *reference* that we use to understand something else. The reference can be an actual experience (an event), a person, an idea. A referent can be something real and actual or imaginary and vicarious.

Frame terms: using the metaphor and structuring device of "frames" we can now think in terms of and work with something. This creates our frame terms.

Frame wars: when we conflict with another person, it is typically a conflict of frames.

Frameworks: when a particular frame of mind becomes so solidified in our orientation, it then becomes our characteristic mindset or attitude, this transforms it into one of the very basic frameworks of our mind and personality, thereby giving it even more power and influence over us.

Future pacing: process of mentally practicing or rehearsing an event; a key process for installing a program and ensuring the permanency of an outcome.

Game: a set of actions that play out some concept or idea for some purpose, e.g. to "win" something, another emotion, stroke, transaction, etc. A frame-generated realm that describes and creates our virtual reality or matrix.

Game consciousness: awareness of a game, whom it works, who sets it, how it invites people into it, the states it elicits, etc.

Generalization: process of representing a whole class of experiences based on one or a few specific experiences.

Gestalt: the overall configuration, impression or feel of thoughts and feelings; the whole of an experience that is more than the sum of its parts.

In-frame: living, feeling, seeing, experiencing, etc. from within a frame of reference or frame of mind. Living in a virtual reality governed and informed by our ideas, ideals, concepts, beliefs, and values, etc. *See also* **Matrix**.

Kinesthetic: describing sensations, feelings, tactile sensations on the surface of the skin, proprioceptive sensations inside the body; includes vestibular system or sense of balance.

Matching: adopting characteristics of another person's outputs (behaviour, words, etc.) to enhance rapport.

Matrix: a metaphorical way to think about the "world" or universe of discourse that we create perceptually, mentally, and emotionally via our frames. As we build meta-levels of the mind, we tend to become "paradigm-blind" and to see the world in terms of our ideas and concepts. Thus, the Matrix arises.

Meta: combining form used to denote something "above or beyond" something else and therefore "about" it; applied to a relationship of levels, as when a thought is *about* another thought, a feeling *about* a feeling, a thought *about* a feeling, etc.

Meta-detective: the ability to *step aside* from our thinking and feeling and to recognize our thoughts and feelings, their layers, etc.

Meta-model: a linguistic model of distinctions that identifies language patterns that obscure meaning via distortion, deletion and generalization, questions that clarify imprecision to enrich a person's model of the world.

Meta-Programs: the mental and perceptual programs for sorting and paying attention to things; perceptual filters governing attention.

Meta-State: A meta-state arises for the first T-F (Think-Feel) about our Thought-Feelings. In this, our conscious awareness *reflects back* onto itself (self-reflexive consciousness) to create T-F at a higher logical level. This generates a state-about-a-state (a Meta-State). Such meta-states relate to, or reference, a previous state. So, rather than relating to something about the world, they relate to something *about* (@↓) some previous "thought," "emotion," concept, understanding, or Kantian category. Hence a meta-state describes a higher level of abstraction @ an abstraction. This creates a conceptual state.

Meta-stating: bringing a mind–body state to bear upon another state, accessing a higher logical level to organize, drive, and modulate a lower state.

Modal operators: a linguistic distinction in the meta-model indicating a person's "mode" for operating (mode of necessity, impossibility, desire, possibility, etc.).

Model: a pattern, example, or description of how something works.

Modeling: the process of observing and replicating the actions, skills, knowledge, and states of someone (typically an expert). Modeling discerns the sequence of internal representations and behaviors that comprise the structure of a skill.

Neuro-Semantics®: A model of meaning or evaluation utilizing the meta-states model for articulating and working with higher levels of states and the Neuro-Linguistic Programming (NLP) model for detailing human processing and experiencing; a model that presents a fuller and richer model offering a way of thinking about and working with the way our nervous system (neurology) and linguistics create meaning (semantics).

Nominalization: a linguistic distinction in the meta-model involving a process (or verb) turned into a noun; a process frozen in time.

Outframing: Going above all frames to create a new frame of reference.

Out-of-frame: activities, thoughts, scripts that do not fit a given frame. This creates a loosening of the frame, a threat to the frame. When we step out of a frame of reference, we "break frame" or "lose frame" and so become *out of frame*.

Pacing: gaining and maintaining rapport with another by joining their model of the world, by matching their language, beliefs, values, current experience, etc.; crucial to rapport building.

Rapport: a sense of connection with another, a feeling of mutuality, a sense of trust; created by pacing, mirroring and matching; a state of empathy or second position.

Referent/references: the idea, person, event, belief, etc. that we have in mind and use in our thinking. A reference point identifies a singular idea, person, or event. A reference frame involves understandings of how the points are related.

Reframing: altering a frame of reference by presenting an event or idea from a different point of view or with a different meaning ascribed to it.

Representation systems: sights, sounds, sensations, smells and tastes make up the basic primary RS; language makes up the meta-RS

- VAK: a shorthand for the sensory RS of visual, auditory, and kines-thetic. K also includes smells (olfactory) and tastes (gustatory).

- A_d: Auditory digital—digital representations, i.e. words, language, symbols.

Sensory acuity: awareness of the outside world via the opening of the senses.

Sensory-based description: directly observable and verifiable informa-tion; see-hear-feel language one can test empirically.

State: a state of mind/body, which never occurs in isolation, hence *a mind–body state* driven by ideas and meanings (conceptions and the sig-nificance we attach to things, a neuro-linguistic or *neuro-semantic state*). Our states generate an overall *feel* or gestalt—thus we refer to our states as *emotional states*. We notate thoughts-feelings as T-F, and the state as a circle. A *primary* state relates to or references some object (person, event, thing) out in the world ($\rightarrow$).

State dependency: once we get into a state, the state itself governs our learning, memory, perception, communication, and behavior. We call this *state-dependency.*

Strategy: a sequencing of thinking/behaving to obtain an outcome or create an experience, the structure of subjectivity ordered in a linear model.

Submodalities: representational distinctions within each sensory sys-tem, qualities or features of representations.

Universal quantifiers: a linguistic term in the Meta-Model for words that code things with "allness" (every, all, never, none, etc.).

Unsanity: term used by Korzybski to describe the stage of poor adjust-ment between sanity (well adjusted to the territory) and insanity (totally maladjusted to reality); the "lack of consciousness of abstracting, confu-sion of orders of abstractions resulting from identification … practically universally operating in every one of us" (*Science and Sanity: An Introduction to Non-Aristotelian Systems and General Semantics*, Page 105).

VAK: *see under* **representation systems**.

Value/valuing: the process of deeming something important; a meta-level phenomenon.

Glossary of Frame Games

Acceptance/Appreciation Frame: willingness to just accept and welcome reality on its own terms.

Aim Frame: goal-directed orientation toward your desired outcomes (or Outcome Frame).

As If Frame: the Pretend Frame, as "as if" something were the case and doing so until actions, thoughts, feelings, and so forth, bring that reality into being.

Assertive Frame: forthrightly speaking up in a kind and gentle way.

Backtracking Frame: retracing steps of a line of reasoning, rehearsing the overall theme of a statement to check out understanding.

Being Frame: beyond being a "human doing" to a human being—just enjoying experience.

Boldness Frame: "taking courage" by using one's values and visions to face fears and to move out into the world with a dash of outrageousness in being one's own self.

Cheerfulness/Humor Frame: looking at things through eyes of humor, to find humor in experiences.

Committed and Loyal Frame: willingness to make a decision to be with and for another person.

Courage Frame: facing fears and brave difficulties in spite of threats.

Ecology Frame: Quality-Control Frame. Checking on the health and balance of a frame.

Enchantment Frame: attitude of looking at others and the world through eyes of appreciation and wonder.

Endurance Frame: willing to endure short-term challenges and difficulties for long-term benefits.

Flexibility Frame: willingness to adjust response and vary patterns.

Future Pacing Frame: a time frame that strategically imagines a desired future and puts oneself into that preferred future.

Hidden Success Frame: assuming others have successes and resources, and looking to find them.

Implementation Frame: framing acting on knowledge, concepts, beliefs, etc.

Intentional Stance Frame: imagining and specifying fully your outcome of your outcomes until you get to your highest outcome frames and then using that as your intentional stance.

"It's all Behavior" Frame: extensionalizing concepts into see, hear, feel referents or behaviors, operationalizing terms.

Justice Frame: willing to operate from attitude of fairness and equity for others.

Map Frame: recognizing thoughts, ideas, beliefs, etc. as just a way of mapping things.

Meta-Decision Frame: deciding to decide, and to decide with clarity, wisdom, focus, etc.

No Failure/Only Feedback Frame: classifying all responses and communications as "feedback" rather than failure.

Orientation Frame: where we stand with each other; where we are in relation to our goals

Pain Frame: the aversion frame that causes us to move away from something.

Persistence Frame: continuing to pursue a goal through tough times, persisting, patiently, bouncing back from troubles.

Personal Warmth Frame: recognizing such qualities as empathy, care, love as a powerful interpersonal frame.

Playfulness Frame: lightening up and being playful.

Pleasure Frame: the attraction frame that describes the mindset and feelings involved in moving toward something.

Positive Intention Frame: assuming that every behavior and communication arises from someone trying to accomplish something of value for themselves.

Power Frame: accessing/owning the four basic powers: thinking, emoting, speaking, and acting.

Propulsion System Frame: operating from a strong aversion toward "dis-values" and simultaneously being strongly compelled toward desired outcomes and states.

Relevancy Frame: inquiring about relevancy: Is this relevant? How? In what way? How does this relate to the subject?

Responsibility To/For Frame: distinguishing accountability ("for") and relationship ("to").

Responsiveness Frame: responsive to another person.

Self-Acceptance Frame: accepting self as having innate and unconditional dignity.

Solution Frame: focusing on solutions rather than problems, difficulties.

Systems Frame: recognizing the systemic factors involves in processes that involve many interactive parts; viewing things from a holistic and systemic mindset that takes the larger system into account.

Time Frames: recognition of the different frames we can use to encode "time."

Vitality Frame: recognizing the importance of physical health and well-being for a healthy mind.

Vulnerable and Open Frame: willingness to disclose oneself openly to another.

Win/Win Frame: approaching others in a cooperative mode seeking to find ways so that everybody can win Collaborative Frame Game.

The Author

Dr L. Michael Hall is an entrepreneur who lives in the Rocky Mountains in Colorado. As a psychologist he had a private psychotherapeutic practice for many years, and then began teaching and training—first in communication (assertiveness, negotiations, relationships), then in NLP. He studied NLP with one of its co-founders, Richard Bandler, in the late 1980s, wrote several books out of that experience, and has since become quite prolific in authoring more than two dozen NLP books.

Hall's doctorate is in cognitive-behavioral psychology. His dissertation dealt with the *languaging* of four psychotherapies (NLP, REBT [Rational Emotion Behavioural Therapy], reality therapy, logotherapy) using the formulations of general semantics. He addressed the Interdisciplinary International Conference (1995) presenting an integration of NLP and general semantics.

Books by the Same Author

Dragon Slaying: Dragons to Princes (1996, 2000, 2nd edition)

Figuring Out People: Design Engineering With Meta-Programs (with Bobby G. Bodenhamer) (1997)

Frame Games: Persuasion Elegance (2000)

Games Slim People Play (2001)

Instant Relaxation: How To Reduce Stress At Work, At Home And In Your Daily Life (with Debra Lederer) (2000)

Languaging: The Linguistics of Psychotherapy (1996)

"Meta-State Magic" (*Meta-States Journal*, Volume I, II (1997, 1998)

Meta-States: Managing the higher levels of your mind (1995, 2000 2nd edition)

Mind-Lines: Lines For Changing Minds (with Bobby G. Bodenhamer) (1997)

NLP: Going Meta—Advance Modeling Using Meta-Levels (1997/2001)

Patterns For "Renewing the Mind" (with Bobby G. Bodenhamer) (1997)

Personality Ordering & Disordering Using NLP (2001)

The Secrets of Magic: Communication Excellence for the 21st Century (1998)

Secrets of Personal Mastery (2000)

The Sourcebook of Magic (with B. Belnap) (1997)

Speak Up, Speak Clear, Speak Kind: Assertive Communication Skills (1987)

The Spirit of NLP: The Process, Meaning And Criteria For Mastering NLP (1996)

The Structure of Excellence: Unmasking the Meta-Levels of Submodalities (Hall and Bodenhamer) (1999)

Time-Lining: Patterns For Adventuring In 'Time' (with Bobby G. Bodenhamer) (1997)

The User's Manual For The Brain (Bodenhamer and Hall) (1998)

BOOKS CAN BE ORDERED THROUGH
Neuro-Semantics Publications
P.O. Box 8
Clifton CO. 81520
United States of America

The Society & Institutes of Neuro-Semantics®

Hall and Bodenhamer trademarked "Meta-States," "Neuro-Semantics," "Meta-NLP," and "Frame Games" and have initiated the International Society of Neuro-Semantics, which as of 2002 has five National Societies and 17 Institutes around the world. See—

www.neuro-semantics.com
www.neurosemantics.com
www.runyourownbrain.com

Training Available

Basic Meta-State training
Accessing Personal Genius (three-day basic). Introduction to Meta-States as an advanced NLP model. This training introduces and teaches the Meta-States Model and is ideal for NLP practitioners. It presupposes knowledge of the NLP model and builds the training around accessing the kinds of states that will access and support "personal genius."

Basic Meta-States in two other simplified forms

1. Secrets of Personal Mastery: Awakening Your Inner Executive. This training presents the power of Meta-States *without* directly teaching the model as such. The focus instead shifts to personal mastery and the executive powers of the participants. Formatted so that it can take the form of one, two, or three days, this training presents a simpler form of Meta-States, especially good for those without NLP background or those who are more focused on Meta-States applications than the model.

2. Frame Games: Persuasion Elegance. The first truly user-friendly version of Meta-States. Frame Games provides practice and use of Meta-States in terms of frame detecting, setting, and changing. As a model of frames, Frame Games focuses on the power of persuasion via frames and so presents how to influence or persuade yourself and others using the levels of thought or mind that lie at the heart of Meta-States. It is designed as a three-day program, and the first two days present the model of frame games and lots of exercises. Day Three is for becoming a true Frame Game Master and working with frames conversationally and covertly.

Meta-States Gateway Trainings

1. Wealth Building Training (Meta-Wealth). The focus of this training is on learning how to think like a millionaire, to develop the mind and meta-mind of someone who is structured and programmed to create wealth economically, personally, mentally, emotionally, relationally, etc. As a Meta-States application training, Wealth Building Excellence began as a modeling project and seeks to facilitate the replication of that excellence in participants.

2. Games Great Sales People Play (Meta-Selling). Another Meta-States application training, modeled after experts in the fields of selling and persuasion and designed to replicate those skills in participants. An excellent follow-up training to Wealth Building, since most people who build wealth have to sell their ideas and dreams to others. This training goes way beyond mere persuasion engineering, as it uses the Strategic Selling model of Heiman, which is also known as relational selling and facilitation selling, among others.

3. Mind-Lines: Lines for Changing Minds. Based upon the book by Hall and Bodenhamer (1997), now in its third edition, Mind-Line Training is a training about conversational reframing and persuasion. The Mind-Lines model began as a rigorous update of the old NLP "sleight of mouth" patterns and has grown to become the persuasion language of the Meta-State moves. This advanced training is highly and mainly a linguistic model, excellent as a follow-up training for Wealth Building and Selling Excellence. Generally a two-day format, although sometimes three and four days.

4. Accelerated Learning Using Neuro-Semantics and NLP (Meta-Learning). A Meta-State application training based upon the NLP model for "running your own brain" and the Neuro-Semantic (Meta-States) model of managing your higher executive states of consciousness. Modeled after leading experts in the fields of education and cognitive psychologies, this training provides extensive insight into the Learning States and how to access your personal learning genius. It provides specific strategies for various learning tasks as well as processes for research and writing.

5. Defusing Hotheads: A Meta-States and NLP application training for handling hot, stressed-out, and irrational people in fight/flight states. Designed to "talk someone down from a hot angry state," this training provides training in state management, first for the skilled negotiator or manager, and then for eliciting another into a more resourceful state. Based upon Hall's book, *Defusing Strategies* (1987), this training has been presented to managers and supervisors for greater skill in conflict management, and to police departments for coping with domestic violence.

6. Instant Relaxation: Another practical NLP and Meta-States application training designed to facilitate the advanced ability to quickly "fly into a calm." Based in part upon the book by Lederer and Hall (*Instant Relaxation*, 1999), this training does not teach NLP or Meta-States, but coaches the relaxation skills for greater "presence of mind," control over mind and neurology, and empowerment in handling stressful situations. An excellent training in conjunction with Defusing Hotheads.

Basic NLP training

1. Meta-NLP™ NLP Practitioner Training: A training that produces an introduction to the NLP model and all of the essential skills involved in NLP, including calibrating, state awareness and management, anchoring, time-lines, Meta-Model, hypnotic language, submodalities, and Meta-Programs.

2. Meta-NLP™ Master Practitioner Training: A training that more extensively provides training in the three meta-domains of NLP— the Meta-Model, Meta-Programs, and Meta-States—as well as trance, time-lines, mind-lines (sleight-of-mouth reframing patterns), strategies, and modeling with an emphasis on developing the *spirit* of NLP.

Advanced Neuro-Semantic Training

Advanced Modeling Using Meta-Levels: Advanced use of Meta-States by focusing on the domain of modeling excellence. This training typically occurs as the last four days of the seven-day Meta-States Certification. Based upon the modeling experiences of L. Michael Hall and his book, *NLP: Going Meta—Advanced Modeling Using Meta-Levels*, this training looks at the formatting and structuring of the meta-levels in resilience, "uninsultability," and seeing opportunities. The training touches on such things as the modeling of wealth building, fitness, women in leadership, and persuasion.

Advanced Flexibility Training: An advanced Neuro-Semantics training that explores the riches and treasures in Alfred Korzybski's work, *Science and Sanity*. Originally presented in London (1998, 1999) as "The Merging of the Models: NLP and General Semantics," this training now focuses almost exclusively on developing advanced flexibility, using tools, patterns, and models in General Semantics. Recommended for the advanced student of NLP and Meta-States.

Neuro-Semantics Trainers' Training: An advanced training for those who have been certified in Meta-States and Neuro-Semantics (the seven-day program). This application training focuses the power and magic of Meta-States on the training experience itself—both public and individual training. It focuses first on the trainer, to access his/her own top training states, and then on how to use Meta-States or set the frames when working with others in coaching or facilitating greater resourcefulness.

TO CONTACT THE AUTHOR, WRITE:
L. Michael Hall, Ph.D.
P.O. Box 8
Clifton CO 81520
Michael@neurosemantics.com

970 523-7877

Index

USA & Canada *orders to:*

Crown House Publishing
P.O. Box 2223, Williston, VT 05495-2223, USA
Tel: 877-925-1213, Fax: 802-864-7626
www.crownhouse.co.uk

UK & Rest of World *orders to:*

The Anglo American Book Company Ltd.
Crown Buildings, Bancyfelin, Carmarthen, Wales SA33 5ND
Tel: +44 (0)1267 211880/211886, Fax: +44 (0)1267 211882
E-mail: books@anglo-american.co.uk
www.anglo-american.co.uk

Australasia *orders to:*

Footprint Books Pty Ltd.
Unit 4/92A Mona Vale Road,
Mona Vale NSW 2103, Australia
Tel: +61 (0) 2 9997 3973, Fax: +61 (0) 2 9997 3185
E-mail: info@footprint.com.au
www.footprint.com.au

Singapore & Malaysia *orders to:*

Publishers Marketing Services Pte Ltd.
10-C Jalan Ampas #07-01
Ho Seng Lee Flatted Warehouse, Singapore 329513
Tel: +65 256 5166, Fax: +65 253 0008
E-mail: info@pms.com.sg
www.pms.com.sg

South Africa *orders to:*

Everybodys Books
Box 201321 Durban North 401, South Africa
Tel: +27 (0) 31 569 2229, Fax: +27 (0) 569 2234
E-mail: ebbooks@iafrica.com